W9-AOJ-284

06/24
STAND PRICE
$ 5.00

Cracked it!

06/24
STAND PRICE
$ 5.00

Bernard Garrette • Corey Phelps
Olivier Sibony

Cracked it!

How to solve big problems and sell
solutions like top strategy consultants

Bernard Garrette
HEC Paris School of Management
Jouy-en-Josas, France

Corey Phelps
Desautels Faculty of Management
McGill University
Montreal, QC, Canada

Olivier Sibony
HEC Paris School of Management
Jouy-en-Josas, France

ISBN 978-3-319-89374-7   ISBN 978-3-319-89375-4   (eBook)
https://doi.org/10.1007/978-3-319-89375-4

Library of Congress Control Number: 2018944260

© The Editor(s) (if applicable) and The Author(s) 2018
This work is subject to copyright. All rights are solely and exclusively licensed by the Publisher, whether the whole or part of the material is concerned, specifically the rights of translation, reprinting, reuse of illustrations, recitation, broadcasting, reproduction on microfilms or in any other physical way, and transmission or information storage and retrieval, electronic adaptation, computer software, or by similar or dissimilar methodology now known or hereafter developed.
The use of general descriptive names, registered names, trademarks, service marks, etc. in this publication does not imply, even in the absence of a specific statement, that such names are exempt from the relevant protective laws and regulations and therefore free for general use.
The publisher, the authors, and the editors are safe to assume that the advice and information in this book are believed to be true and accurate at the date of publication. Neither the publisher nor the authors or the editors give a warranty, express or implied, with respect to the material contained herein or for any errors or omissions that may have been made. The publisher remains neutral with regard to jurisdictional claims in published maps and institutional affiliations.

Cover illustration: alashi/DigitalVision Vectors/Getty

Printed on acid-free paper

This Palgrave Macmillan imprint is published by the registered company Springer Nature Switzerland AG
The registered company address is: Gewerbestrasse 11, 6330 Cham, Switzerland

Business leaders praise Cracked It!

"When dealing with a major business issue, every decision maker is facing his own cognitive biases, rooted in experience and personality. In *Cracked It!*, the authors not only remind us of the importance of challenging even obvious solutions or ideas, by taking a step back, thinking differently, and walking in the other's shoes – be it a customer or an audience – but they also provide practical, value-creating and proven insight."

—Stéphane Richard, *Chairman and Chief Executive Officer, Orange*

"The future is no longer what it used to be. The business world is undergoing unprecedented disruption. Every problem is more complex. *Cracked It!* will be the bible of the true problem solvers."

—Daniel Bernard, *Former Chairman and Chief Executive Officer, Carrefour*

"If you want to master problem solving, buy this book. It will save you from coming to sloppy conclusions and guide you through every aspect of the process of solving a problem. I used it the day after I started reading it."

—Neil Janin, *Chairman, Bank of Georgia, and Senior Partner Emeritus, McKinsey*

"Too often at the Board or executive level, time is wasted looking for solutions to a problem which has not been clearly defined. Garrette, Phelps and Sibony provide a structured approach to defining problems which should prove useful to practitioners."

—Paul M Tellier, *Former Chief Executive Officer, Bombardier and Canada National Railways*

Thought leaders praise Cracked It!

"Too many companies fail because of bad strategy. This book is full of frameworks and tips to help you avoid that fate."

—Adam Grant, New York Times *bestselling author of* Give and Take, Originals, *and* Option B *with Sheryl Sandberg*

"Written by a trio of leading experts on strategy who draw both on decades of rigorous academic research and consulting experience, *Cracked It!* offers a crystal clear approach to frame and solve challenging strategic issues. A must-read for executives, consultants, business school students and leaders in charge of transforming their organizations."

—Laurence Capron, *Professor of Strategy and Dean of Faculty, INSEAD*

"CEOs regularly pay a king's ransom to the top management consulting firms for help in solving their most complex problems. You may not have the consultant's connections or their knowledge of the industry, but this book will help you learn the secrets of their problem-solving process so you can tackle your own problems more effectively."

—Chip Heath, *Coauthor of* Switch *and* The Power of Moments

"Why do smart and experienced executives sometimes make spectacularly bad decisions? This book exposes the flaws in analysis that lie at the root of the problem. Building on deep academic insights and lots of real-world experience, Garrette, Phelps and Sibony lay out a structured problem-solving approach to overcome the many pitfalls that executives fall into. They don't just tell you how to get the analysis right, they also explain how to sell your advice to others. An invaluable guide to anyone who is involved in decision-making in the business world today."

—Julian Birkinshaw, *Author of* Fast/Forward, *Professor and Deputy Dean, London Business School*

"This is a GREAT 'how to' book for tackling strategic problems and becoming a better strategic thinker. It not only describes all the major frameworks used by strategy analysts, but also shows their pitfalls and how to decide when a particular framework will be useful. All of the concepts in the book are also demonstrated with real case studies that bring the process of strategic analysis to life."

—Melissa Schilling, *Author of* Quirky *and Herzog Family Professor of Management, Stern School of Business, New York University*

"Problem solving is a critical skill for managers and entrepreneurs and often underserved in business education. *Cracked It!* does a phenomenal job in presenting a full problem solving framework grounded in sound theory, tested in years of practice and fun to read."

—Franz Heukamp, *Dean, IESE Business School*

Strategists praise Cracked It!

"A fully comprehensive and practical introduction to problem-solving tools and techniques."

—Georges Desvaux, *Senior Partner and Managing Partner, Africa, McKinsey & Company*

"Strategy is problem solving – an important, subtle and pervasive skill for which business practitioners receive little formal training. Garrette, Phelps and Sibony provide a valuable and practical guide to the art, from framing the problem through to communicating and selling the solution, which should be invaluable to practitioners and consultants."

—Martin Reeves, *Director, BCG Henderson Institute*

"A great read for all current and future business leaders! The secret sauce of solving hard problems and selling solutions to drive change is at your doorstep. Just go get it!"

—Eric Gervet, *Lead Partner, AT Kearney, San Francisco office*

"The companies that win will be those that use superior problem solving tools. *Cracked It!* teaches you how. It captures the real world experience of successful problem solving and presents the learnings in an engaging style."

—Rima Qureshi, *Executive Vice President and Chief Strategy Officer, Verizon*

"The ABSOLUTE reference handbook on problem solving! It is clearly unique and it smartly introduces an amazing richness of methods, through cases and easy to understand frameworks. I have to say… I love it!"

—Jean-Baptiste Voisin, *Chief Strategy Officer, LVMH*

"In an uncertain world that defies comprehension, we are forced to make intuitive decisions… but our problem-solving process must be rational. Therein lies *Cracked It!*'s greatest value. Readers will learn how to shape an effective problem-solving process to channel intuition into rationality and avoid the mistakes that ensnare the amateur strategist."

—General Vincent Desportes, *French Army*

Acknowledgments

As strategy professors, we interact with a broad range of audiences, from undergraduate students to MBA participants to senior executives. Despite very different backgrounds and expectations, all of them consistently tell us that they struggle with a common challenge: how to *apply* what they learn.

Our students tell us that the tools and concepts of business management are relatively easy to understand. Analyzing the structure of an industry or assessing whether a company has a cost advantage is not, after all, an extraordinary intellectual challenge for people who often have advanced degrees in non-business fields, not to mention many years of successful experience. When the time comes to apply the same tools to real business situations, reality does not conform to the stereotype presented in the textbooks—or even to the stylized examples presented in case studies. The problems business people face are complex. Situations are ambiguous. Facts are unclear. Expectations change quickly. Whether it is learned in school or on the job, business knowledge provides executives with a treasure trove of frameworks. But it does not help them to recognize and make sense of the problems.

In 2014, we set out to fill this gap by developing a course on problem solving for the core curriculum of the HEC Paris MBA. We soon realized we needed to address aspects of business communication as an integral part of the course, for reasons that will become clear as you read this book. After many iterations and refinements, the course morphed into the method described in this book.

A significant inspiration for this book is the problem-solving method developed and refined over many years by McKinsey consultants. Because the very nature of top management consulting is to help senior executives make sense of the toughest problems they deal with, problem-solving proficiency is at the heart of what McKinsey consultants do. Like almost everything in this extraordinary firm, it is passed on from generation to generation, in the spirit of apprenticeship. Olivier is immensely grateful to the masters who taught him the ropes as a young consultant, but also to all the colleagues, from the partners to the summer associates, who challenged him in countless team meetings over a quarter century.

We are indebted to the hundreds of students and executives who participated in our problem solving and communication seminars over the past few years. Not only did they force us to clarify and refine our thinking continuously, but they also kept telling us that something was missing: the course was long enough to make them aware of the need to hone their problem-solving skills, but too short for them to become familiar with all the tools and techniques required. Where, they asked us, is the book they can read to become better problem solvers? We hope the answer is now in your hands.

Many parts of this book benefited from the input and wisdom of colleagues. To name only a few, we would like to thank Blaise Allaz, Pierre Dussauge, Thierry Foucault, Andrea Masini, Anne-Laure Sellier, and Mathis Schulte, who have been instrumental in extending the scope of our problem-solving views toward their respective areas of expertise. More generally, we are indebted to all our colleagues at our home schools—HEC Paris and McGill— as well as to friends and colleagues from other institutions we collaborate with, such as IESE and Saïd Business School, who engaged in stimulating conversations with us at various stages of the project. We insist that all remaining errors are ours.

We also benefited from research support from HEC Paris, the HEC Foundation, and the Desautels Faculty of Management at McGill University, which we gratefully acknowledge.

Turning a classroom experience into a book is an interesting challenge. We hope this book has retained some of the "hands-on" feel that we strive for in our teaching, while following the conventions that make it possible for a reader to navigate it easily. If we've had any success in this endeavor, our editor Jennifer Worick deserves much of the credit. Isabelle Huynh, our visual editor, helped us convert our cluttered slides into the elegant visuals you will discover. We are also grateful to Stephen Partridge and Gabriel Everington of Palgrave Macmillan for their patient and supportive work.

Working on a book is like any relationship—it requires care and attention, and sometimes, it can become all-consuming. It can provide joy one day, and frustration the next. It can also impact other relationships and benefit from them. Bernard wants to thank Béatrice for her loving care and support, especially in the challenging personal circumstances that surrounded the completion of this work. Corey's wife, Tiffany, and kids, Chloé-Rose and Connor, went through a lot and did a lot to support him during the project, for which he is extremely grateful. Olivier is equally grateful to Anne-Lise, Fantin, and Lélia for their unfailing encouragement and patient support.

Contents

List of Figures

List of Tables

1

The Most Important Skill You Never Learned

On July 16, 2004, Michael Dell, Chairman and Chief Executive Officer (CEO) of Dell Inc., announced that longtime Dell senior executive and Chief Operations Officer Kevin Rollins would take over as CEO of the company formerly known as Dell Computer. Before joining Dell in 1996, Rollins had been a VP and partner at the consultancy Bain & Company, where he advised Dell on its famous direct business model. At the time of Rollins's anointing, Dell was the world's largest and most profitable producer of computers. Its stock closed just above $35, the highest since the bursting of the tech bubble in the summer of 2000. Only two and a half years later, at the beginning of 2007, the situation was very different. Revenue growth had slowed significantly, market share had declined, and HP had knocked Dell out of the top spot as the world's largest computer manufacturer. Dell had also repeatedly missed analysts' earnings estimates, and its stock price had dropped by nearly a third. In late 2006, Dell recalled over four million laptops because batteries were exploding or igniting. A few months earlier, the US Securities and Exchange Commission (SEC) launched an investigation into accounting irregularities relating to the timing and recognition of income and expenses, which led to a restatement of Dell's net income for 2003–06. Finally, an internal employee survey had bluntly signaled declining confidence in Dell leadership.

Dell Inc. had a problem. Shareholders and employees were unhappy with the situation and desperate for a return to better performance. As Chairman and the largest shareholder, Michael Dell "owned" this business problem and had a powerful incentive to solve it quickly. If you were Michael Dell in early 2007, what would you have done to tackle this issue?

© The Author(s) 2018
B. Garrette et al., *Cracked it!*, https://doi.org/10.1007/978-3-319-89375-4_1

Fast and Slow Problem Solving

The problem Dell faced in early 2007 involved a complex set of poorly under-stood factors, which made it hard to define the problem, let alone know how to solve it. Such complex and ill-defined problems are idiosyncratic and infre-quently occur, making it difficult to develop routine solutions or approaches to solving them. Nevertheless, we may be tempted to believe we know all we need to solve Dell's problem. For many of us, the cause of the problem and the solution are apparent: Kevin Rollins is to blame and should be replaced as CEO. Framing the situation this way simplifies the challenge. Instead of a lengthy and difficult task of defining, structuring, and analyzing the problem and then generating and choosing among potential solutions, we just reduce the problem-solving process to a choice between keeping and replacing Rollins. Regardless of what you would advise, you most likely zeroed in on a solution rather quickly.

Daniel Kahneman, psychologist and Nobel laureate in economics, explains in his groundbreaking best seller *Thinking, Fast and Slow* how we have two minds in one brain, constantly in contention over our mental operations.[1] Our default approach to thinking—including about how to solve problems—is fast. This is known as "System 1" thinking. System 1 thinking is largely involuntary, automatic, and unconscious. When thinking fast, we limit our attention to information readily available rather than search for information that could help us better understand the situation, a tendency Kahneman calls "What You See Is All There Is (WYSIATI)." Fast thinking is also associative: the limited information we initially have about a situation (and pay attention to) triggers a rapid and unconscious activation of related ideas we hold in memory, which trigger other associated ideas, and so on. The result of this cascading process is that we can quickly make sense of new situations, even though we have limited information, by constructing coherent stories about what is going on and what we should do. In other words, our brains excel at jumping to conclusions.

In contrast to fast thinking, slow thinking (aka "System 2") is voluntary because it requires effortful attention and conscious deliberation. But this effort is cognitively expensive: mental capacity is a scarce resource, and we need to allocate it to the problem (thus the phrase "paying attention"). Consequently, in solving challenging problems, we often gravitate toward the law of least effort. One way we do this is to rely on the results of the faster and cognitively cheaper System 1 approach to thinking. Our deliberative System 2 thinking then merely endorses System 1's proposals. With sufficient effort and skill, however, slow thinking can be logical, skeptical, and methodical, causing us to search for missing information, question assumptions and beliefs, and utilize tools and frameworks to make sense of a situation, resulting in a much better understanding of it and how to tackle it. But our brains only trigger slow thinking by exception, when fast thinking is ineffective at dealing with the situation at hand. Neuroscience research on problem solving bears this out: the region of the brain that is active when people solve problems quickly, based on beliefs, is distinct from the part that activates using deliberate logic, indicating that different mental processes are competing for control in problem solving.[2]

The temptation in the story about Kevin Rollins and Dell Inc. is to think (too) fast about the problem and solution or to be lazy in our slow, deliberative thinking. When presented with information about Kevin Rollins's tenure as CEO of Dell compared to the Michael Dell era—slowing sales growth, declining market share, missed earnings estimates, falling stock price, and so on—it's easy for us to take it at face value and believe we don't need to know more. Immediately, our brains go to work on detecting the associations among the information. An important point is that Rollins is a CEO. This is likely to trigger a belief most of us hold about leadership: that leaders can (or should) control the fate of the organizations they lead. Consequently, we attribute good performance to good leadership and bad performance to bad leadership. Connecting the dots between this association about leadership and the indicators of poor organizational performance, we quickly develop a coherent story about what's going on, and jump to a solution: fire Rollins.

But would we come to the same conclusion if we questioned the information and searched for more? For example, what if we learned that, despite Dell's declining stock price, it was still outperforming everyone else in the industry? Or that Rollins was widely respected and admired within Dell, even though employee confidence in other senior leaders was declining? What if we had additional insight into the causes of the problem? For example, Dell sourced the faulty batteries from Sony, a supplier that everyone in the industry considered reliable. What if we also learned that Dell lost its top spot in market share after HP acquired Compaq (another major producer of computers)? What if, in investigating Dell's declining market share further, we discovered it was due, in part, to flattening demand from its core enterprise customers and growing demand from end consumers, whom Dell wasn't adept at serving? Or to a decline in the value of customization, which was a core part of Dell's customer value proposition, because rapid advances in computer components resulted in standardized machines that were good enough to satisfy most customers? Would we analyze the problem differently if we discovered

Michael Dell had elevated Rollins to CEO to maintain the firm's strategic focus on enterprise customers and customization, rather than alter the company's business model to adapt to changing competitive conditions (as Rollins had, in fact, wanted to do)? Finally, what if we recognized that some symptoms, such as the SEC's investigation into Dell's accounting practices, resulted from decisions Michael Dell made during his tenure as CEO instead of choices Rollins made?

When we stop presuming we know what's going on, and instead question the sufficiency of the information we possess and search for more, we become more likely to overcome our assumptions and see the problem differently, enabling us to generate different and potentially better solutions. While it would be imprudent (and potentially disastrous) to believe we can develop an effective solution to the problem facing Dell in early 2007 without taking these steps, jumping to a solution was still easy to do.

Therein lies the core problem of problem solving—our tendency to think too fast (or too lazy) and jump to solutions. We spend too little time and effort understanding a problem, believing instead we know all we need. We unleash the associational machine in our minds, reflecting our implicit assumptions about causes and effects, on this limited information to develop a coherent and plausible story about what's going on and why. As Wharton professor Adam Grant explains in his book, *Originals,*[3] people have no trouble turning any information they receive into a coherent narrative, even when the information is random. People can't help seeing signals, even in noise.

The danger is to believe the story we are quick to create, and to take action based on that story. Shakespeare's character Othello is the archetype of this tragic flaw. He resolves to kill his wife Desdemona when he sees in the hands of another woman the handkerchief he gave her as a token of love. This woman received it from Cassio, which suggests that Desdemona had given it to Cassio. As the traitor Iago has convinced Othello that Desdemona and Cassio are lovers, the handkerchief looks like hard evidence. The real story is that Desdemona dropped it inadvertently and Iago planted it in Cassio's lodgings. Because of assumptions and a false narrative, Othello kills Desdemona, who is actually faithful to him, thereby destroying the one worthy of his love. While the consequences may not be as tragic, we all run the risk to jump to conclusions and take action without questioning the implicit assumptions— or the emotions—that dictate the way we interpret events and information.

The remedy is to think about problems more thoroughly, search for missing information, double-check every clue, weigh the pros and cons, and investigate all possible hypotheses. To avoid Othello's mistake, however, we can be vulnerable to becoming Shakespeare's perhaps most famous character, Hamlet. You may recall that Prince Hamlet is the son of the late King of Denmark, and his uncle Claudius (the King's brother) has usurped the throne by killing the King and marrying the widow Queen. The drama is about Hamlet's reluctance to avenge his father. Hamlet wants to be sure Claudius is guilty and kill him under legitimate circumstances. His endless hesitations paralyze him and drive him to commit irreparable mistakes. At the end of the play, the entire Danish royal family kill one another and Denmark surrenders to Norway, its archenemy.

So, are you Othello or Hamlet? Are you more likely to think—and act— too fast, or to get mired in analysis paralysis? While jumping to conclusions and actions is a widespread fault in individuals, analysis paralysis is frequent in large, bureaucratic organizations that pile up studies and reports before taking any action or no action at all. On the one hand, being fast or lazy in our thinking allows us to economize on scarce and expensive mental resources, but the resulting solutions are often poor and ineffective. On the other hand, slow thinking and thorough investigation are necessary to tackle complex business problems—the focus of this book—but the reflection process might create delays in decision-making and thwart action. For organizations and institutions to be both effective and efficient, they need people who can overcome these challenges to solving complex business problems. These people must be as thorough as Hamlet and as action oriented as Othello, without jumping to conclusions like the latter or being stuck in a loop of endless questioning like the former. Conventional wisdom suggests these people should be chosen for their intelligence, experience, and expertise. But as we'll see, being smart, experienced, and well-trained may not be enough. A systematic problem-solving method is also necessary.

Problem Solving and the Expertise Trap

We all solve problems. We couldn't make it through a day without tackling the steady flow of challenges life throws at us: "What's the most efficient route to avoid a traffic jam and get to work on time?" "Where do I take my out-of-town friend to dinner?" "How do I lose the pounds I put on during the holidays?" Technology can help solve our problems, but not always. Problem solving is a dominant form of how we think and one of our most complex intellectual activities. It's a core part of what makes us human.

While we all solve problems, managers and consultants are professionals— they're hired and paid to do so. Iconoclastic management scholar Henry Mintzberg, one of the first to study what managers do, found they spend much of their time solving problems.[4] Leadership consultancy Zenger Folkman recently surveyed over 300,000 managers and found that problem solving was the second most important competency at all management levels.[5] The OECD Survey of Adult Skills showed that complex problem-solving skills are essential for fast-growing, highly skilled managerial, professional, and technical occupations.[6]

Management consulting firms, such as McKinsey, Boston Consulting Group, and Bain, *exist* to solve business problems. As Harvard professor Clayton Christensen recently observed, "Management consulting's fundamental business model has not changed in more than 100 years. It has always involved sending smart outsiders into organizations for a finite period and asking them to recommend solutions for the most difficult problems confronting their clients."[7] No wonder that according to an internal McKinsey staff paper, problem solving is viewed as the most important skill for success in the firm.[8] As part of their recruiting, management consultants carefully assess the problem-solving skills of their applicants through anxiety-inducing "case interviews": during the interview, candidates are given a short description of a challenge facing a disguised client company and tasked with solving the problem. Some firms also use formal problem-solving tests: according to consulting prep website IGotAnOffer.com, only one-third of qualified applicants pass McKinsey's test.

So how good are the professionals at solving challenging problems? We can look to research on expertise and problem solving for insight. Experts have developed in-depth knowledge within a particular domain through extensive study and practice, and have mentally organized their knowledge for easy recall and use. Managers and consultants typically specialize in particular functional or industrial areas for much of their careers, developing expertise in these areas. Research has found that for problems within their domain of expertise, experts have advantages over novices: they have more richly developed mental models of different problems and can better recognize and understand problems, often by using analogies to past problems.[9] Experts also use more effective problem-solving strategies in their areas of expertise, more carefully evaluate potential solutions against constraints, and more effectively monitor their problem-solving progress by refining solutions.[10]

These advantages of expertise explain why research shows, for example, that when compared to novice accountants, seasoned tax accountants can more readily draw on their understanding of tax law and accounting conventions to solve a particular client's tax problem.[11] They also explain why a lean manufacturing expert can walk into a manufacturing plant and quickly spot opportunities to increase efficiency by reducing work-in-process inventory that plant employees missed.

Expertise, however, is likely to be irrelevant to solving the problem facing Dell in 2007 and could even hamper it. This is because expertise comes with constraints. Even though experts are better problem solvers than novices within their areas of expertise, when they tackle problems outside their expertise or when task conditions in their fields change, they often perform like novices … *or worse*. Experts' rich and detailed mental models can constrain their ability to understand problems and search for solutions when working outside their fields of expertise. Mental models are rigid and resistant to change, particularly when associated with successful outcomes. Experts can become trapped by their expertise. Psychologist and Rice University professor Erik Dane finds that the more expertise and experience people gain, the more entrenched they become in a particular way of viewing the world.[12] Compared to novices, experts also are overconfident in their ability to understand problems outside their areas of expertise, leading them to develop worse solutions.[13]

Finally, reasoning by analogy can also lead experts to develop poor solutions when faced with new but seemingly familiar situations. When reasoning by analogy, a person starts with a new, unfamiliar target problem to solve. She then considers other source settings she knows well and compares them to the target through a process of similarity mapping. By finding a source problem she believes has similar characteristics as the target, she identifies a candidate solution that solved or could have solved the source problem. The whole process may be summed up like this: "I've seen something like this before, so what worked there may work here." While analogical reasoning can be a valuable source of insight and creativity, it can lead to poor solutions when problem solvers develop analogies based on superficial similarities instead of deep causal traits. When problem solvers have deep experience in a particular domain, their knowledge is salient and easy to recall, which can lead them to pay more attention to characteristics of the new setting that seem similar and ignore those that are different, and to develop superficial analogies and poor solutions.[14] Experience can be a poor guide when working outside your area of expertise or when the nature of your work changes.

Complex Problems and "Unknown Unknowns"

Expertise is a double-edged sword. Even relevant expertise is insufficient for some problems. Like the Dell example, many business problems are complex, ill-defined, and non-routine. Complex problems' many interrelated causes make them difficult to understand. An ill-defined problem is one where the current situation, desired outcome, and path between the two are difficult to articulate. Complex problems are often initially ill-defined and typically non-routine. A non-routine problem has idiosyncratic characteristics: we face them infrequently and lack the opportunity to develop experience and expertise in solving them. The complexity of business problems often requires the integration of various domains of knowledge, exceeding the expertise of all but the polymath problem solver.

As problem complexity increases, solvers are more likely to face "unknown unknowns," further challenging the value of expertise.[15] Long before US Defense Secretary Donald Rumsfeld made the term famous in his 2002 press conference, the notion of unknown unknowns (commonly called "unk-unks") was familiar to project management and engineering professionals.[16] Although a cumbersome phrase, an unknown unknown simply means that a problem solver faces uncertainties in solving a problem she is unaware of. Faced with complex problems, we rarely know the right questions to ask. As Rumsfeld put it, "There are things we don't know that we don't know." The more we are unaware of the factors that produce a problem, the more likely we are to be surprised when events happen that cause our solution efforts to fail.

Consider the case of entrepreneurship. Entrepreneurs identify valuable customer problems to solve in exchange for money. The extent to which an entrepreneur recognizes an important and widely held problem and develops a solution—a product or service—that is better than rival offerings increases the chances the venture will be profitable. Important and valuable customer problems are often complex and poorly understood by entrepreneurs. Instead of recognizing their ignorance and investing in learning from potential customers so they can discover what they don't know, research shows that entrepreneurs often abide by the *field of dreams* principle: if you build it, they will come. CB Insights, a data analytics firm that tracks global venture capital investing, recently conducted a postmortem of over 200 failed startups and found the leading cause of failure (over 40 percent) to be insufficient market acceptance. These ventures developed offerings that didn't effectively solve customers' problems.

Banco Davivienda in Colombia is a case in point. In 2009, bank executives in Bogotá identified what they believed was a big problem worth solving: nearly 40 percent of the population had no bank account. In response, the bank introduced a stripped-down, inexpensive, and easy-to-use account that relied on the bank's retail branch network. Despite aggressive promotion, there was little customer acceptance and the initiative was deemed a failure and abandoned. Project team members evaluated the failure and realized they'd done little to understand the nature of the problem they were trying to address. Instead, they let their knowledge of existing customers and solutions distort their understanding of the problem.

Just because something is unknown, however, doesn't mean it's unknowable. Many unknowns are unknown because problem solvers fail to spend the time, effort, and resources to recognize the unknown aspects of a problem. In response to their failed effort, members of the Banco Davivienda project team acted like cultural ethnographers to better understand the challenges the unbanked faced with financial transactions. They immersed themselves in the daily lives of the unbanked by spending weeks living in the poor neighborhoods where their target customers lived, observing, and engaging in conversations. The team developed personas of prototypical customers that summarized the primary financial tasks they performed, and the motivations, behaviors, and frustrations associated with these tasks. From these personas, the team identified previously-unknown dimensions of the challenge the unbanked faced. The primary challenge was the enormous time it took—sometimes as much as a full day of travel and waiting—just to get cash and make a payment.

With this new understanding of the unbanked customer problem, coupled with knowing that nearly all Colombians have mobile phones, the team conceived of a different solution—a mobile phone-based wallet that would allow customers to send and receive payments from merchants without ever needing to visit a branch or use an ATM card. But there were still challenges. Even with their efforts to recognize unknown unknowns, the Davivienda team had to resolve now-known sources of uncertainty. As DaviPlata's executive director Juan Carlos Rojas Serrano observed, "DaviPlata was born without knowing exactly the scope of what we were about to embrace." The team has since resolved these uncertainties and the DaviPlata product has been adopted by hundreds of thousands of Colombians and rolled out to neighboring countries.[17]

What this discussion of expertise and unk-unks tells us is that, when facing complex business problems, having experience and expertise in the domain of the problem can be helpful, but there are limitations. Probably the most important limitation is that experience and expertise can create an illusion of understanding. In facing complex problems with unknown unknowns, experts may not recognize their ignorance and instead assume they know all they need to tackle the problem. As the Davivienda example suggests, such an approach can lead to poor solutions. Research shows that expertise can lead to overconfidence in the assessment of difficult decisions, exacerbating the WYSIATI tendency of fast thinking, and resulting in an unwillingness to investigate and analyze the problem. Expertise is necessary for complex business problem solving, but not sufficient.

The Need for a Disciplined Problem-Solving Process

If we can't rely solely on experts and expertise to solve complex business problems, what else can we do? Psychological research suggests raw intellectual horsepower can help. In a recent comprehensive analysis of 47 studies involving nearly 14,000 participants, people's general intelligence explained almost one-fifth of the variation in their effectiveness at solving complex problems.[18] While intelligence matters, over 80 percent of complex problem-solving effectiveness is explained by other factors—smarter is better, but it isn't enough. This helps to explain why management consulting firms don't just strive to hire smart people and develop their expertise in specific areas, but also invest considerable resources in building their problem-solving skills through formal training and on-the-job coaching.

The ability to solve complex business problems is essential for managers and consultants and the organizations that employ them. This capability will become more important and valuable as organizations increasingly rely on fluid, cross-functional, and multi-disciplinary teams to tackle new business challenges. Even if your organizational context remains a traditional functional one, it's likely that at some point you'll be asked to lead or participate in a cross-functional problem-solving effort (if you haven't done so already). Your career success may depend on how well you contribute to solving such complex problems—your functional expertise, while valuable, won't be sufficient.

Because of the insufficiency of expertise and intelligence for complex problem solving, it may not be surprising that organizations find it difficult to recruit people with this skill set. Recruiters polled by the *Financial Times* consistently rank "the ability to solve complex problems" among the top five skills that matter most in MBA graduates.[19] Bloomberg (publisher of *Bloomberg Businessweek*) surveyed organizations that recruit MBA graduates and found that, across the industries surveyed, the second-biggest skills gap recruiters faced was with candidates' problem-solving skills.[20] Another survey of company recruiters showed that the biggest skills gap in new college graduates was in problem solving and critical thinking.[21] Organizations need effective complex problem solvers, but they tell us that our schools and universities aren't adequately developing this competency.

It's unlikely that technology will help us overcome this skills gap. Although technologies help us with many challenging problems, rapid advances in big data analytics, artificial intelligence (AI), and robotics won't make problem-solving skills any less relevant or important. Many analysts are predicting the opposite. Rather than substitute for human labor and jobs, automation enabled by big data, AI, and robotics is likely to place a bigger premium on human problem solving. The World Economic Forum's 2015 Future of Jobs Report predicted that 36 percent of all jobs across all industries would require complex problem solving as one of their core skills by 2020—by far the most important skill identified in the report.[22] The OECD Adult Survey data shows a similar increase in the demand for complex problem-solving skills across professions and countries.[23] Now and into the future, the ability to solve difficult problems and communicate their solutions will only increase in importance and value.

If expertise, intelligence, and technology aren't enough for solving complex business problems, then how can we do better? There isn't much we can do in the short term about our expertise, and even less we can do about our general intelligence. When we face non-routine complex problems, we can't rely solely on our expertise. We need to know *how* to reason, in a generalizable way, to solve complex problems, without falling prey to analysis paralysis. We also need to harness expertise and intelligence and overcome our powerful temptation to jump to ill-informed solutions. What we need is a disciplined and generalizable problem-solving method and a set of useful tools for each step of the process.

A disciplined method can help. Strategy consultants turn rookies into trusted advisors and then into CEOs partly by teaching them robust, general-purpose problem-solving techniques. Research confirms that solving problems isn't just a matter of raw intellectual horsepower: an analysis of 70 studies that investigated the influence of training methods on creative problem solving found that providing training in specific processes and techniques improved problem-solving performance.[24] Following a method matters for problem-solving performance.

*   *   *

Decades of social science research has identified a set of barriers to effective problem solving. If we want to be better at it, then we must understand these impediments and how to overcome them. In the next chapter, we'll introduce you to the most pernicious pitfalls of problem solving. In Chap. 3, we'll present a method to help you defeat them, and in later chapters, we'll walk you through how to use the method.

Chapter 1 in One Page

- Like our thinking, our problem solving can be "fast" or "slow":

  - *Fast: WYSIATI ("What You See Is All There Is"); associative thinking; stories*
  - *Slow: logical; skeptical; methodical; investigative*

- Many business problem solvers over-rely on "fast" thinking and quickly jump to an apparently coherent interpretation of the situation and a possible solution:

  - *The new CEO looked like he was to blame for Dell's problems, but when you consider the case carefully …*
  - *Othello kills Desdemona because he jumps to the conclusion she is unfaithful.*

- The opposite problem, "analysis paralysis," is dangerous too:

  - *Hamlet hesitates to avenge his father.*

- Expertise ≠ problem solving: experts rely on mental models from their domain of expertise, but can fail to recognize the limits of their expertise and become "trapped by expertise" when conditions change.

- Complex, ill-defined problems usually contain important unknowns we know of …

  - *Banco Davivienda invested heavily in understanding the needs of the unbanked.*

- … and some we're not aware of:

  - *There are things we don't know that we don't know, "unknown unknowns."*

- Human resource leaders and recruiters consider complex problem-solving skills essential:

  - *IQ explains only one-fifth of variance in problem-solving effectiveness.*
  - *Problem-solving skills will be more, not less, essential in the future.*

- Therefore, mastering an effective problem-solving method is a key asset.

Notes

1. Kahneman, D. (2011). *Thinking, Fast and Slow*. New York: Farrar, Straus and Giroux.
2. Evans, J.St.B.T. (2003). In Two Minds: Dual Process Accounts of Reasoning. *TRENDS in Cognitive Sciences*, *7*(10), 454–459.
3. Grant, A. (2016). *Originals: How Non-Conformists Move the World*. New York: Viking.
4. Mintzberg, H. (1973). *The Nature of Managerial Work*. New York: Harper & Row.
5. Zenger, J., & Folkman, J. (2014, July 30). The Skills Leaders Need at Every Level. *Harvard Business Review Online*. Retrieved from https://hbr. org/2014/07/the-skills-leaders-need-at-every-level.
6. Organisation for Economic Co-operation and Development. (2016). *The Survey of Adult Skills: Reader's Companion, Second Edition*. Paris: OECD.
7. Christensen, C.M., Dina D., & van Bever, D. (2013). Consulting on the Cusp of Disruption. *Harvard Business Review, 91*(10), 106–115.
8. Davis, I., Keeling, D., Schreier, P., & Williams, A. (2007). *The McKinsey Approach to Problem Solving*. McKinsey Staff Paper, No. 66. July.
9. Pretz, J.E., Naples, A.J., & Sternberg, R.J. (2003). Recognizing, Defining and Representing Problems. In J.E. Davidson & R.J. Sternberg (Eds.), *The Psychology of Problem Solving* (pp. 3–28). Cambridge, UK: Cambridge.
10. Nokes, T.J., Schunn, C.D., & Chi, M.T.H. (2010). Problem Solving and Human Expertise. *International Encyclopedia of Education, 5,* 265–272.
11. Marchant, G., Robinson, J., Anderson, U., & Schadewald, M. (1991). Analogical Transfer in Legal Reasoning. *Organizational Behavior and Human Decision Processes, 48*(2), 272–290.
12. Dane, E. (2010). Reconsidering the Tradeoff Between Expertise and Flexibility: A Cognitive Entrenchment Perspective. *Academy of Management Review, 35*(4), 579–603.
13. Wiley, J. (1998). Expertise as Mental Set: The Effects of Domain Knowledge in Creative Problem Solving. *Memory & Cognition, 26*(4), 716–730.
14. Gavetti, G., Levinthal, D.A., & Rivkin, J.W. (2005). Strategy Making in Novel and Complex Worlds: The Power of Analogy. *Strategic Management Journal, 26*(5), 691–712.
15. Feduzi, A., & Runde, J. (2014). Uncovering Unknown Unknowns: Towards a Baconian Approach to Management Decision-Making. *Organizational Behavior and Human Decision Processes, 124*(2), 268–283.
16. Graham, D.A. (2014, March 27). Rumsfeld's Knowns and Unknowns: The Intellectual History of a Quip. *The Atlantic*. Retrieved from https://www. theatlantic.com/politics/archive/2014/03/rumsfelds-knowns-and-unknowns-the-intellectual-history-of-a-quip/359719/.

17. Furr, N., & Dyer, J. (2014). *The Innovator's Method*. Boston: Harvard Business Review Press.

Rojas Serrano, J.C. (2012). DaviPlata: 'Self-Service' Financial Inclusion. In *Management Innovation eXchange*. Retrieved from http://www.managementexchange.com/story/daviplata-financial-inclusion-all-using-self-service-transactional-product-going-kyc-kyc-know-

18. Stadler, M., Becker, N., Gödker, M., Leutner, D., & Greiff, S. (2015). Complex Problem Solving and Intelligence: A Meta-Analysis. *Intelligence, 53*, 92–101.

19. Moules, J., & Nilsson, P. (2017, August 31). What Employers Want from MBA Graduates – and What they Don't. *Financial Times*. Retrieved from https://www.ft.com/content/3c380c00-80fc-11e7-94e2-c5b903247afd.

20. Levy, F., & Cannon, C. (2016, February 9). The Bloomberg Job Skills Report: What Recruiters Want. *Bloomberg Business Week*. Retrieved from https://www.bloomberg.com/graphics/2016-job-skills-report/.

21. PayScale Human Capital. (2016). *2016 Workforces Skills-Preparedness Report*. Retrieved from https://www.payscale.com/data-packages/job-skills.

22. World Economic Forum. (2016). *The Future of Jobs: Employment, Skills and Workforce Strategy for the Fourth Industrial Revolution*. Retrieved from http://www3.weforum.org/docs/WEF_Future_of_Jobs.pdf.

23. Organisation for Economic Co-operation and Development. (2016). *op. cit.*

24. Scott, G., Leritz, L.E., & Mumford, M.D. (2004). The Effectiveness of Creativity Training: A Quantitative Review. *Creativity Research Journal, 16*(4), 361–388.

2

The Five Pitfalls of Problem Solving

As Chap. 1 demonstrates, spontaneous approaches to solving problems can end badly, especially when we rely on assumptions we don't question (or even acknowledge), and jump to conclusions. In this chapter, we use five real-life cases to explore the primary pitfalls of assumption-based problem solving.

Case 1: When the Music Industry Went Out of Tune

Anyone old enough to have bought CDs probably remembers the first time they downloaded an MP3 file over the Internet. For most people, this took place in the last few years of the past century. As Witt wrote in his account of these years, *How Music Got Free*,[1] 1997 was the year MP3 file-sharing went viral among US college students. Napster, the website that made peer-to-peer file-sharing mainstream, debuted in 1999. One year later, it had 20 million users downloading 14,000 songs a minute. "MP3" had become the most searched-for term in Internet search engines, surpassing even "sex."

Even the least business-savvy observer could tell the business of music was under pressure, and the record industry wasn't blind to the threat. It fought an all-out battle against the file-sharing revolution. The first line of defense (and most vulnerable point of attack music executives discovered) was in the recording studios and CD manufacturing facilities. It had become shockingly frequent for a new album to be available on file-sharing sites weeks before its release in stores, something pirates could only accomplish if helped by insiders. The record companies took elaborate measures to reduce theft, including

© The Author(s) 2018
B. Garrette et al., *Cracked it!*, https://doi.org/10.1007/978-3-319-89375-4_2

airport-style security screenings for all plant employees leaving the work premises every day.

This proved ineffective. "Inside jobs" continued: one CD factory manager smuggled 2000 albums out of a North Carolina facility over eight years. Regardless, if anyone could walk into a record store at 8 a.m. on the day a CD was released, rip it, and post it online to the entire world minutes later, security measures were futile. The recording industry soon concluded it had to stop the file-sharing itself.

Since file-sharing was illegal, music executives did what honest citizens do in such a situation: they called in law enforcement. Unfortunately, despite intense lobbying, this produced no results. Neither the Department of Justice nor Congress seemed to have any appetite for siding with millionaire executives in prosecuting teenagers playing with computers in college dorms. It didn't help that the music industry was deeply unpopular on Capitol Hill, having mightily resisted Congress's attempts to regulate explicit lyrics. Recording studios were equally unconvincing in arguing that file-sharing was doing massive economic damage, given that in 2000, their revenues were still growing, and the highly concentrated recording industry remained hugely profitable. As a later investigation and settlement would reveal, this profitability was bolstered by illegal price collusion. The recording industry made an unconvincing victim.

Since playing defense didn't work, recording studios went on the offensive, despite the risk of alienating younger consumers. In 2000, they sued MP3 operators left and right. While the Recording Industry Association of America (RIAA), their industry association, sued manufacturers of MP3 players, 18 record companies jointly sued Napster.

This momentous lawsuit, *A&M Records vs. Napster*, ended in a clear legal victory for the record companies. The outcome came swiftly by the standards of legal battles, and in July 2001, Napster was unplugged. But it was a pyrrhic victory. The years 2000–09 were a "decade horribilis" for the record companies, who saw two-thirds of their revenues evaporate. The battle they had fought—and won—wasn't the right one.

Pitfall 1: Flawed Problem Definition

At the heart of this disaster was the way the music industry viewed file-sharing. To music executives, file-sharing was piracy, pure and simple. That it took place online didn't make it different from selling bootleg CDs in the night markets of Bangkok in the 1980s or trading homemade cassette tapes in the

1970s. Downloading MP3 files was theft on a grander scale than anything the industry had known before, and it called for harsher measures and greater resources. But it was the same old problem.

This assumption was implicit and industry executives didn't seriously question it. They framed the problem that MP3 and Internet technologies posed essentially as: "How do we stop (or drastically reduce) the illegal sharing of music files to protect the business of selling CDs?"

A very different and more productive question could have been: "How can we make money in a world where technology is changing the distribution of music?" One company—Apple—asked this question. When Apple launched the iPod in January 2001, followed by the iTunes store in 2003, it created a new business model for digital music distribution. The iTunes music store sold tracks, not albums, created a seamless and portable experience for consumers, and introduced digital rights management (DRM) to limit piracy. This didn't make piracy disappear, just as travelers' checks didn't eliminate bank robberies. But it created a large and profitable business. Sales of music downloads took off, peaking at $4 billion in 2012 (when they started to erode under the pressure of subscription-based alternatives such as Spotify and Tidal). The real business opportunity for Apple wasn't in the sale of music tracks, but of iPods: with over 50 million units sold annually from 2006 to 2010, Apple generated annual revenues of around $8 billion and laid the groundwork for the iPhone and its phenomenal success.

The music industry did briefly try to play this game, too. By 2002, the record labels made costly and short-lived attempts to launch music distribution services such as PressPlay and MusicNet. But even as they launched these services, their obsession with fighting piracy and protecting the sales of albums remained paramount: for instance, MusicNet downloads self-destructed after 30 days, and PressPlay didn't let you burn more than two tracks from the same artist to a CD. With such "stunningly brain-dead features," as *PC World* called them in its list of the "Worst Tech Products Ever Released," no wonder the services didn't take off.

The contrast between the record companies and Apple illustrates the importance of stating the right problem. The problem as the music industry defined it wasn't one it could solve. As soon as technology made it possible to compress a music track into a digital file of a few megabytes, and Internet access became widespread, it should have been clear that forcing consumers to buy entire albums for $14 was a dying business model. In the USA, CD sales fell from $18.2 billion in 2000 to $1.5 billion in 2015, a 92-percent drop. By failing to recognize the disruptive power of technology, music industry executives condemned themselves to solving the wrong problem and fighting the wrong battles.

Not that, had they defined the problem differently, the outcome would have been rosy. Under any scenario, the digital revolution would have reduced the total profit pool of the industry. But it is striking that industry incumbents sponsored none of the major business models that emerged. When you frame the question as an unsolvable problem, it's hard to see opportunities.

Flawed problem definition is the first pitfall of problem solving, and conversely, stating the problem effectively is the first step ("State") in the 4S problem-solving method we'll introduce in the next chapter. Chapter 4 expands on this to show you how to develop an effective problem statement.

Case 2: The Grameen–Danone Strengthening Yogurt

In October 2005, Franck Riboud, CEO of Danone, a multinational corporation with €13 billion revenues in dairy products, beverages, and baby food, had a lunch meeting in Paris with Professor Muhammad Yunus, father of the microfinance concept and head of Grameen Bank. Their conversation that day was memorable: Yunus mentioned it in his 2006 Nobel Prize acceptance speech and referred to it extensively in the prologue of his book *Creating a World Without Poverty*[2] to exemplify "the power of a handshake."

Yunus and Riboud discussed the problem of child malnutrition in poor communities, especially in Bangladesh, Yunus's homeland and one of the world's poorest countries. They realized that their two organizations could join forces to find innovative solutions. Danone produced high-quality and healthy food, especially for babies and children. Thanks to its leadership in nutrition-related R&D, Danone could develop an adequate and affordable product. Danone was also highly regarded for its strong commitment to corporate social responsibility. Grameen (which means "village" in Bengali) had no competence in food or nutrition, but had direct access to potential users. The Grameen Bank had extended its microfinance services to the poorest and most remote areas of the country, and Yunus's reputation as a hero of the poor was unquestionable. Grameen had diversified its activities in several other industries (e.g., in mobile telecom through Grameenphone). All Grameen branches were "social businesses"—philanthropic enterprises that generated "no loss nor dividend," but just enough to cover their operational costs. Riboud was open to try the social business approach in a country such as Bangladesh, where Danone didn't operate yet.

The Yunus–Riboud meeting led to the creation of a yogurt-producing joint venture called "Grameen Danone Foods Limited" (GDFL), the first example of a social business involving a multinational corporation.

Things moved fast after the initial October 2005 handshake. Within three days, a small team designed the business model for GDFL. Then, in March 2006, Franck Riboud traveled to Bangladesh and launched GDFL officially. Four months later, GDFL purchased a plot of land in Bogra, a city of 200,000 about 190 miles northwest of the capital Dhaka. After a triumphal plant inauguration featuring soccer superstar Zinedine Zidane, the venture produced its first yogurt in February 2007 under the Shoktidoi (strengthening yogurt) brand name.

The venture's performance, however, didn't live up to the founders' expectations.[3]

First, the choice of product proved problematic almost immediately. Shoktidoi is a dairy product, and its storage and transportation require refrigeration, which is a problem, given Bangladesh's climate and lack of infrastructure. Marketing a dry or stable grocery product that doesn't require refrigeration would have been more effective and efficient, but Danone had divested its biscuit and grocery businesses several years earlier, in a move to refocus on "healthier" dairy products. Another option was dried baby food, which Danone made, but thought selling it to poor women was too controversial and risky. European food companies still vividly remembered the mishaps of Nestlé with baby milk powder in developing countries some 30 years earlier. Nestlé had spent years recovering from accusations of deterring poor mothers from breastfeeding their babies.

Besides a lack of refrigeration, which made yogurt difficult to store and distribute, another challenge was that milk is considered almost a luxury item in Bangladesh. Both the supply and the price of milk are volatile, which made the cost of Shoktidoi too high and too unstable, making it too expensive for poor communities.

Customer perceptions were also problematic. Danone spent a lot on R&D to include the necessary nutrients in the product. Shoktidoi was to be marketed as a child nutrition solution whose benefits would appear only with regular use. However, parents bought the yogurt as an occasional and affordable treat, limiting its health impact. All things considered, yogurt was far from an optimal choice.

Marketing in rural areas was another challenge. Building on Grameen's microfinance experience (microloans are distributed by "Grameen ladies"),

GDFL created a team of independent female sales representatives—Shokti Ladies—to sell Shoktidoi door to door. The company believed this was the only way to reach poor communities in remote rural areas. Creating such a salesforce would also create jobs for poor women, further contributing to GDFL's poverty alleviation objective.

Danone executives quickly realized the Shokti Lady network was unsustainable. The number of women employed by GDFL varied dramatically, in line with variations in the supply of milk and the resulting changes in the product's price. While 273 Shokti Ladies were active in February 2008, only 17 remained in September of the same year. GDFL had to launch a new hiring campaign from scratch. Over the years, the rural salesforce remained weak and volatile, hovering around 500 Shokti Ladies from 2010 on. The underlying problem was that most Shokti Ladies didn't stay for long because they couldn't earn a decent living by selling Shoktidoi.

More fundamentally, the whole rural marketing initiative never took off. As early as 2008, GDFL marketed Shoktidoi through small general stores to increase sales volumes. In June 2009, shops accounted for 80 percent of sales of Shoktidoi. By using this distribution network, GDFL marketed to the urban middle class much more than to the rural poor. This allowed for higher prices and traditional marketing techniques, such as TV advertising campaigns and product extensions (e.g., flavored yogurts and drinks).

Thanks to this new revenue stream, GDFL developed the business slowly—but it never achieved its objectives of alleviating childhood malnutrition. In 2015, eight years after production started, and after several strategic reviews and reorganization initiatives, GDFL sold around 2000 tons of yogurt, which accounted for only two-thirds of the plant's capacity. Supermarkets in urban areas accounted for the vast majority of sales and the impact on poor communities was marginal.

Despite these outcomes, Danone and Grameen executives argue that GDFL is a success because of what they learned from this bold experiment. The mere existence of GDFL and Danone's commitment to its development triggered an intense wave of motivation in Danone employees. Creating and marketing products that contributed to the health of the greatest number of people became an integral part of Danone's strategy. The GDFL experience also paved the way for the creation of Danone Communities, a non-profit initiative sponsored by the company now considered one of the most successful social business networks worldwide.

Pitfall 2: Solution Confirmation

GDFL's difficulties didn't stem from a poorly defined problem. Both Yunus and Riboud set out to deal with a significant problem that was both well identified and well documented. According to the United Nations Children's Fund (UNICEF), nearly half of all deaths in children under five are attributable to malnutrition, which translates into the loss of about three million young lives every year.[4] This is a serious problem that is currently unsolved, but not unsolvable: data show that the number of malnourished children has declined significantly over the past 25 years.

Yunus and Riboud wisely made the problem manageable by focusing on a specific country, Bangladesh, and even on a particular region in the country where the problem was especially salient. When they considered the issue, 40 percent of children in Bangladesh suffered from stunted growth, one of the highest rates in the world. By limiting the scope of their joint venture, Yunus and Riboud narrowed down a significant global issue to a problem they could own. Danone also committed significant resources to the initiative and implemented GDFL at incredible speed—considerably faster than typical investment decisions.

On the flip side, this remarkable effectiveness drove GDFL into the *solution confirmation pitfall*. Rather than beginning with the problem—child nutrition—and analyzing it to find a relevant and cost-effective solution, Danone and Grameen started from the potential solutions they had to offer. The choice of sales channel was driven by the assumption that Grameen Bank's distribution system could be replicated for the venture. Despite the difficulties they experienced in using this approach, which challenged the validity of this belief, GDFL never gave up and tried to relaunch the same salesforce concept again and again. Similarly, on the product end, the assumption was that the solution was somewhere in Danone's existing product portfolio. No one seriously challenged this assumption. As baby food was deemed too risky, the only plausible option seemed to be yogurt. However, other options existed. A good example is ready-to-use therapeutic food (RUTF), which is now improving the lives of hundreds of thousands of African children under the aegis of both the World Health Organization (WHO) and the UNICEF.[5] The product—peanut butter mixed with dried skim milk, vitamins, and minerals—provides sufficient nutrient intake for complete nutrition recovery. It can be stored at home for three to four months without refrigeration, even at tropical temperatures.

Candidate solutions are powerful components of any problem-solving process. There is a difference between using them as hypotheses to be tested and simply assuming they're correct. In a rigorous problem-solving process, Yunus and Riboud's product and distribution solutions would have been viewed as working hypotheses to be validated using factual evidence. In this case, as in many others, a laudable action orientation and the sponsorship of senior executives conspired to turn these hypotheses into unchallenged beliefs. In the next chapter, we'll introduce the role of hypotheses and candidate solutions in the second step of the 4S problem-solving approach: "Structuring" problems. We'll discuss the pros and cons of hypothesis-driven problem structuring in Chap. 5 and consider an alternative approach using issue trees instead of hypotheses.

Case 3: The Call Center Story

As human resource (HR) director of CallCo, a large operator of call centers, Lisa[6] faced a tough problem: how could she find good people?

For CallCo, as for most talent-driven companies, recruiting was an arduous process. Ads had to be placed, resumes sorted, tests organized, and interviews held. At the end of this process, fewer than 10 percent of the applicants received an offer, and even fewer joined. To keep up with its planned growth, CallCo was continually raising its targets and increasing the size and scope of its recruiting.

Lisa saw several problems. Her first concern was with the quality of the hiring decisions. While experienced call-center supervisors conducted multiple interviews, they would often disagree on a candidate, and there was no sure-fire way to tell whose judgment was better. As a sophisticated HR professional, Lisa knew that decades of academic research showed that interviews are poor predictors of on-the-job success. She knew there must be a better way.

Second, Lisa saw signs that the company's recruiting might be biased: she couldn't miss the fact that the proportion of minorities CallCo recruited was much lower than in its pool of applicants. This raised the disturbing possibility that CallCo wasn't only missing good talent, but exposing itself to reputational and legal challenges if it was discriminating against minority candidates.

Lisa's third concern was equally important—and even more urgent: the cost of recruiting and training people was out of control. The recruiting process itself was expensive, mostly because of the time supervisors had to dedicate to interviews. Then, once they joined, operators had to undergo a period of training and on-the-job coaching before they could be productive. The problem was that many of the new hires didn't stay long enough for CallCo to recoup the cost of hiring and training them. With a staff turnover of over 30 percent (and even more among new hires), CallCo wasted almost half of its investment on people who didn't stay.

After some research, Lisa identified that BigHRData, a provider of HR analytics solutions, offered a promising solution to her problem. BigHRData's model relied on an online personality questionnaire submitted to applicants. The same personality profile would be administered to CallCo's employees, both new and more seasoned. Using machine-learning algorithms, BigHRData could then discern the personality traits associated with a longer tenure in the company—and select applicants with those characteristics. As more applicants and new hires populated the database, the algorithms would become smarter at predicting who would stay and who would go, helping CallCo get better at selecting the right people.

This solution had the potential to address all three of the problems Lisa had identified. By using BigHRData's models as a first filter before the interview process began, CallCo's supervisors would meet with higher rated interviewees, reducing the number of interviews per offer. Using data, as opposed to the manual screening of resumes, ensured an unbiased selection, which provided a solid line of defense against potential accusations of discrimination. Most important, BigHRData had impressive references from companies who had implemented its solution and who had achieved an increase in the one-year retention rate of new hires.

Pitfall 3: Wrong Framework

Lisa wondered whether she should join the long list of BigHRData's clients. But something troubled her. After some thinking, she put her finger on it— BigHRData was forcing her to think of the problem in a specific way, to use a specific lens: it offered a *framework* to address the HR issue, and this framework used unstated, disputable assumptions.

The first assumption is that an online personality questionnaire measures something meaningful—personality. Not all personality tests are reliable: with some tests, if the same person takes them twice, the result may be very different. Another issue is whether applicants can easily game the desired personality traits and the questionnaires that measure them.

Even if personality can be reliably measured through a quick online test, BigHRData's approach implies a second assumption: that personality is an important driver of the high turnover at CallCo. Employees may be leaving CallCo for many reasons: because the pay is too low, or their supervisor is a poor manager, or they found a better job somewhere else … Shouldn't Lisa explore these possibilities before she buys into the idea that employee personality predicts tenure at CallCo?

Lisa's focus—her problem statement—centers on the recruiting process, not on the reduction of turnover. But if a solution is predicated on a link between recruiting and turnover, the assumptions about that link should be explicit. It's possible there is a correlation between certain personality traits and tenure at CallCo. The data BigHRData is processing is probably not meaningless. But by focusing *exclusively* on that link, BigHRData's solution is adopting a framework—a way of reasoning—that links personality to outcomes such as tenure at CallCo. To choose this framework is to exclude other causal factors from the analysis—factors that may be much more important.

To discover these factors, Lisa conducted exit interviews with employees leaving CallCo. She found that the leavers unanimously found their jobs at CallCo deeply unsatisfactory, due to low pay, poor working conditions, and brutal management. According to those leaving, employees who remained at CallCo shared this dim view—but just couldn't secure a better job elsewhere.

Although she was reluctant to draw conclusions from a few interviews, Lisa thought about what BigHRData's personality model would recommend in this context. If it worked as advertised, it would identify the personality traits of those CallCo employees that no other employer wanted to hire, and look for these same traits in different applicants! This could result in lower turnover, which might account for the success of the model in other companies. But what would it do to job performance—a factor that had been, so far, absent from the discussion? How would it affect CallCo's ability to develop some of its operators, over time, into supervisors and managers? Was this the solution Lisa was looking for, or would it do more harm than good?

Using the wrong framework—the mistake Lisa narrowly avoided—is the third pitfall of problem solving. In this example, as in most other business situations, *different frameworks* can be applied to the same problem. The assumption implicit in BigHRData's framework is that "job tenure is a function of personality." The alternative Lisa formulated after her exit interviews assumes instead that "job tenure is driven by multiple factors, including job satisfaction." While these aren't mutually exclusive, they can lead to very different conclusions.

Frameworks are like theories—they're a way of seeing and understanding our world. They carry with them implicit assumptions about what causes what. They tell us what to pay attention to in a particular situation—what variables are important—and they provide us with a story to explain and understand it. But frameworks, like theories, have an insidious nature: by suggesting what we should attend to, they also tell us what to ignore. Frameworks frame reality. We see and pay attention to what's in the frame(work), but ignore what's outside of it. As the literary theorist and philosopher Kenneth Burke put it, "A way of seeing is also a way of not seeing."[7] Our choice of frameworks can blind us to important aspects of a problem, leading us to develop ineffective and costly solutions.

This cognitive bias goes by at least two names: "the law of the instrument," coined by Abraham Kaplan[8] (another philosopher), and "Maslow's hammer," after the eminent psychologist Abraham Maslow (of "the hierarchy of needs" fame). Maslow captured the essence of the bias when he stated, "I suppose it is tempting, if the only tool you have is a hammer, to treat everything as if it were a nail."[9]

The key point the CallCo story illustrates is that we must recognize the assumptions implicit in the conceptual frameworks we use to understand and solve problems. If we don't, the pitfall we face is allowing our problem-solving efforts to be led astray by the wrong frameworks. Because frameworks are a crucial tool in structuring business problems, we'll devote a second chapter—Chap. 6—to the "Structure" step of the 4S method.

Case 4: New Strategy at J.C. Penney

On June 14, 2011, the American department store chain J.C. Penney announced that Ron Johnson, head of Apple's wildly successful retail stores, would become Penney's new CEO.[10] The stock market reacted to the news with glee by bidding up Penney's share price 17.5 percent, adding over $1 billion to its market capitalization. Johnson had been brought in to turn around the ailing retailer, which saw its sales steadily erode from their peak in 2006 and its razor-thin return on sales bounce between 1 percent and 3 percent compared to the 4–5 percent returns generated by its rivals. As a result, Penney's stock price had fallen to $30 per share just before the announcement from a high of $82 in March 2007.

Johnson began his tenure as CEO on November 1, 2011, and quickly pursued dramatic changes. His solution to Penney's declining fortunes consisted of two pillars, which would be reflected in a rebranding initiative. First, Johnson would eliminate Penney's obsession with sales promotions and price discounts—there were nearly 600 sales in 2011 alone—and replace it with a simple, everyday low-pricing approach. Messy clearance racks and confusing price tags would be eliminated. Second, Johnson would transform Penney's from a crowded and cluttered department store selling many of its own labels organized by product category, such as "men's suits," to a collection of 100 boutiques spaciously organized by brand, such as Levi's and Martha Stewart, with a kind of town square in the middle. As part of this makeover, store employees were encouraged to dress in their own style and many were outfitted with hand-held checkout devices. The company communicated these dramatic changes as part of a major rebranding effort. It unveiled an updated corporate logo in which "J.C. Penney" became "jcp," launched an aggressive ad campaign emphasizing Penney's new "fair and square pricing," and embarked on a direct marketing campaign using style guides that highlighted new trends and ensembles of different brands.

These changes represented a dramatic departure from what Penney's customers expected from the century-old retailer. Johnson publicly unveiled them at a jcp launch gala held in New York City in January 2012. To implement this new strategic vision, he would invest hundreds of millions of dollars. The return on this investment became clear in February 2013 when Penney's announced its 2012 results. They were awful. The firm's revenues had plunged by $4.3 billion from the previous year, and same-store sales had fallen 25 percent. Penney's recorded a $1 billion loss, and its stock price fell to $18, less than half its value from the year before. Cash on hand dropped from $1.5 billion to $930 million, leading Standard & Poor's to cut the company's debt rating to CCC+, deep in junk bond territory. By April 2013 Johnson was out as CEO, only 18 months after he started. He was replaced by the CEO he had replaced—Mike Ullman—who quickly rolled back Johnson's changes.

Pitfall 4: Narrow Framing

What went wrong? Probably many things, but the problem definition pitfall doesn't appear to be among them. Johnson had over two decades of experience in managing national retailers, likely giving him an intuitive understanding of the key drivers of performance. The board of directors had examined J.C. Penney's performance problem before Johnson's arrival and concluded that Johnson's profile fit the bill. This suggests they agreed the company needed a complete overhaul of the consumer proposition and a new CEO to implement it. It seems plausible that Penney's truly needed a strategic turn-around, starting with a redesign of the in-store experience.

There are clear signs that Johnson fell into the solution confirmation trap. Both his merchandising strategy—branded products sold at undiscounted prices in cool-looking stores—and the way he promoted it, with Steve Jobs-style keynote speeches, seem lifted from the Apple playbook. And once his mind was set on making this Apple-style strategy work for J.C. Penney, Johnson paid no attention to signs it was failing. Those who questioned the strategy or advised him to slow down its execution were dismissed, because, Johnson assured, "skepticism takes the oxygen out of innovation." Skeptics had, however, ample reason to be worried: the company missed its sales targets in the first quarter of 2012, saw a 19.7 percent stock price drop in a single day in May, was criticized in June by analysts who claimed consumers didn't understand the pricing strategy, and saw archrival Macy's gleefully announce market share gains and record profits. It took a real believer to ignore the alarm bells ringing and stay the course. Clearly, Johnson was one.

If Johnson's bold strategy had succeeded, we would, in hindsight, celebrate his courage and steadfastness in imposing it. Sure, the CEO was passionate about the strategy and relentless in his desire to execute it aggressively: isn't that the leadership any ambitious strategic transformation requires? The real issue isn't *how* Johnson pursued the strategy, it's that the strategy just didn't work.

This is puzzling. Johnson was an experienced, highly successful retail executive, described by some press reports as "an industry icon" who "turns anything he touches to gold." When he moved to J.C. Penney, he left a lucrative job leading the retail arm of the world's most admired company, betting his career, his reputation, and some of his fortune (Johnson invested $50 million in J.C. Penney warrants) in the process. How could such an extraordinary player place such a huge bet on a strategy that was so wrong?

Press reports shed some light on this mystery. Johnson may have correctly identified the problem as one of consumer appeal, but he spent little time and effort investigating its causes. Outgoing CEO Ullman noted in an update to Penney's board of directors that Johnson hadn't asked a single question about how the business was operating when they met. Johnson decided from the start that the crux of Penney's issue was its consumer proposition. But why, exactly, were consumers dissatisfied with J.C. Penney? What did they like and dislike about the store? It seems Johnson didn't know and didn't try to find out. In 2012, Johnson told *Businessweek* magazine: "I thought people were just tired of coupons and all this stuff. The reality is all of the couponing we did, there were a certain part of the customers that loved that ... So our core customer, I think, was much more dependent and enjoyed coupons more than I understood." That the CEO of J.C. Penney didn't understand that its core customers loved coupons and discounts demonstrates his understanding of the problem was, at best, superficial.

Perhaps Johnson, under time pressure, decided he had no time to learn everything about the preferences of his consumers. Even if that were true, Johnson could have deployed his new strategy in a gradual, learn-as-you-go manner, for instance, by running small-scale pilot tests in a few stores to gauge customer acceptance of his everyday low-pricing and boutique-centric format. Johnson, however, acknowledged no uncertainty about his solution. He just assumed he was right and moved quickly to implement the new approach nationwide, spending nearly $120 million on the Levi's boutiques alone according to one press report. Asked if he would test these ideas before rolling them out, Johnson reportedly scoffed, "We didn't test at Apple."

Johnson's misfortune illustrates the *narrow framing pitfall*. When we tackle a complex and multifaceted problem that we superficially understand, it can seem intractably broad. In these cases, it's tempting to frame the problem narrowly to make it look like one we've worked on before. We can then reason by (superficial) analogy to quickly identify a solution instead of investing in thoroughly understanding the problem. Although this approach to generating a solution is efficient, it can have disastrous consequences, as it did in the case of Ron Johnson and J.C. Penney.

Johnson ignored his superficial understanding of Penney's customers and quickly jumped to an Apple-inspired solution—undiscounted, branded merchandise sold in a hip setting by quirky salespeople supported by a fresh, minimalist brand. The assumption, which proved to be wrong, was that Penney's customers are similar to Apple Store customers. This assumption also explains why Johnson didn't see a need to pilot-test his solution. If Apple Store and Penney's customers are similar, what worked at Apple will work at J.C. Penney. Johnson's faith in the validity of his assumption seems to have blinded him to the downside risk of his solution.

When we face complex, human-centered problems that we understand poorly, such as the one Ron Johnson faced at Penney's, we should avoid framing them by analogy with others situations. Instead, we should invest in understanding problems from the perspective of the people who experience them. Doing so can help us identify opportunities for solutions that we would otherwise miss. We should also resist the temptation to zero in on one solution, and instead generate multiple potential solutions to the problem at hand. We can then avoid "betting the farm" on one idea that may not work by prototyping and testing potential solutions to identify the best one.

The design thinking path to problem solving, which we'll introduce in the next chapter, addresses these objectives. In Chaps. 8 and 9, we'll explore the design thinking process in depth and show how it relates to the "State," "Structure," and "Solve" stages of the 4S method.

Case 5: A Fat Chance for Sugar

Research shows the main cause of obesity, diabetes, and coronary heart disease is the overconsumption of sugar—not fat. British scientist John Yudkin made this discovery in the late 1950s. He made the point public in his book *Pure, White and Deadly*,[11] which received significant attention in the 1970s, although policy-makers largely ignored his findings. When Yudkin died in 1995, his research had long been forgotten.[12]

In 2009, Robert Lustig, a pediatric endocrinologist at the University of California San Francisco, surfaced Yudkin's work in a video titled "Sugar: The Bitter Truth."[13] In a 90-minute talk that garnered over 7.6 million views on YouTube, Lustig summarizes his research and offers a compelling demonstration that fructose, a form of sugar ubiquitous in packaged foods and soft drinks, is the "poison" that is causing the worldwide obesity epidemic. While Yudkin's prophetic book presented the same insights, Lustig admitted he'd never heard of Yudkin before completing his research.

Meanwhile, for 40 years, nutritionists and public health authorities issued dietary guidelines focused on reducing saturated fat consumption and downplayed the role of sugar. The evidence that obesity, diabetes, and heart disease were on the rise despite significant cuts in the consumption of meat, butter, eggs, and cheese in most developed countries didn't disrupt the consensus view that fat was bad. While everyone was arguing openly against fat, which is relatively innocuous, the packaged food and beverage industry was surreptitiously saturating our diet with harmful sugar. Today, nutritionists struggle to reverse a health disaster they didn't predict and actually might have precipitated.

So, how did they get it so wrong for so long? One of the main reasons is that the correct story was communicated awkwardly, while the erroneous story was communicated persuasively.

First, the wrong story was simpler to understand, which made it easier to tell and sell. Most of us intuitively trust the claim that you get fatter if you eat more fat. The semi-scientific version of the same story is that a calorie is a calorie, no matter where it comes from, so you get fat because you overeat, no matter what you eat, and don't exercise enough.[14] This belief is wrong since some food items, such as alcohol and sugar, are addictive and don't satiate hunger, making them much more harmful than others. Behind the scenes, food and beverage companies, who widely introduced high-fructose corn syrup in their products (soft drinks in particular), fueled this misconception by funding studies that confounded the impact of fructose with a larger set of dietary factors that correlate with obesity and sickness.

Second, empirical evidence and shrewd communication supported the fat hypothesis, which helped it gain traction in both the scientific community and the political sphere. The story began in the mid-1950s, when US President Eisenhower suffered a heart attack. Unlike most politicians, Eisenhower insisted on making his illness public. His chief physician gave a press conference, instructing Americans on how to avoid heart disease: stop smoking and cut down on fat and cholesterol. This advice was rooted in the research of University of Minnesota professor Ancel Keys, who posited that an excess of saturated fats raises cholesterol, which clogs coronary arteries, leading to heart disease.[15]

Keys was brilliant, charismatic, and combative. The US president and his physician publicly supported his views. This combination led to persuasive communication at a crucial moment. The epidemic of heart disease was gaining momentum, especially among middle-aged men. Doctors and patients were relieved to hear that a simple and practical solution would solve the problem. The scientific community called for Keys to validate his hypothesis. To do so, he gathered data on the health and diet of 12,770 middle-aged men in Italy, Greece, Yugoslavia, Finland, the Netherlands, Japan, and the USA from 1958 to 1964. Although the resulting "Seven Countries Study" seemed to confirm his hypothesis, it may have been one of the first misuses of "big data" in scientific history. The study suffered from serious limitations. First, the choice of countries was flawed. While including five countries from Continental Europe, Keys left out the two largest: France and West Germany, which both exhibited a relatively low prevalence of coronary heart disease despite a diet rich in saturated fats. Second, while Keys found a correlation between dietary fat and heart disease, he couldn't establish causation or rule out other possible causes.

Keys was effective at convincing other scientists and policy-makers. He was also clever at gaining institutional support and power. He placed his allies in the most influential societies and associations in the American healthcare community, which made him able to direct research funding in the direction he wanted. His hypothesis became a dogma. The US Congress created a committee that issued dietary guidelines based on Keys's results. These guidelines spawned offspring in most Western countries. For the first time in the history of nutrition, governments told their citizens not to have a balanced diet (i.e., eat reasonable quantities of everything), but to ban (or at least reduce) the intake of a particular nutrient.

A third explanation for the widespread belief that dietary fat, not sugar, caused obesity and heart disease was Yudkin's relative lack of persuasiveness in the way he communicated the rival theory that incriminated sugar. This wasn't due to lack of status or credibility. Yudkin was internationally recognized as the UK's leading nutritionist. The US congressional committee in charge of creating dietary guidelines even auditioned him! But he failed to convince them and most other institutions.

Yudkin's core argument was relatively straightforward. He knew that people had been carnivorous since the beginning of humankind, and that even breast milk was rich in saturated fat, which never generated wide-scale health problems. In contrast, refined sugar had been part of people's diets for only a few hundred years, which made it a better suspect to explain modern health disorders.

However, the underpinning theory that linked sugar to sickness was more difficult to convey. It rested on insights from biochemistry and was counter-intuitive: how can sugar generate more harmful fat in the body than fat itself? Understanding this paradox required advanced knowledge in biology, chemistry, and anatomy.[16] The empirical evidence also came from cumbersome laboratory experiments rather than from large sample studies.

Ancel Keys compounded the communication problem by fighting his rival ruthlessly. He called Yudkin's theory "a mountain of nonsense," and accused him of issuing "propaganda" for the meat and dairy industries. He ridiculed both the man and his findings. Yudkin never responded in kind. He was soft-spoken and mild-mannered, unskilled in the art of controversy and political combat. His writing was fastidious, precise, and undemonstrative. He was an excellent scientific investigator, but much less adept at telling a compelling story.

The convincing story came four decades later, thanks to Lustig's video, a masterpiece of scientific communication that emphasizes simple and striking messages. Lustig starts by making his counterintuitive conclusion very clear. He then debunks the rival theory rationally and effectively. He uses compelling examples and metaphors to bolster his message. For example, he shows that sugar is almost as harmful as alcohol (a sugar derivative, chemically speaking), and asks the audience whether they would give a Budweiser instead of a Coke to their kids. Lustig dives into the details of his scientific demonstration through somewhat complicated charts, but never loses sight of the big picture and his core message. Finally, he discusses the economic and political implications of his view and ends with a call to arms against the evil of sugar. A great video!

Pitfall 5: Miscommunication

This example illustrates the crucial importance of communication for motivating action. Being right isn't enough. Solving the problem is worthless if you can't convince decision-makers to adopt the solution. Yudkin's example shows that poor communication of a good recommendation leads to frustration, wasted time, and inaction.

This happens far too often in organizations. How many consulting reports have been skeptically received, then archived and forgotten, producing no tangible impact? Was the recommendation irrelevant or was it poorly communicated? Who knows—and does it matter? An unconvincing recommendation is as ineffective as an irrelevant solution.

This isn't a novel idea; advice abounds on how to communicate ideas effectively. While Yudkin's failure illustrates the perils of poorly communicating the correct solution, Keys's example shows the opposite problem: how brilliant communication of the wrong answer is even more harmful than poor communication because it leads to misguided and even detrimental actions. This is why focusing on communication techniques in isolation from problem solving is a risky endeavor. While books and methods for improving business communication are plentiful and useful, the value of our approach rests in the connection between rigorous problem solving and convincing communication. Consequently, the fourth step in the 4S method is "Sell," which we'll cover in Chaps. 10 and 11.

* * *

Examples of experienced business people who make surprising and costly mistakes in problem solving abound. Most errors arise from one or several of the five pitfalls we've just discussed. First, a flawed problem definition can lead to irrelevant solutions. Second, the confirmation bias can lead problem solvers to believe a solution is valid without testing it and ignore evidence that it won't work. Third, choosing the wrong framework to understand a problem can blind us to important aspects of the issue, leading us to develop ineffective and costly solutions. Fourth, narrow problem framing can stimulate superficial analogies, resulting in inappropriate solutions. Finally, even if we overcome the first four pitfalls, valuable solutions don't sell themselves. A poorly communicated solution is as ineffective as an irrelevant solution. In the next chapter, we introduce the 4S method (State, Structure, Solve, and Sell) to help you overcome these pitfalls.

Chapter 2 in One Page

- Problem-solving pitfall 1: flawed problem definition:

  - *The music industry viewed file-sharing as piracy rather than a strategic disruption of music distribution. Defining the problem as "how to stop piracy" made it impossible to solve.*

- Pitfall 2: solution confirmation:

  - *Grameen–Danone joint venture: The two CEOs had a candidate solution that went unchallenged despite its obvious drawbacks.*

- Pitfall 3: wrong framework:

  - *To improve hiring decisions, the call center company is tempted to use machine-learning algorithms to select job applicants for the personality traits of current, longer-tenured employees. But does the underpinning framework, which links personality with tenure, favor better hiring decisions?*

- Pitfall 4: narrow problem framing:

  - *Ron Johnson failed in his bold strategy to revamp J.C. Penney department stores, framed by analogy with the Apple store.*

- Pitfall 5: miscommunication:

  - *As demonstrated in the "fat vs. sugar" example, poor communication of a good solution leads to frustration, waste of time, and inaction.*
  - *Brilliant communication of an erroneous idea can be even more harmful.*

Notes

1. Witt, S. (2015). *How Music Got Free: The End of an Industry, the Turn of the Century, and the Patient Zero of Piracy.* New York: Viking.
2. Yunus, M. (2007). *Creating a World Without Poverty: Social Business and the Future of Capitalism.* New York: Public Affairs.
3. Garrette, B., & Karnani, A. (2010). Challenges in Marketing Socially Useful Goods to the Poor. *California Management Review, 52*(4), 29–47.
4. UNICEF. (2017). *Undernutrition Contributes to Nearly Half of All Deaths in Children under 5 and Is Widespread in Asia and Africa.* Retrieved from http://data.unicef.org/topic/nutrition/malnutrition/#.
5. World Health Organization. (2016). *Maternal, Newborn, Child and Adolescent Health.* Retrieved from http://www.who.int/maternal_child_adolescent/topics/child/malnutrition/en/.
6. "Lisa" is a composite of several situations. Identifying details have been changed.
7. Burke, K. (1935). *Permanence and Change: An Anatomy of Purpose.* New York: New Republic Inc.
8. Kaplan, A. (1964). *The Conduct of Inquiry: Methodology for Behavioral Science.* San Francisco: Chandler Publishing Co.
9. Maslow, A.H. (1966). *The Psychology of Science.* New York: Harper & Row. p. 15.
10. Sources for the JC Penney story include: Reingold, J. (2014, March 20). How to Fail in Business While Really, Really Trying. *Fortune.com.* Retrieved from http://fortune.com/2014/03/20/how-to-fail-in-business-while-really-really-trying/.

    Reingold, J. (2012, March 7). Ron Johnson: Retail's New Radical. *Fortune.com.* Retrieved from http://fortune.com/2012/03/07/ron-johnson-retails-new-radical/.

    Martin, S. (2011, May 19). How the Apple Stores Model of Retail Defied the Odds. *USA Today.* Retrieved from https://usatoday30.usatoday.com/tech/news/2011-05-18-apple-retail-stores_n.htm.
11. Yudkin, J. (1972). *Pure, White, and Deadly: How Sugar Is Killing Us and What We Can Do to Stop It.* London: Penguin Books, reprint 2012.
12. Leslie, I. (2016, April 7). The Sugar Conspiracy. *The Guardian.* Retrieved from https://www.theguardian.com/society/2016/apr/07/the-sugar-conspiracy-robert-lustig-john-yudkin.
13. Lustig, R. (2009). *Sugar: The Bitter Truth.* University of California Television. Retrieved from https://www.youtube.com/watch?v=dBnniua6-oM.
14. Lustig, R. (2013, April 29). Still Believe a 'Calorie Is a Calorie'? *The Huffington Post.* Retrieved from https://www.huffingtonpost.com/robert-lustig-md/sugar-toxic_b_2759564.html.
15. Leslie, I. (2016, April 7). *op. cit.*
16. Lustig, R. (2012). *Fat Chance: The Hidden Truth about Sugar, Obesity, and Disease,* London: 4th Estate.

3

The 4S Method

How can we overcome the pitfalls described in the previous chapter to be better problem solvers and solution sellers? In this chapter, we'll introduce a process that can help. We call it the 4S method because it consists of four stages—State, Structure, Solve, and Sell. We'll explore these stages in Chaps. 4, 5, 6, 7, 8, 9, 10 and 11, and we'll apply the method to an actual case in Chap. 12.

Where Does the 4S Method Come from?

Before we introduce the 4S method, we'll explain its origin. If you're only interested in learning about the method instead of where it comes from, you can skip this section.

PSAC: The Problem-Solving Approach of Consulting

The core of the problem-solving method we present here has been developed and refined over many years by McKinsey & Co, one of the oldest and most respected strategy consulting firms, and emulated by other consultancies, such as Bain and the Boston Consulting Group.[1] The Problem-Solving Approach of Consulting (PSAC) isn't usually taught outside of consulting firms, and the ability of strategy consultants to "crack" tough business problems in unfamiliar fields is a large part of the consulting industry's mystique. Perhaps because of this mystique, some components of PSAC have found their way into everyday business lingo. Many executives are familiar with

© The Author(s) 2018
B. Garrette et al., *Cracked it!*, https://doi.org/10.1007/978-3-319-89375-4_3

terms such as "hypothesis-driven problem solving" or "MECE" problem decompositions (which we'll define in Chap. 5). University and business school students who practice "case cracking" hoping to impress consulting-firm interviewers also strive to become familiar with these tools, sometimes at the risk of focusing on isolated parts of the problem-solving approach without grasping its overall structure.

As its origin suggests, PSAC is a practical approach, and rarely makes its intellectual underpinnings explicit. These foundations are based on Aristotelian logic and Cartesian method and on their modern incarnations, including the practice of "critical thinking" taught in many universities. PSAC is grounded in pure logical reasoning: for instance, it assumes that facts are part of an objective reality, and that all honest observers will agree upon that reality once presented with the evidence. It assumes one thing can't be true if its opposite is true. It also presumes that causal links between events can be established and verified, and that the necessary and sufficient conditions for a proposition to be true can be identified (we'll discuss these in Chap. 5). These are principles with which the overwhelming majority of executives agree. Some epistemologists and cultural anthropologists may object, but, in our experience, very few CEOs do.

Logical thinking is a powerful tool in any setting, and business is no exception. By pushing their clients to formalize their reasoning, by rigorously testing the links in the causal chain of that reasoning, and by insisting on evidence to back up each link in that chain, strategy consultants—or any skilled user of formal logic—can sometimes overturn preconceived ideas or challenge accepted practices. Often, it's possible to conclusively prove, using logic and facts, that one course of action is inappropriate, or (less often) that one recommendation is demonstrably the best. Logic is a powerful way of communicating conclusions to a rational audience. This idea is reflected in the "pyramid principle" of communication, which we'll present in Chap. 10. In sum, PSAC is powerful, pragmatic, and tested. It provides a sound foundation for a general-purpose problem-solving approach.

PSAC does, however, suffer from some limitations. Two of these limitations have been the focus of serious challenge from other schools of thought. We'll briefly examine each.

Hypothesis-Driven Thinking and Cognitive Science

One of the tenets of formal logic is the concept of formulating and testing hypotheses. It is how scientists conduct scientific research: develop a hypothesis, grounded in theory; design an experiment to test it; and subject the results to challenge and debate with peers. PSAC borrows a page from the scientist's handbook and suggests that the method of choice to move the problem-solving effort forward efficiently is to formulate hypotheses, then test them. This approach is logically defensible and highly efficient: by zeroing in quickly on a possible solution, consultants avoid the painful process of exploring all the possible (but unlikely) answers, a trap they deride as "boiling the ocean." This is "hypothesis-driven problem solving," an approach that newcomers to consulting firms (and their clients) initially regard as disconcerting, but quickly find addictively powerful.

There is, however, a difficulty that practitioners of hypothesis-driven problem solving must overcome. Logic dictates you should be able to test hypotheses independently of the way they're formulated: it should not, in principle, make a difference whether you hypothesize that "this product will sell more than $100 million" or "this product will sell less than $100 million." Regardless of the formulation, the same evidence should lead you to the same conclusion. Proving a hypothesis and disproving its opposite are logically equivalent and should be practically identical.

Unfortunately, this neutrality is very difficult to achieve. As Francis Bacon put it in 1620, "Man prefers to believe what he prefers to be true."[2] William James echoed this when he wrote, "A great many people think they are thinking when they are merely rearranging their prejudices." This is what cognitive scientists call the *confirmation bias*.[3] Because of confirmation bias, we are much more likely to seek evidence that confirms our hypotheses and much more likely to believe such evidence once we find it, than we are to search for, and pay attention to, *disconfirming* evidence. The confirmation bias explains, for instance, why voters who support opposite parties can watch the same political debate and confidently conclude that "their" candidate has won: they unconsciously pay more attention to the points their preferred debater has scored and ignore the ones made by her opponent. This can severely distort our assessment of facts and mistakenly lead us to conclude our hypothesis was supported.

Consultants aren't immune to this bias, but they've developed at least three safeguards against it. First, as outsiders, they have, in principle, no vested interest in the recommendation: there may be a hypothesis on the table, but it's not *their* hypothesis. Being neutral doesn't eliminate confirmation bias, but being politically or financially biased would make it worse. Second, consultants work in teams and are trained to challenge one another. McKinsey's core values, for instance, include a "non-hierarchical atmosphere" and the "obligation to dissent." These guiding principles help ensure that a team member blind to his own confirmation biases will be called out by a colleague.

The spirit of collaboration that such social norms foster is an integral component of the problem-solving apparatus. Finally, consultants learn and practice PSAC continually. Rookies are taught that their task, once a hypothesis is formulated, is to work diligently to *either prove or disprove* it, with no preconceived idea of what the answer will be. Experienced consultants are regularly reminded of this. These safeguards don't guarantee that consultants won't fall in love with their own hypotheses. But the risk is much greater when the safeguards are removed. Our experience shows that when corporate executives attempt to apply this method in their companies—because they are former consultants or they've been trained by them—they often struggle with the challenge of fighting confirmation bias and its ramifications.

Consider, for instance, the case we introduced in the previous chapter involving Danone and Grameen, and put yourself in the shoes of an executive tasked with implementing the vision of the two CEOs. Can you see the flaw in the candidate solution? Maybe … but the odds are stacked against you. First, you're probably not a member of that team by accident: as a longtime employee selected for this high-visibility project, you may also believe in the vision of fresh dairy products as the remedy for child malnutrition. Second, it doesn't take a Machiavelli of corporate politics to realize that the CEOs' vision isn't a mere "hypothesis" to be skeptically challenged. In most organizations, there is no such thing as "a hypothesis to be proven or disproven"—proposals have proponents, precedents, and histories, and those who evaluate them know it. Third, as someone tasked with implementing the vision your bosses have put forward (and achieving its life-saving benefits), you're under considerable pressure, a condition that reduces your ability to think creatively.[4] Fourth, if you disproved the hypothesis, what would you do next? You'd have no report to write, no action to recommend, and perhaps no way of achieving the objectives assigned to you. Your criticism of the solution might even be regarded as an attempt to find excuses for not reaching the new business' growth targets. Finally, even if you were the lone skeptic on a team of true believers, you'd probably quickly decide that it's not your job to challenge other team members' confirmation biases, and just "go with the flow" despite your doubts—a powerful phenomenon sometimes called *groupthink.*[5]

The upshot is that hypothesis-driven problem solving is a powerful tool—so powerful it can be dangerous. It is, by design, a risky method that pushes us in a direction we are already prone to take. Outside of consulting firms—and sometimes within them—there is a real risk that it will lead to some of the pitfalls we described in Chap. 2, especially the "solution confirmation trap."

This is a difficult challenge to overcome, but there is an antidote—which is also part of PSAC. Alongside *hypothesis-driven* problem solving, many strategy consultants practice *issue-driven* problem solving. This version of logical problem solving eschews the formulation of hypotheses, and treats problems as "open questions." This isn't a guarantee against confirmation bias: your hypotheses may creep into your definition and structuring of the problem, leading you to define your problem narrowly, which constrains the solution. This is the "narrow framing trap" of Chap. 2. However, when you avoid the explicit formulation of hypotheses, you prevent some of the worst cases of the "solution confirmation pitfall." Therefore, this approach, while more difficult to master, is often preferable. We'll discuss in Chap. 5 when to use an issue-driven approach, and when it's safe to rely on the more expeditious hypothesis-driven approach.

Solution Generation and Design Thinking

The second important limitation of PSAC is that some problems just seem to resist it. Some critics of the consulting approach (and the consulting profession) see this as the result of a lack of creativity in the problem-solving method (and in those who deploy it). PSAC, they claim, is a mechanical process, routinely applied by like-minded consultants who come from the same backgrounds, wear the same gray suits, and produce the same uninspired, formulaic solutions. No wonder the flashes of insights that produce novel solutions never seem to emanate from consulting firms.

This criticism is, in our view, misguided—or at least too broad. While there are brilliantly creative consultants, many problems don't require much creativity. Although contemporary business culture sometimes seems to view innovation as an absolute good to be pursued at all costs, creativity in problem solving isn't universally desirable. We expect experts such as doctors, air traffic controllers, or auto mechanics to identify and solve problems, but we don't expect them to be creative. Sometimes, creativity is even illegal, as the sarcastic phrase "creative accounting" suggests. Much business problem solving consists of identifying tried-and-tested solutions to complex problems, not in finding novel solutions to them. Experienced practitioners of PSAC call this temptation "reinventing the wheel": the tendency to look, at all costs, for a new, out-of-the-box answer to a problem that has an acceptable off-the-shelf solution.

Critics of PSAC, however, have a point: some problems don't lend themselves to being disaggregated and solved by logic and facts in the linear way consultants prescribe. Some problems are hard to state precisely, because problem solvers don't understand them well enough. Some are hard to structure logically because problem solvers don't understand their causes. And some are hard to solve using facts alone because they require active idea generation. This is likely to be the case when the problem is complex and poorly understood, and when the solution must be designed for and used by people. The challenge of redesigning the customer experience at J.C. Penney, described in the previous chapter, is a good example of such problems.

Over the past 20 years, the school of thought known as "design thinking" has proposed a compelling approach to address problems of this kind. While various flavors exist, the core process is most closely associated with the Silicon Valley design firm IDEO and the Hasso Plattner Institute of Design at Stanford University (commonly known as the Stanford d.school). Design thinking has emerged as a powerful problem-solving toolkit that integrates both creative and analytical approaches. Although developed for the design of physical artifacts, design thinking has evolved to address intangibles such as services, processes, and larger organizational systems and strategies.[6]

Why has the reach of design thinking expanded? There are a few reasons. One is its growing use by a variety of organizations, including for-profit, non-profit, educational, governmental, and non-governmental. Reflecting its broad applicability, problem solvers in these organizations are finding new and useful applications of human-centered design beyond material artifacts. For example, the Designing Out Crime research center, a partnership in Australia between the New South Wales Department of Justice and the University of Technology Sydney, uses design thinking to help solve complex crime and social problems. A related reason is that design thinking works—it helps problem solvers tackle highly complex and poorly understood problems in ways that more traditional analytical methods don't. The intensive use of design thinking by companies also improves their financial performance. The Design Management Institute's Design Value Index shows that a stock portfolio of 16 design-centric companies outperformed the Standard & Poor's (S&P) 500 by 228 percent over the period 2006–16. Many organizations have established design thinking service units and some, such as IBM and Intuit, are reinventing their cultures and operations around design thinking. Management consulting firms are also investing in this capability by acquiring design services firms. In the past few years, Deloitte bought Doblin, Accenture acquired Fjord and 2nd Road, and McKinsey acquired Lunar.

Design thinking is concerned with how people experience human-created artifacts because these artifacts represent solutions to problems. At their most basic, problems signal unsatisfied needs and wants. They arise from dissatisfaction with existing solutions. In *The Sciences of the Artificial*, his landmark book on problem solving and design, Nobel laureate Herbert Simon argued that design is concerned with how things ought to be and with devising artifacts to attain goals.[7] Designers devise courses of action aimed at changing existing situations into preferred ones by deliberately creating new artifacts as solutions. For a problem to be solved, a solution must be designed.

From a logical and philosophical standpoint, design thinking is distinct from the other approaches we've discussed. Hypothesis-driven and issue-driven problem solving are both forms of *deductive reasoning*. Both approaches require the problem solver to have a theory—an understanding of cause-and-effect relationships—about the general causes of the problem being solved. In contrast, design thinking is a form of *abductive reasoning*. As defined by the American philosopher Charles Sanders Peirce, abduction takes place when you use a limited set of observations to generate the most plausible and parsimonious explanation for the data—an explanation which may be incorrect, and must be tested and validated. Design thinkers do this when they suppress their assumptions about the problem, and instead, use insights generated from observations of users to develop hypotheses about solutions. These hypotheses are then iteratively tested in the form of prototypes to converge toward the best-fitting solution. As Roger Martin argues in *The Design of Business*, "Designers live in Peirce's world of abduction; they actively look for new data points, challenge accepted explanations, and infer possible new worlds."[8]

Design thinking is a powerful approach to solve *some* problems, but not *all* problems (just like the traditional PSAC method is effective in many, but not all situations). The key is knowing which approach to select and when. The 4S method provides a guide.

An Overview of the 4S Method

Figure 3.1 summarizes the 4S method. The flowchart may look complex at first, but it's easy to follow. It combines the approaches we introduced above in a pragmatic manner. It will help you decide which of three possible paths to take to solve a problem: the hypothesis-driven, issue-driven, or design thinking path.

A simple example will help illustrate this reasoning.

A new CEO—let's call her Tracy—has been appointed at Solar, a multi-business, family-owned industrial company that sells packaging products to large corporate customers. Over the years, Solar acquired firms that

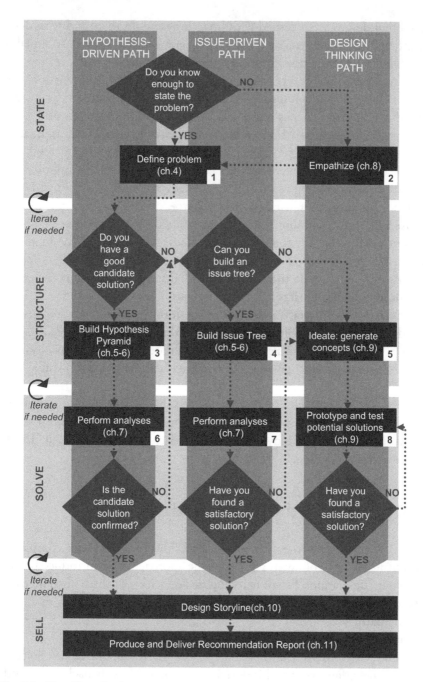

Fig. 3.1 The 4S method

specialize in different packaging technologies to provide a full range of packaging solutions to its corporate customers—a classic example of customer-centric diversification. When Tracy joins, the corporation is profitable overall, but two of its business units—Pluto and Uranus—are in the red. Members of the management team have differing viewpoints about the money-losing businesses. Several of them believe that their problems are due to a temporary decline in market demand, and believe the problem will resolve itself as soon as the economy improves. A few claim that the problems are purely operational, and assert that better manufacturing effectiveness could restore profitability. Others, however, believe such a turnaround to be impossible: they suggest selling or even closing Pluto and Uranus—despite the risk of labor unrest associated with such a move.

Tracy must decide on the most appropriate course of action (a problem-solving task) and sell the solution to the Board (a communication task). How could she think about the steps in that process, using the 4S method?

State: A Problem Well Posed Is Half-Solved

The importance of a good problem statement can't be overstated. Einstein said, "If I had an hour to solve a problem, I'd spend 55 minutes thinking about the problem and 5 minutes thinking about solutions." As we saw in Chap. 2, the "flawed problem definition" is a pitfall problem solvers should be aware of.

The first step for Tracy is to state the right problem. At this stage, Tracy has a clear question ("What to do with Pluto and Uranus?"), a set of symptoms (losses), and even some proposals for possible answers. This may seem like it's enough to state the problem. But it's not. Many more elements are needed for a complete problem statement. The first question may not be "What is the problem?" but "Do I know enough to state the problem?"

In Tracy's case, what don't we know, but need to know to define the problem? For instance, we don't know the extent of the bleeding. The problem isn't the same if the losses of Pluto and Uranus threaten the viability of the corporation and are an urgent problem, or if they are only a minor concern. Likewise, we don't know what Tracy's objectives are: perhaps the family owners expect her to create maximum shareholder value, even if it means shrinking the company, or maybe they're more concerned about keeping the corporation intact for reasons of social responsibility, prestige, or other considerations.

These are just examples. As we'll see in Chap. 4, writing a full problem statement requires you to examine five elements of the problem—abbreviated in the acronym TOSCA (Trouble, Owner, Success criteria, Constraints, Actors). If Tracy tries to write a full-fledged problem statement (Box 1 in the flowchart in Fig. 3.1), she'll find she doesn't know enough about the problem yet.

This realization should lead Tracy to discover more about the problem. There are two ways to do that. Sometimes, basic data gathering and rigorous thinking may be sufficient to define the problem properly. In this case, some data on recent business results are needed. Tracy will want to spend time at the production sites of Uranus and Pluto, meet with customers, and talk to board members about their objectives. This is the minimal level of inquiry required to state almost any problem of reasonable complexity.

Frequently, however, this won't be enough to develop a full problem statement. It will then be valuable to borrow from the design thinking toolkit and use techniques known as *empathy* (Box 2). In the design thinking path, a problem solver invests in *empathizing* with users by observing them, engaging with them, and immersing herself in their situation. This helps her discover their needs and learn how they experience the problem: how they think and feel about it, the context in which they experience it, and the constraints they face. During this phase, problem solvers develop rich insights about users, which they can use to state the problem better, reframing how they understand it by viewing it from different users' perspectives. We'll explain these techniques in Chap. 8.

Structure: The Architecture of Problem Solving

As soon as we state the problem, it's tempting to list actions Tracy could take to solve it immediately. Not surprisingly, this is what members of her executive team propose. Business people have knowledge and judgment, and they typically look at situations through the lens of their experience.

Tracy could decide that one idea her colleagues propose is an attractive candidate solution, and treat that idea as a hypothesis to be tested. That is, she can adopt a *hypothesis-driven* approach (pictured in the leftmost column of the flowchart).

The hypothesis-driven approach starts from an idea—a hypothesis—about what the solution might be and then tests it. Suppose, for instance, that Tracy hypothesizes that Solar should sell Pluto and Uranus. Logically, for this hypothesis to be true, many things must be true. For instance, the unit to be sold must be readily separable from the rest of the business, there must be a buyer at an acceptable price, and so on. If she chooses this approach, Tracy should list these conditions, and disaggregate them into smaller requirements. This is what we'll call a "hypothesis pyramid" (Box 3 on Fig. 3.1). Tracy and her team can then move to the "solve" stage to perform the analyses to test all these hypotheses.

However, as we've seen, the hypothesis-driven approach increases the risk of confirmation bias and exposes you to the solution confirmation pitfall. Before using this approach, Tracy must ask herself whether she has good reason to be *highly confident* in a given hypothesis. In our example, this doesn't appear to be the case. The fact that different colleagues have radically different hypotheses should give Tracy pause.

In such a situation, the alternative is to go for an "issue-driven" path, following the second column in the flowchart. An issue-driven approach requires you to break down the problem into smaller components with an *issue tree* (Box 4). An issue tree is a way to structure the problem thoroughly, to look at its different facets systematically, without a preconceived idea of what the solution might be. The benefit of this approach is that you can avoid the solution confirmation pitfall.

The downside is that building an issue tree is more difficult and more time-consuming than building a hypothesis pyramid. In Chaps. 5 and 6, we'll introduce techniques that will help you overcome this challenge, and especially the role of *frameworks* in building issue trees. Frameworks are essential shortcuts for someone building an issue tree because they provide pre-packaged decompositions of typical, recurring business problems. For example, Tracy's issue tree may include a branch that asks whether Uranus operates in an attractive industry: that is a question that Porter's five forces framework[9] can help address. Likewise, if Tracy must analyze the business portfolio of Solar, a strategic business portfolio matrix can be useful. Frameworks enable you to think faster. However, as we'll see in Chap. 6, this convenience has a cost: frameworks also constrain your thinking. A framework encapsulates a theory to solve a class of problems, and to use a framework is to espouse a theory and the assumptions that underlie it.

If you succeed at decomposing the problem and turning it into an issue tree, then you can move onto the "Solve" phase and analyze the issues. You may, however, struggle to build an issue tree. Unlike Tracy's problem, which she could readily turn into an issue tree (we'll show how in Chap. 5), not all problems are amenable to decomposition. Solving a product design problem, imagining a new advertising campaign, or designing a bold new strategy for an ailing company are tough business problems. But you'll probably find them difficult to break down with a hypothesis pyramid or an issue tree.

Instead of a traditional decomposition, these kinds of problems call for an *ideation* phase (Box 5). Design thinking practitioners use what they learned about *what is* (in the "State" phase) to then imagine *what should be*. They begin this effort by understanding the problem space. They then build on this understanding to synthesize an essential set of *design imperatives* that an effective solution must address. These imperatives represent the benefits a solution must provide users. They serve as a guiding vision for the ideation, prototyping, and testing phases. Together, the imperatives constitute a model of what should be, guiding the search for solutions. Once imperatives are established, designers generate a wide variety of ideas for solutions.

Solve: Between Analysis and Creativity

We've now seen three routes Tracy can follow to get to the "Solve" stage: hypothesis driven, issue driven, and design driven. The next steps will depend on her entry point.

Let's first assume that Tracy adopted a hypothesis-driven approach. Her next task is to test her hypothesis with the requisite analyses (Box 6). If, for instance, she hypothesizes that Uranus should be sold, she'll need hard facts to back up each statement into which her central hypothesis breaks down. Two outcomes are possible:

- Tracy may reject the hypothesis altogether if she finds clear evidence it was wrong. In that case, she'll naturally be tempted to formulate a different hypothesis: "If X doesn't work, let's try something else." Given the dangers of hypothesis-driven reasoning, however, that is a risky approach. A better strategy is to switch gears and adopt an issue-driven approach (moving to the middle column in the flowchart). Sometimes, it may even be necessary to return to the first stage in the problem-solving process and revisit the problem statement.
- The other possibility is that the hypothesis will be confirmed. Wholesale confirmation is, however, rare. More often, analyzing the hypothesis will cause changes or refinements to it. For instance, Tracy may conclude that Uranus should be sold, but Pluto shouldn't. The question Tracy must answer eventually is whether this resulting, refined hypothesis meets the success criteria she specified in her initial problem statement. If it doesn't, she'll consider the hypothesis rejected, with the same consequences as in the previous paragraph. If the resulting solution meets success criteria, she'll proceed to the "Sell" stage.

The second case we must consider is the one where Tracy chose the issue-driven route from the onset. She, therefore, enters the "Solve" stage with an issue tree that breaks down her problem into discrete parts to be analyzed separately. For instance, her issue tree may include the question, "What are market prospects for Uranus?" This question calls for a specific piece of analysis, probably using market research. It may ask, "What would be the value of Uranus as a stand-alone entity?" This question calls for some financial valuation work. In general, an issue tree will lead you to do all the same pieces of analysis as a hypothesis pyramid, and more: unlike the hypothesis pyramid, which zeroes in on the key analyses that prove or disprove your hunch, a good issue tree leaves no stone unturned. Box 7 in the Fig. 3.1 flowchart shows the step of conducting these analyses.

All these analyses may point Tracy toward a solution. Suppose, for instance, that the data unambiguously show that Pluto's problems are caused by declining quality. It takes little effort to propose that Pluto needs a quality improvement program. Once proposed, Tracy will ask herself whether it meets the success criteria she had predefined; if it does, she'll need to sell the program to her board.

However, with an issue tree, there is no guarantee the solution will just emerge like this. Issue trees disaggregate problems, but not all problems can be solved by being disaggregated. For instance, disaggregation may reveal that Pluto's difficulties stem from growing customer dissatisfaction, resulting from unattractive products, changing preferences, and the launch of superior competitive products. In such a case, the issue tree yields a complete diagnosis, but doesn't, by itself, suggest a solution. What can Pluto do to make its products great again? You won't answer this question by splitting the problem into smaller problems. You need fresh ideas.

Fresh ideas are precisely what the design thinking approach can generate. If the problem-solving process gets "stuck" on the issue-driven path, it may be useful to move back from Box 7 to Box 5 in the flowchart. Generating solution imperatives and solution ideas will allow Tracy to propose how Pluto's offering can be improved.

Once ideas are generated, they must be tested. This is when the "designer" (i.e., the problem solver on the design thinking path) leaves the realm of abstraction and returns to the concrete world to translate ideas into tangible prototypes to be tested with real-world users. In this *prototyping and testing* phase (Box 8), designers choose promising potential solutions and represent them in tangible form so users can interact with them. Prototypes embody designers' hypotheses about desirable solution characteristics, which are then tested by users in the final phase. User feedback about prototypes helps designers choose the final solution for implementation. Tim Brown, CEO of IDEO, summed it up this way in his book *Change by Design:* "The mission of design thinking is to translate observations into insights and insights into products and services that will improve lives."[10] Ultimately, one or several solutions should emerge that satisfy the problem statement's success criteria. If that doesn't happen after a reasonable amount of trial and error, a rethink of the problem statement may be in order.

Some proponents of creative problem solving might argue these last steps are the only valuable ones, and that building the issue tree was just a waste of time. We disagree. First, when Tracy started building the issue tree and analyzing issues, she had no way of knowing whether an issue-driven approach would generate an acceptable solution (but as we showed, it often does). The analysis Tracy conducted based on her issue tree informed her thinking. It narrowed down the solution space for her creative search: if the challenge is to make the product great again, she'll get creative about that, not about boosting employee motivation. And the analysis may have planted the seeds of ideas that will be helpful in the creative stage. Rather than substitute for each other, the analytical and creative approaches are complements.

To summarize, Tracy has three paths to a potential solution, which form the three columns in the flowchart:

- She can have a hypothesis from the beginning and test it to confirm its validity.
- She can start without a hypothesis, and find after she disaggregates the problem with an issue tree, that a viable idea emerges from her analysis.
- Or she can generate ideas using specific ideation techniques, because she couldn't build an issue tree or because the issue tree she built didn't generate a solution.

Sell: Choose the Approach That Suits Your Audience

Regardless of the path taken, Tracy has now settled for a solution she believes is the best. Her next task is to convince the Board to approve her plan. It is time to switch gears from problem-solving mode to communication mode.

As we mentioned in the discussion of the "miscommunication pitfall" in Chap. 2, this switching of gears raises an important question. If communication is a different exercise from problem solving, why are we covering both in this book? There are innumerable books and training programs on how to communicate your ideas effectively that don't cover the problem-solving stage, and some are excellent.[11] So why not just stop at a "3S" method? The pragmatic answer is that almost anyone who reads this book looking to become more effective at solving problems will also need to sell the solution, which makes a "one-stop shop" approach appropriate. More importantly, while solving a problem and selling the solution are distinct stages, they should be integrated for at least two reasons.

First, business problem solvers usually can, and should, interact with their audience throughout the problem-solving process. In our example, Tracy must talk to the board not only when she has found a solution, but from the very beginning of the problem-solving process, to state the problem correctly. She may well involve board members in the "Structure" and "Solve" stages of the process too. It's likely she'll give the board interim progress reports in which she presents emerging findings, shares ideas on possible solutions, and gets feedback about the board's thoughts and concerns. In short, her communication task starts at the very beginning of the problem-solving process. Sometimes, a fully baked solution must be sold to a "virgin" audience—for instance, when an advertising agency pitches a campaign to a new client. But communication approaches that are based on this premise are not generally appropriate for a problem solver within an organization.

There's a second reason to consider communications in the problem-solving phase, and vice versa: it ensures the two are sufficiently distinct and communication concerns don't "contaminate" the search for a solution. Finding the best solution is one task, selling it is another, and shouldn't start before you're sure the problem is solved. With the fat vs. sugar debate we described in the previous chapter, Ancel Keys did exactly the opposite: because he thought he knew the solution, he didn't use his empirical work as a problem-solving device to test his hypothesis. Instead, he used it as a sales pitch to convince decision-makers. This aggravated the analytical mistakes he made in the Seven Countries Study, by leading him to focus on countries that supported his view and disregard those that could have proven it wrong. The confirmation bias led him to confuse problem solving and solution selling. This confusion is summed up by the adage: "Never let the facts get in the way of a good story."

Letting the need for a good story pollute the search for a solution frequently traps business problem solvers. Anyone who's been tasked with finding a solution to a tough problem is, understandably, anxious about the "selling" part—the final "pitch" that completes the effort. Whenever you discover something, like an untested candidate solution, it's natural to ask yourself "How will I explain this?" But, as the example of Ancel Keys shows, jumping to selling an untested idea can result in the adoption of a poor or even harmful solution. Contrast this with what Lustig did in "Sugar: The Bitter Truth." Unlike Keys, he didn't let the need for telling a good story hinder finding the best answer. But unlike Yudkin, he didn't try to walk his audience through all the steps of a complex problem-solving effort. In Chaps. 10 and 11, we'll explain how to switch from problem-solving to solution-selling mode, and how to develop efficient and persuasive presentations of your solutions.

*   *   *

Like any linear description of a complex process, the overview we've presented is a simplification. The four stages of the 4S method are sequential, but, in practice, you won't work through them rigidly. Sometimes you'll double back to previous stages. The problem-solving process is inherently iterative. For example, you'll often revise a problem statement based on what you learn during your efforts to structure it. Refining the problem statement is a crucial part of structuring and solving a problem. Likewise, the way you structure the problem is likely to change after some analysis. In a hypothesis-driven approach, the facts will lead you to revise your hypothesis, while in an issue-driven approach, they'll lead you to think of different ways to slice and dice the issues. The 4S flowchart (Fig. 3.1) shows additional feedback loops.

Fundamentally, the 4S method encourages you to switch from an intuitive, informal, and automatic approach to solving and selling problems, to a reasoned, structured, and manual approach. Rather than solve problems based on what may instinctively come to mind, which leads to the pitfalls we discussed in the previous chapter, you deliberately and rigorously attend to stating, structuring, and solving them and selling your solutions.

Our goal in this book is to help you become better at solving challenging business problems and effectively selling your solutions to those who need them. In the chapters to come, we'll show you how the 4S method works, and how to use it to achieve this goal.

Chapter 3 in One Page

- The 4S method is based on the problem-solving approach of strategy consulting (PSAC), but addresses its two limitations:

  - *"Hypothesis-driven" in corporate setting → risk of confirmation bias, groupthink*
  - *Not all problems are amenable to disaggregation → some require creative thinking*

- The 4S method has three paths: hypothesis driven, issue driven, and design thinking.

- Each path covers the four stages: State, Structure, Solve, and Sell.

- *State* the problem, after learning enough about it:

  - *When you don't know enough, this requires using empathy techniques.*

- *Structure* the problem, depending on the path you're on:

  - *With a hypothesis pyramid (if you are highly confident in the candidate solution)*
  - *With an issue tree (if you don't have a good candidate solution, but can decompose the problem)*
  - *With ideation based on solution imperatives (if decomposing the problem is ineffective)*

- *Solve* the problem:

  - *By performing the analyses required (first two paths)*
  - *By prototyping and testing solutions (design thinking path)*

- *Sell* the solution, focusing on the answer and your audience, not on how you solved the problem.

- The 4S method is iterative and not rigidly sequential.

Notes

1. This doesn't imply that the approach applies only to strategy problems. Indeed, much of the work "strategy" consulting firms do isn't concerned, strictly speaking, with strategy. The term "strategy consulting" is shorthand for "CEO-level, premium management consulting," and "strategy" consultants use essentially the same problem-solving approach when solving organizational, operational effectiveness, or marketing problems.
2. Bacon, F. (1620). *Novum Organum, XLIX.*
3. Nickerson, R.S. (1998). Confirmation Bias: A Ubiquitous Phenomenon in Many Guises. *Review of General Psychology, 2*(2), 175–220.
4. Friedman, R.S., & Förster, J. (2001). The Effects of Promotion and Prevention Cues on Creativity. *Journal of Personality and Social Psychology, 81*(6), 1001–1013.
5. Janis, I.L. (1982). *Groupthink: Psychological Studies of Policy Decisions and Fiascoes.* Boston, MA: Houghton Mifflin.
6. Liedtka, J. (2017). Evaluating the Impact of Design Thinking in Action. *Academy of Management Best Paper Proceedings.* Beckman, S.L., & Barry, M. (2007). Innovation as Learning Process: Embedding Design Thinking. *California Management Review, 50*(1), 25–56.
7. Simon, H.A. (1969). *The Sciences of the Artificial.* Cambridge: MIT Press.
8. Martin, R.L. (2009). *The Design of Business: Why Design Thinking Is the Next Competitive Advantage.* Cambridge, MA: Harvard Business Press.
9. Porter, M.E. (1980). *Competitive Strategy.* New York: Free Press.
10. Brown, T. (2009). *Change by Design: How Design Thinking Transforms Organizations and Inspires Innovation.* New York: HarperBusiness.
11. Heath, C., & Heath, D. (2007). *Made to Stick: Why Some Ideas Survive and Others Die.* New York: Random House.

4

State the Problem: The TOSCA Framework

The first S in the 4S method stands for "state the problem." To introduce it, we'll stray from the exciting but sometimes dry world of business problems and consider a critical situation familiar to opera lovers: the challenge Tosca faces in the second act of the eponymous Puccini masterpiece.

Here are the facts:

- Mario, Tosca's lover, has been arrested and will be executed tomorrow.
- Tosca is understandably worried.
- She would like nothing more than to get Mario out of jail alive before tomorrow and escape with him.
- Tosca, however, is a virtuous woman, and there are things she won't do, even to save her lover.
- Unfortunately, Scarpia, the chief of police, is the key player here, and what he wants from Tosca is what she isn't willing to give.

The problem Tosca faces is thorny, but crystal clear: "How do I get Mario out of jail alive, without yielding to Scarpia?" The "resolution" of this problem illustrates what game theorists call a prisoner's dilemma, in which two adversaries would benefit from cooperating, but are tempted to betray each other. In Puccini's opera, Tosca promises Scarpia that, if he saves Mario by staging a mock execution, she'll give herself to him; but when the time comes, she kills Scarpia instead. Alas, Scarpia also betrayed Tosca: Mario's execution was real. A crisp problem, a disastrous "solution"—this makes for great tragedy.

Most business problems are not this neatly defined. Thankfully, they don't end quite as badly, either. Formulating problems this sharply, however, is a

© The Author(s) 2018
B. Garrette et al., *Cracked it!*, https://doi.org/10.1007/978-3-319-89375-4_4

valuable discipline. Before stating the core question, a problem solver must ask five questions that Tosca's situation illustrates—and that spell the acronym TOSCA:

- *Trouble*: What makes this problem real and present? (Mario's arrest)
- *Owner*: Whose problem is this? (Tosca's)
- *Success criteria*: What will success look like, and when? (Escape)
- *Constraints*: What are the limits on the solution space (e.g., resources, time-line, and context)? (Virtue)
- *Actors*: Who has a say in the way we solve this problem, and what do they want? (Scarpia, who wants a night with Tosca.)

Once we answer the TOSCA questions, it becomes possible to state the core question that will guide the problem-solving effort.

To illustrate and explain this process, let's revert to the example we used in Chap. 2 to show the perils of a flawed problem definition: the music industry facing digital piracy.

Trouble: What Makes This Problem Real and Present?

The reason any problem solver embarks on a problem-solving journey (and perhaps the reason you picked this book) is a perceived problem or opportunity. We call this initial perception the "trouble," to distinguish it from the real problem that will emerge from the problem statement phase.

The basic definition of "trouble" is a gap between an observation and an aspiration. If you aspire to grow revenues and revenues decline, that is trouble. But by the same definition, "trouble" can also be a perceived opportunity. For instance, if your revenues are growing 10 percent a year and you have reason to believe it is possible to double that growth rate. It's the discrepancy between aspiration and reality, the dissatisfaction, which defines trouble.

This definition implies that both terms—the aspiration and the reality—must be defined carefully. Consider the case of the music industry. The trouble seems obvious—people are illegally downloading millions of files. But what is the aspiration? Is it zero illegal downloads? Or fewer illegal downloads than legal ones? This question seems odd for an apparent reason: a music industry executive doesn't define the aspirations in terms of downloads—whether they're legal or not. The executive defines them in terms of revenues.

Around 1999, the revenues of the music industry are still growing at a healthy clip. Illegal downloads aren't, in and of themselves, the trouble. They are a symptom, or more accurately a precursor, of future trouble: future revenue decline. The music industry probably has a revenue growth aspiration, and it is rightly concerned about the impact that illegal downloads will have on future revenues.

As this example shows, the trouble isn't always as obvious as it seems. A few tips are helpful in formulating it:

- *Be specific.* Don't accept "fake problems"—vague gripes you can't possibly "solve." If you're running a customer service center, "we must create a results-oriented culture" isn't trouble, nor a problem that can be solved. "Twenty percent of customer calls remain unanswered" is trouble, and may (or may not) be the symptom of a culture problem.
- *Don't let interpretation (or solution ideas) creep into your definition of "trouble."* For instance, someone who says "Our product has lost consumer appeal" is providing an interpretation, not describing a symptom. A description that stays at the symptom level might be, for instance, "Our product has lost five points of market share over the past year." This matters because the problem may not be the product's appeal: the market share loss may be due to many issues, such as a competitor's moves or a decline in distribution.
- *Ask "Why now?"* If the gap between reality and aspirations is a generic, eternal one—for example, "We would like to increase revenues," it is unlikely to provide a good basis for a problem statement. When the "trouble" as formulated would have been the same five years before and would be the same five years hence, asking why it hasn't been acted upon before and why it has become pressing now will often reveal valuable insights.

Is "Trouble" a Diagnosis?

When we ask about the trouble, we focus on the symptoms. Some readers—both practitioners and experts—may be surprised by this approach: a common prescription in problem solving is to go *beyond* the symptoms to interpret the problem's cause. In many types of problem solving, this step—diagnosis—is a crucial one: doctors diagnose a disease before prescribing a treatment, and consultants often borrow medical vocabulary and start projects with a diagnostic phase.

This approach, however, isn't the only possible one. Presuming you can make a diagnosis is equivalent to adopting a hypothesis-driven problem-solving approach. A diagnosis is much more than a problem statement: the diagnostician may claim he is just defining the problem, but he's already offering a solution.

For a physician, this makes sense. Diseases belong to pre-existing categories, which are continuously updated in medical reference books. A physician's education consists, in part, of learning to recognize them—and then to verify, through clinical examination or tests, that her initial diagnosis is correct before recommending a treatment. Pattern recognition and hypothesis testing are appropriate problem-solving approaches in medicine.

But is it always the case in business problems? When we attempt to diagnose business problems, we implicitly assume they're like diseases, and just like physicians, we can classify them into preexisting, universal "pathologies." Often, this assumption is justified. For instance, a sudden and unexplained dip in your bank account may be symptomatic of a pathology called theft. Likewise, unwanted variability in a manufacturing process is a well-specified, measurable problem, and has a finite number of possible causes. But the medical analogy becomes misleading, and the hypothesis-driven approach detrimental, when problems are more complex. A defining feature of complex problems, in business and elsewhere, is that, unlike diseases, they don't always belong to well-defined, preexisting categories with recognizable symptoms and proven therapies.

This distinction is critical for problem solvers. The observation of trouble is the first step in stating the problem. It's an excellent time to ask yourself whether you're dealing with a well-known problem that belongs to a recognizable class of situations that calls for standardized remedies. If so, you'll continue to state the problem with a clear candidate solution already in mind. You'll take a hypothesis-driven approach, and proceed down the first column in the 4S flowchart (Fig. 3.1). If you don't have a strong hypothesis about a possible reason for the perceived trouble, you should keep an open mind.

The risk is in wrongly believing you recognize a problem you know, just like a physician misdiagnosing a disease. This is the "flawed problem definition" trap into which the music industry fell: it falsely diagnosed illegal file-sharing as one more instance of a well-known pathology called piracy. The industry couldn't see what aspect of the problem was new and how to tackle it. Many experienced problem solvers fall into this trap. Perversely, the more experienced we are, the more likely we are to recognize a new situation as a familiar one and make a misguided diagnosis.

Therefore, the bar for adopting a hypothesis-driven approach should be a high one. You should define trouble as a symptom, without attribution to a known diagnosis, unless you have reason to be confident that you can make an appropriate diagnosis (and propose a candidate solution). More simply: when in doubt, stick to trouble.

Owner: Whose Problem Is This?

Observing symptoms leads to the "owner" question: whose job is it to take care of the symptoms? This question is sometimes obvious: no one but Tosca will bother to save Mario. Conversely, some issues—including serious ones—are no one's problem. Many people, for example, believe that global business today is dominated by a culture of short-termism that presents a real danger for capitalism and society, but that is a problem without a clear owner. Often, political and societal problems of this sort don't have a clear owner or have multiple owners with conflicting, irreconcilable objectives. Such problems are sometimes called "wicked" problems and don't lend themselves to the problem-solving approach described here.[1]

Few business problems, however, are "wicked." Most problems don't have a single, obvious owner, but they can be stated *from the perspective* of a particular owner; and that choice will bear on the way the problem is defined. In our example, whose problem is piracy? Who, exactly, is "the music industry?" Are we talking about the RIAA, the industry body that represents it? The RIAA has a mission to further the industry's interests, and as a neutral party, it represents all players equally in theory. But its mission is lobbying, and not much else. Its resources and skills most likely match its mission. If it is the problem owner, the solution space is limited to things it can do—lobbying, advertising, and so on. The RIAA may well define success as "doing something about piracy that gets my members off my back."

Let's assume the problem owner is the head of one of the large music labels. The range of possibilities now feels very different. Lobbying is still an option, but a label, alone or with other parties, can do many more things, such as changing its product and pricing strategy, or launching new business models. If you discuss problem definition with this owner, they will probably define success as "doing something that saves *my* business from the deadly threat posed by piracy—whether or not the rest of the industry follows suit."

As this example shows, asking who owns the problem can sometimes lead to an illuminating discussion. The identity of the problem owner shapes the potential solution space, and hence the problem definition. In practice, you rarely have a choice: either you own the problem or someone is posing the challenge to you. But in all cases, being explicit about problem ownership is essential.

Identifying the problem owner has another important consequence. As we'll see, problem definition is an iterative process, and only stops when you reach a definition that is "good enough." Likewise, later in the process, we'll consider the problem solved when the solution is "good enough." But who will be the judge of a "good enough" problem statement or solution? The problem owner. If you don't know who's on the hook to solve the problem, you can never define or solve it.

Success Criteria: What Will Success Look Like, and When?

One virtue of having identified a problem owner is that there is someone you can ask the most critical question in problem solving: *what do you want?*

This question is unlikely to elicit the answers you hope for—at least until you probe. Let's assume from here onward that the owner of the music industry problem is the top management team of one of the record labels. Had you asked them, back in 1999, "what they wanted," they would probably have answered something like "stop this piracy." However, this is merely a restatement of the "trouble," the situation that triggered the question. It doesn't get to the actual objectives the owners are pursuing.

The standard advice to get past this point is to ask "why" as often as needed (typically five times). This can be tricky. Trying it with a music industry executive in 1999 might trigger this conversation:

"We want to stop this piracy!"
  "Why?"
  "To protect our sales, of course."
  "Why?"
  "Because kids who download free music don't buy our CDs anymore. Are you dumb?"
  "Why?"
  "Get the hell out of here!"

This doesn't mean that probing for reasons is irrelevant: *why* kids prefer to download music rather than buy CDs is a crucial issue (and price isn't the only answer). But asking why isn't always specific enough to get to the right question.

A more productive way to ask "why" is to ask *what success will look like*. An effective way to ask this question is as follows: *"We are in the future and this problem-solving effort has been a great success. What is the date, and what do we see?"* This creates an open-ended discussion about *success criteria*. Let's role-play this approach with the same music industry executive:

> "We are in the future, having dinner together to reflect on this project and celebrate its success. What is the date?"
>
> "Well, I guess it's at least three years from now. We aren't going to solve this problem overnight, are we?"
>
> "I guess not. And how do we know we've succeeded?"
>
> "Well, if we're having dinner together, it means I still have a job, for starters!"
>
> "Good to know dinner will be on you. What else?"
>
> "We've solved the piracy problem."
>
> "Sure. But how do you know? How do you measure it?"
>
> "Obviously, our revenues are growing again. If we've stopped this piracy, we've restored the growth trajectory we were on before it started."

With this simple line of questioning, you got somewhere: the critical success metric is revenues. It's not how many files are downloaded, or how many people are thrown into jail for sharing them. This approach leaves room for a very different—and more productive—discussion.

Another benefit of asking the question in this way is that it will call out a frequent (and shoddy) practice: defining the problem by its proposed solution. Here, an executive might say, "The problem is that we need to make it more difficult to download pirated CDs," or even "We need to raise our game on theft prevention." This frequent mistake leads straight into the "solution confirmation pitfall" we illustrated in Chap. 2 with the Grameen–Danone story: when we define a problem so it suggests the solution, we're in great danger of blindly confirming that conclusion.

As with many mistakes, problem owners usually commit this one with the best intentions. Isn't that what we call being "results-oriented"? Don't good bosses instruct employees to "come to us with solutions, not with problems"? And yet, to properly define a problem, we must resist the urge to solve it too quickly. To focus on stating the problem, we need first to *ignore* the possible solutions. Asking the "success criteria" question is a tool to do just that.

An important question when considering success criteria is whether they should include a specific, quantifiable target. When such a number is chosen, there's always a lot of discussion around it, and for good reason: it can be difficult at the beginning of the problem definition process to set an ambitious yet realistic aspiration level. In our example, if we continued the conversation with the music industry executive, the executive might be compelled to specify an annual revenue growth of 5–7 percent as the target. This is an understandable, but probably unrealistic, perspective. In hindsight, no strategy could have maintained the music industry's previous trajectory of growth and profitability in the face of digital disruption.

Because of this difficulty, there are two schools of thought on whether targets should be quantified. One approach is to give up quantification and formulate the question with an open-ended target that recognizes uncertainty. In the music example, such a target might be "maximize revenues while maintaining ROS" (return on sales—profit as a percentage of sales).

Some argue, however, that in an organizational context, this may not be enough to push the problem-solving squad to think hard enough. Picking an aspirational number, even if it is arbitrary, has real benefits. It focuses the mind, stretches the thinking, justifies allocating resources to the problem-solving effort, and generally raises aspirations. This approach is often attractive, provided you're prepared to revisit your target as you discover new facts—the initial target may have been set too high or too low.

Constraints: What Are the Limitations and Trade-Offs?

Let's assume you've identified the Trouble, Owner, and Success criteria. A picture of the problem you're trying to solve is emerging. But in solving any problem, there are limits to what you can do. Be aware of these constraints.

You should define constraints from the perspective of the problem owner. But asking the question "Do you face any constraints?" will probably not get you far. A practical approach is to consider three types of constraints.

First, there are always *constraints on the success criteria*, arising from conflicts with other objectives and commitments. Although achieving success as you define it is your primary objective, it's rarely your only one. For instance, when the record label defines revenues as the critical success metric, it implicitly assumes it must maintain a minimum level of profitability. For this year, and perhaps the next one, the label may be committed to achieving specific revenue and profit targets. Such commitments are a constraint on the possible solution. These constraints qualify the success criteria—success is success, but it can't be achieved at all costs. You should identify these trade-offs as early as possible in the process.

Second, the owner's resources and capabilities may also impose *constraints on the solution*. We mentioned that if the owner were the RIAA, its limited capabilities would rule out certain types of solutions. With a record label as owner, capability constraints are different but important. One capability gap is the absence of any "digital" skills in the organization.

Third, there are often *constraints on the problem-solving process* itself: for instance, limitations to the time and budget that can be devoted to solving the problem, or confidentiality constraints that prevent you from accessing people and information you would like to involve. Setting up a visible problem-solving effort may sometimes worsen the problem by giving it visibility. "Panicky music industry sets up emergency task force to address rampant piracy" is a headline the problem owner doesn't want to generate.

Discussing constraints early on can save you time and effort. Exploring solutions only to discover later they're incompatible with constraints you hadn't identified earlier can be costly. But take your initial discussion about constraints with a grain of salt. If you identify too many constraints, you may end up defining the problem as "just making the trouble disappear without changing anything else." That's usually mission impossible. Few problems would get solved if their owners didn't, at some point, relax some of the constraints they face.

The music industry, for instance, should realize that restoring past levels of revenue growth *and* profitability is unrealistic. But this realization will probably not happen in the first discussion. The need to reevaluate constraints, and possibly to relax them, is one of the reasons to revisit the problem definition periodically throughout the problem-solving process.

Actors: Who Are the Stakeholders?

Finally, the "owner" is usually not the sole person dealing with a problem and its consequences. The owner must contend with other stakeholders, who rarely have the same objectives (i.e., success criteria). This might be just another constraint to deal with, but because it's a crucial element of the problem definition, it's worth treating it separately. While constraints are usually stable or at least predictable, actors are reactive: they can deliberately respond to our recommendations in supportive or detrimental ways. It's therefore indispensable to understand their objectives and the stakes they have in the problem.

Stakeholder analysis is a useful technique to identify, systematically, the stakeholders and their objectives. The music industry, for instance, invested considerable time and effort trying to get Congress to pass legislation to crack down on illegal file-sharing. A stakeholder analysis might have revealed that few members of Congress wanted to be seen as persecuting teenagers and stifling technological innovation, just so the music industry could continue to sell CDs at $14 apiece. A contributing factor was that the music industry had done nothing to endear itself to lawmakers, having fiercely resisted their attempts to police explicit lyrics.

Write the Core Question

Now that you've completed the five TOSCA steps, you can write the *core question* you'll answer. It should be a question, not a statement—"We must stop piracy" isn't a question. But beyond this simple requirement, there are many degrees of freedom in formulating the core question, and there is usually no single "best" way to define a problem.

The essential choice you must make at this stage is *question scope*. Like any question, a problem definition can be an open question ("How can we stop piracy?") or a closed one ("Should we launch a music download service?"). A closed question entails a narrower scope than an open one. However, the critical choice isn't the grammatical form of the question but its scope.

Take, for example, a company considering an acquisition to enter a new market. An obvious (closed) question would be: "Should we proceed with this deal, at the price and terms currently offered?" A slightly broader scope, still with a closed question, would be: "What is the maximum price we would be prepared to pay for this company?" But you could also open the aperture of your inquiry by asking, for instance, "What approaches are possible, including but not limited to acquiring Company X, to enter this market?" Whether you phrase it in this open way or as a closed question ("Is acquiring Company X the best way to enter this market?"), you will have broadened the question scope considerably.

The harder the problem is and the earlier you are in the problem-solving process, the more likely it is that a broad question scope will be preferable. But the only absolute requirement is that the question scope follows the TOSCA steps you've listed. These steps can serve as a checklist to verify that the core question meets the tests of a good problem definition:

- Does the question address the *trouble* that got you to consider the problem in the first place? In the music industry case, the symptoms include pirated downloads, but also the fast-growing availability of broadband Internet and the emergence of various providers of digital playback devices. A problem definition that doesn't mention these symptoms would be a generic question about growth and profitability, not a statement of the urgent problem you're facing.
- Is the question phrased from the perspective of the *owner*? For instance, asking "Why do teenagers download music illegally?" is a broad, interesting, important, and relatively difficult question. It will play a part in the problem-solving process, as we'll see when we discuss problem structuring. But it's not asked from the perspective of the music industry executive. It can't be our problem statement.
- Would answering this question meet *success criteria*? This is equivalent to asking whether the question reflects the specific metrics and time horizon in your success criteria. For instance, "How can we face the digital music threat?" doesn't explicitly address the success criteria. To do so, you might ask a question that starts with "How can we restore an x-percent revenue growth rate in three years' time?"
- Does the question recognize the *constraints*? As just phrased, for instance, it doesn't: sharply cutting CD prices would probably result in revenue growth, but would violate a key constraint. Adding a profitability constraint to the problem definition question addresses this.
- Does the question consider relevant *actors*? It is usually impractical to list all the stakeholders in a core question, but you must identify the key players. Here, for instance, one prominent "actor" whose behavior matters is the consumer illegally downloading music.

Going through this list might lead you to a core question like this: "In a context where young consumers are increasingly downloading pirated music files, and knowing that enablers of that behavior—broadband access and digital playback device—are bound to become more accessible, what actions can we take that would result in restoring an X-percent revenue growth rate, with a minimum return on sales of Y percent, in three years' time?"

Figure 4.1 offers a worksheet for applying the TOSCA checklist to your problem.

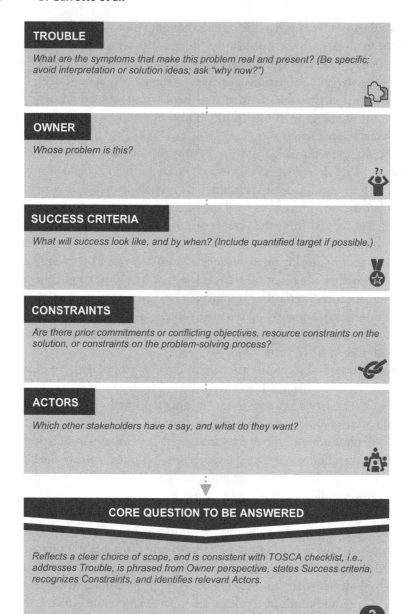

TROUBLE

What are the symptoms that make this problem real and present? (Be specific; avoid interpretation or solution ideas; ask "why now?")

OWNER

Whose problem is this?

SUCCESS CRITERIA

What will success look like, and by when? (Include quantified target if possible.)

CONSTRAINTS

Are there prior commitments or conflicting objectives, resource constraints on the solution, or constraints on the problem-solving process?

ACTORS

Which other stakeholders have a say, and what do they want?

CORE QUESTION TO BE ANSWERED

Reflects a clear choice of scope, and is consistent with TOSCA checklist, i.e., addresses Trouble, is phrased from Owner perspective, states Success criteria, recognizes Constraints, and identifies relevant Actors.

Fig. 4.1 TOSCA problem statement worksheet

Singing TOSCA as a Choir

In describing the steps in the problem definition process, we've made them appear sequential and reasonably straightforward: spot the trouble, verify the owner, define success, identify constraints, list actors—and then, write the question. In reality, the process is more complicated.

The first reason is easy to see: the steps aren't sequential, but overlap with one another. It's hard to define "trouble" accurately without an identification of the owner. It's difficult to determine success without acknowledging the constraints. Identifying actors you initially neglected may lead you to revisit success criteria, and so on. You'll probably need to write your core question not just once, but several times, and come back to the problem owner several times to test it. When the owner agrees that the problem will be solved if you bring the answer to that question, you'll know you have a solid problem statement.

But rewriting the question doesn't stop at the problem statement phase. Your problem owner, who decides if your problem definition is relevant, may change her mind—because of new facts you bring, or because she thinks about the same facts differently. Stating the problem is an iterative process of discovering or shaping a question, which doesn't stop when the solving phase begins.

This iterative process isn't performed alone by a problem solver holding a problem statement worksheet and a pen. For each component of TOSCA, many people will have different opinions, insights, and perspectives to contribute. These views may be complementary or entirely at odds with one another, but they are bound to differ. To state a problem well, you must integrate these various perspectives into your problem statement.

To do so isn't an additional step in the problem statement process. It's a mindset—an attitude of openness, an ability to see the same problem simultaneously from several angles. Design thinking experts call it "empathy": to state a meaningful problem, you must put yourself in the shoes of various constituents, including the problem owner, and the other actors whose worldviews, choices, and behaviors shape the problem and may contribute to its solution.

To illustrate this, let's look at the music industry again. From the perspective of the recording label executive, the problem is well defined. But what does it look like to a college student storing illegally downloaded files on a computer hard drive in his dorm room? Asking that question would reveal that the price of CDs, although a component of the problem, isn't the whole issue. At their peak, Napster and other file-sharing sites provided a user experience—immediacy, ease of use, excitement—that was hard to match. These consumers also were frustrated at the time by the lack of user-friendly devices to play digital music away from their computers. Apple's iPod and iTunes later succeeded primarily because they offered an attractive user experience (and the music industry's attempts to provide legal downloading alternatives failed because they provided a ridiculously unwieldy one). Without empathizing with all the actors, the problem statement can't be complete.

At the problem statement stage of the 4S process, a practical way to "empathize" (i.e., to see the problem from the points of view of several stakeholders) is to contact them and ask them how they view the problem. Usually, this means conducting problem definition interviews: early in the problem-solving process, you can meet multiple stakeholders, and ask them the TOSCA questions. What is the trouble, in *your* view? Whose problem do *you* think it is? What would success look like *to you*? And so on. The more diverse the interviewees and their viewpoints, the better.

However, interviews are sometimes not enough to get to real needs and wants, particularly if some stakeholders are unwilling or unable to express them. Recall, for instance, the story of Ron Johnson in Chap. 2, and his admission that he didn't understand the needs and preferences of J.C. Penney shoppers, particularly regarding promotions. In such cases, careful observation of the actors' behaviors may reveal their needs and expectations. Design thinking practitioners call this approach *immersion*. Whenever you don't know enough about actors to state the problem, consider putting yourself in their shoes—or immersing yourself in their situation. We will further discuss empathy and immersion techniques in Chap. 8.

Whether it is achieved through problem definition interviews or immersive techniques, empathizing with stakeholders will be beneficial in several ways. It will help you refine your problem statement, the primary objective. But it will also give you ideas for the next stage in the problem-solving process, as interviewees will almost always volunteer what they think the solution is. Finally, it may be a good way to build goodwill with stakeholders.

*   *   *

If you take only one thing away from this chapter, it should be that there is no "right" problem definition, although there are many wrong ones. Each coherent problem statement (i.e., each problem definition question consistent with a TOSCA set) is a frame on the problem, and multiple frames can coexist. Crafting a problem statement is an iterative process, and a collegial effort involving various stakeholders with different perspectives. As the problem-solving effort proceeds and you gather facts and generate options, you'll continue to refine your problem statement. The structuring stage of the problem-solving process, which we'll examine next, will be instrumental in helping you reflect on and refine your problem statement.

Chapter 4 in One Page

- To state the problem, use the *TOSCA checklist* to formulate the *core question*.

- *Trouble*: a gap between a situation and an aspiration (problem or opportunity):
  - Defined in specific terms, including the answer to the "Why now?" question
  - Usually a symptom, not an interpretation or a diagnosis
  - *Music industry: trouble = declining sales, not "piracy"*

- *Owner*: the person asking for this problem to be solved and who will judge a good problem definition and a good solution:
  - *Music: is the "owner" the industry or the CEO of one music label?*

- *Success criteria*: spell out "what success will look like":
  - Should not predefine the solution
  - May include a quantified target (if you're prepared to revise it)
  - *"We are in the future and the problem has been solved. What is the date, and what do we see?"*

- *Constraints* include:
  - Preexisting objectives and commitments that constrain the success criteria
  - Resource and capability limitations that constrain the solution scope
  - Time, budget, skill, or confidentiality issues that constrain the problem-solving process

- *Actors* are important stakeholders whose objectives you must understand.

- *The core question* can be open or closed, and its scope can be narrow or broad, but it must be compatible with all the elements of TOSCA.

- Problem statement is iterative and collaborative:
  - Empathize with stakeholders through problem-definition interviews and immersion
  - Integrate the perspectives of multiple actors
  - Revisit the problem statement periodically throughout the problem-solving process

Note

1. Rittel, H.W.J., & Webber, M.M. (1973). Dilemmas in a General Theory of Planning. *Policy Sciences*, *4*(2), 155–169.

5

Structure the Problem: Pyramids and Trees

In 2007 Amazon launched Kindle Direct Publishing (KDP) in the USA. Using this service, writers could post their e-books in Kindle format on all Amazon websites for free and price them anywhere from $0.99 to $200, keeping 70 percent of net revenues. KDP was an immediate success. Digital self-publishing had arrived.

Aspiring writers use such platforms to turn their manuscripts into e-books or print-on-demand books and sell them on the Internet. Digital self-publishing has helped commercialize hundreds of thousands of books that otherwise wouldn't have been. Indeed, traditional publishers receive thousands of manuscripts annually and select only a handful for publication. Despite this selectivity, they are surprisingly bad at spotting best sellers, contributing to an industry-wide fear of missing the next *Harry Potter*. Dozens of publishers rejected the little sorcerer's story before Bloomsbury finally published it.

Librinova is a start-up that successfully launched a digital self-publishing platform in France in 2014.[1] Any writer can pay to join the Librinova platform and access a range of services to edit, produce, and commercialize their book, in both print-on-demand and digital formats. Readers can buy these books through online bookstores such as Amazon. Publishers can use the platform to spot potential best sellers and target them for traditional publication. Librinova's competitive advantage is that it acts as literary agent for books that are self-published on its platform and sell over 1000 copies, helping authors to publish them conventionally. While other platforms just support writers in editing and marketing their books, Librinova sells writers the dream of being

© The Author(s) 2018
B. Garrette et al., *Cracked it!*, https://doi.org/10.1007/978-3-319-89375-4_5

published by an established publishing house and having their books on display in the bookshop windows of the Latin Quarter in Paris.

By 2018, over 1000 writers had joined the platform and established publishers had picked up 40 books for publication. After two successful funding rounds, investors pushed Librinova to expand internationally. Most digital platforms, such as Uber or Airbnb, pursue aggressive international expansion. The aim is to grow the platform quickly to leverage network effects, triggering a "winner takes all" dynamic in which the platform becomes a de facto standard, locking out rivals.[2]

Let's suppose the founder and CEO of Librinova has asked you for advice on how to expand internationally. To tackle this issue, you need first to define and state the problem. The TOSCA framework from the previous chapter will help:

- The Trouble: shareholders are pushing for internationalization, while publishing activities are essentially domestic, with little synergies across countries. Because of linguistic and cultural differences, each nation has its own publishing industry, with local writers, readers, and publishers. International players are exceptions.
- The Owner of the problem is the founder and CEO of Librinova.
- Success can be defined as quenching the investors' thirst for international growth in a profitable way, for example, by launching a viable self-publishing platform in a foreign country within the next 12 months.
- Constraints are strategic, financial, and organizational: self-publishing is difficult to internationalize, and the company is small, purely domestic, with limited human and financial resources.
- Other than the CEO, the key Actors are the pushy investors and potential international partners. Traditional publishers in target countries are critical: if they don't adopt Librinova's platform, its competitive advantage vanishes.

You might state the core question as: *Which international expansion strategy—when, where, and how—should Librinova use to respond to shareholder pressure?*

Following the 4S approach, after stating the problem, you'll structure it in either a hypothesis-driven or an issue-driven way. Let's explore these two approaches in sequence.

Hypothesis-Driven Problem Structuring

International expansion is not a novel problem. Many start-ups, including digital platforms that connect providers and buyers, have gone through it. The typical hurdle is that some activities tend to be domestic by nature, which requires building operations from scratch in each country. For example, in each geography, Uber must attract drivers and travelers, both of whom are locals, and perform purely local transactions. Even though the same algorithms and platform architecture can be used everywhere, cross-country synergies are weak, hampering internationalization. This issue is particularly salient in book publishing.

Librinova has examined possible internationalization strategies. One scenario is to collaborate with De Marque, a Canadian company operating in the wholesaling and distribution of digital books. De Marque and Librinova already are commercial partners: De Marque distributes Librinova e-books through online bookstores in Europe, Canada, and the USA. Librinova also knows that De Marque has considered launching its own self-publishing platform in Canada, a project that stalled due to lack of skills and technology. A joint initiative would solve that problem and leverage the partners' complementary capabilities: Librinova's capabilities in self-publishing would help De Marque diversify into a growing arena, while De Marque's connections with the local publishing industry would help Librinova create a sister platform in Canada.

This sounds like a good candidate solution for Librinova's problem. Now, your mission, if you choose to accept it, is: discover whether teaming up with De Marque in Canada is a good option. Since you see no particular reason why the CEO would be wrong, the most interesting part of the study is not to confirm the idea, but to explore it and develop some interesting insights and recommendations on how to implement it. What a relief! Instead of looking into all possible geographies (Why not go for Europe or Asia?) and all possible entry strategies (Why not look for an acquisition target in Canada or elsewhere?), you have a good starting point from which to work.

This is a typical situation. Problem owners typically pose business problems so they point to potential solutions, at least in broad terms. Most have given some thought to the problem at hand and have conducted preliminary research. Experience also plays its part: having solved similar problems in the past helps get directly to the point and identify good candidate solutions. In such contexts, the problem solver's task is to validate the solution, examine its various aspects, refine it, and recommend an action plan for implementation.

But how do you do that in practice?

Building a Hypothesis Pyramid

In this approach, you'll consider the potential solution as a hypothesis and challenge it in all its possible dimensions. Just because you have an idea does not mean it's correct—the whole point of the exercise is to validate that. To do so, you'll build a *hypothesis pyramid* from the top down. You'll start with your leading hypothesis and break it down into sub-hypotheses that are conditions for it to be true. You might also break these first-level conditions into sub-sub-hypotheses, until they are specific enough to be proven or disproven by analyses, facts, and data (Fig. 5.1). When you've performed all the required analyses, you can climb back up the pyramid and say whether the leading hypothesis is right or wrong, or more interestingly, what is right and wrong in it, and to what extent.

If you work in a team, the hypothesis pyramid is an efficient way to allocate the analytical work within the team. This chapter focuses only on how to build a hypothesis pyramid. We'll discuss how to gather the data and carry out the analyses in Chap. 7.

The Librinova case can help illustrate this approach. You can structure the problem around the hypothetical solution that the CEO is considering: Librinova should collaborate with De Marque to launch a sister platform in Canada. This candidate solution is your leading hypothesis at the top of the pyramid (Fig. 5.2). What are the conditions for it to be true?

This hypothesis combines three choices: the choice of country (Canada), the choice of entry mode (collaboration with a local partner to create a sister platform, rather than organic entry or acquisition), the choice of partner (De

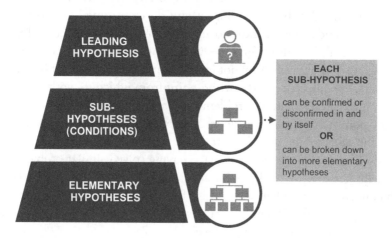

Fig. 5.1 The hypothesis pyramid

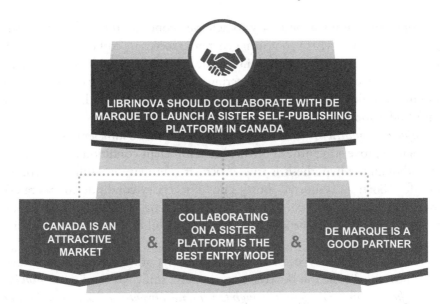

Fig. 5.2 First level of a hypothesis pyramid on the Librinova case

Marque rather than someone else). You must check if these three choices are correct: Canada must be an attractive market, collaboration on a sister platform must be the best entry mode, and De Marque must be a good partner. Otherwise, Librinova should reconsider the idea and look into another country, another entry mode, or another partner. These three sub-hypotheses are conditions that must hold (be true) for the main hypothesis to hold.

Necessary and Sufficient Conditions

The Librinova example points to a key principle in building a hypothesis pyramid: at any level of the pyramid, a hypothesis must be supported by sub-hypotheses sitting at the lower level. What we mean by "supporting" is that each sub-hypothesis is a condition for the focal hypothesis to be true. To avoid mistakes here, we must explore a distinction you may remember from your math classes between *necessary* and *sufficient* conditions.

Necessary conditions are conditions that cannot be wrong if the hypothesis is true. For example, "Socrates is mortal" is a necessary condition for "Socrates is human." Similarly, "earning a net operating profit on sales" is a necessary condition for "achieving economic profit." However, necessary conditions can be true while the hypothesis is wrong: "Socrates is mortal" can be true even if Socrates is not human—for example, if Socrates is your dog. Similarly, a positive operating profit is necessary to achieve economic profit, but it doesn't guarantee that the return your firm generates exceeds its cost of capital, which is the definition of economic profit. In the Librinova example, Canada must be an attractive market to justify entering it. This is a necessary condition. But Librinova could decide not to go to Canada—for example, if they realize they can't find a good partner there.

Sufficient conditions work the other way around. A sufficient condition is enough to prove a hypothesis is true, but a sufficient condition can be wrong even though the hypothesis is true: "Socrates is human" is a sufficient condition for "Socrates is mortal," but it's not a necessary condition for Socrates's mortality. Expanding a company's client base abroad is sufficient to increase its export sales, but export sales can increase for other reasons, such as variations in currency exchange rates.

You can use both types of conditions in a hypothesis pyramid, provided you know the distinction between necessary and sufficient conditions: *proving one sufficient condition right is enough to validate a hypothesis, while proving one necessary condition wrong is enough to reject it.*

From a purely logical standpoint, you'd love to find a single "killer" sufficient condition to confirm your hypothesis or a single "killer" necessary condition to reject it. In the Librinova case, the three conditions we listed are all necessary: proving one of them wrong is enough to reject the leading hypothesis. Conversely, finding a single piece of evidence that would be sufficient to demonstrate the validity of the alliance with De Marque would save you a lot of work.

In practice, however, you'll encounter two challenges. The first is that *accepting or rejecting the leading hypothesis isn't your only objective.* It's more often a means to solve a business problem as thoroughly as you can. Even if you could validate a sufficient condition that confirms the candidate solution immediately, you wouldn't stop there. You would try to find other sufficient conditions that could lead to alternative but compatible ways to solve the problem. For example, increasing sales can be achieved through growing the client base in the domestic market, increasing the average revenue per client, or penetrating new foreign markets. Each of the three conditions is sufficient to increase sales, but you would have to consider all of them and find others, if possible. The hypothesis-driven approach, if properly conducted, won't necessarily lead to a quick confirmation (or disconfirmation) of your hypothesis, but can enlarge the scope of solution options.

The second challenge is that *sufficient conditions are rare in business problems.* In the Librinova hypothesis pyramid, we don't have any sufficient conditions, but we do have a list of necessary conditions. This is typical because finding a single sufficient condition to validate a complex plan is usually impossible. As you disaggregate the leading hypothesis into more elementary sub-hypotheses that are "searchable"—concrete and specific enough to be (in)validated by evidence—you'll identify many conditions that are necessary, but none that is sufficient. Such necessary conditions are what detectives call "clues" and doctors "symptoms." A red rash, especially behind the ears and on the neck, is a symptom of measles. The symptom is a necessary indicator that appears as a consequence of the disease, but it alone cannot confirm the diagnosis. Many things other than measles, such as a dermatologic disorder, can cause a red rash. More conditions are needed to ensure measles is the correct diagnosis.

For example, if you consider taking over a company, you must check at least two necessary conditions: first, that the value created by the expected synergies is significant and offsets the likely acquisition premium, and second, that the target company's shareholders will sell their stock at such a premium. This helps you identify two sources of evidence you'll need to obtain: (1) you'll need to assess the potential synergies between the two firms and estimate if they'll offset the anticipated premium, and (2) you'll need to estimate the minimum acquisition premium which is acceptable to the target firm's shareholders. Failing one of these two necessary conditions is enough to make the deal unattractive. They are necessary, but not sufficient.

When you list a set of necessary conditions in a hypothesis pyramid, you can't be completely sure that validating these conditions is enough to validate the leading hypothesis. You have a nice bunch of clues, but there might be something missing. Working with a hypothesis pyramid is both a fact-finding and logical challenge: you must make sure the necessary conditions are verified and that, taken together, they are sufficient to validate the hypothesis.

The Rule of MECE

Let's get back to the Librinova example. You must confirm all three necessary conditions to validate the leading hypothesis. But this isn't enough. You must also check that the combination of these three necessary conditions is sufficient to validate the hypothesis. Otherwise, you might be missing another condition that could throw a wrench into the logic. As a logical requirement, the conditions should be *collectively exhaustive.*

"Collectively exhaustive" means we've identified all possible conditions to provide logical support for the hypothesis. A trick to make sure that a list of items is collectively exhaustive is to determine whether an "others" category exists. If you think of categorizing car bodies into five categories (sedans, station wagons, convertibles, coupes, minivans), ask yourself whether a sixth category called "others" would be empty or not. For the categories to be collectively exhaustive, we must be able to assign any and all cars to one of the categories. Another way to check for collective exhaustiveness is to assume that all the conditions you've listed hold, and still try to argue against the leading hypothesis: what objections can you find? Suppose that the three conditions you've listed for the Librinova–De Marque alliance are confirmed. Is there another reason Librinova shouldn't proceed? Maybe it has better options: expanding abroad might be easier in neighboring countries, such as Belgium, Germany, or Spain, rather than overseas.

In addition to being collectively exhaustive, the conditions must not overlap. In other words, they should be *mutually exclusive.* If the car body categories are mutually exclusive, then a car cannot be assigned to more than one category. The three conditions we have listed in the Librinova pyramid are mutually exclusive. Indeed, each one is self-contained and can be investigated as such. Proving any one wrong would be enough to reject the hypothesis altogether; there would be no need to look into the other conditions. Conversely, proving one right provides only a piece of support for the hypothesis, but this is a solid and independent piece of support. Once you've checked one condition, you can move to the next and assess whether it also holds, without conducting the same analyses twice.

The combination of these two checks—collective exhaustiveness (sufficient together) and mutual exclusivity (non-overlapping)—is often abbreviated as MECE (pronounced "missy"): mutually exclusive and collectively exhaustive. MECE is a fundamental notion and a pillar of good problem solving and solution selling. We'll continue to refer to it throughout the book. A MECE list is like a solved jigsaw puzzle: the pieces fit with no overlap, and their combination covers the whole picture.

Checking for "MECEness" reveals that our three conditions for the Librinova–De Marque alliance are not collectively exhaustive: we didn't compare the candidate solution with alternatives that might prove more attractive. We must add a fourth sub-hypothesis: "Collaborating with De Marque to launch a sister platform in Canada is the best available option" (Fig. 5.3). Now that we have split the leading hypothesis into four collectively exhaustive sub-hypotheses, we've identified four, not just three, streams of research: one on assessing the Canadian market, one on looking into the pros and cons of collaborating on a sister platform, one on evaluating De Marque as a partner, and one on alternative international expansion strategies. If you

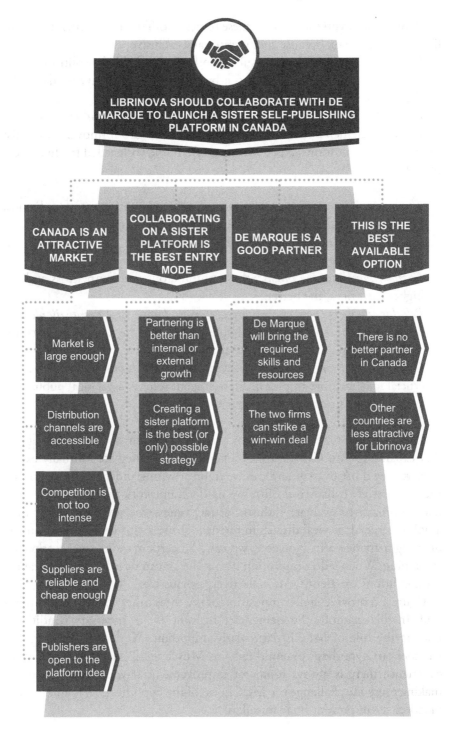

Fig. 5.3   More complete hypothesis pyramid on the Librinova case

work on a team, you can allocate these topics to different team members with little risk of overlap, because they're mutually exclusive.

The next step is to make each sub-hypothesis searchable by splitting it into elementary hypotheses you can check by collecting and analyzing data. The resulting hypothesis pyramid is depicted in Fig. 5.3.

To test the first sub-hypothesis (Canada is an attractive market), you must look into the elements that make a market attractive for Librinova. We can list five necessary conditions, based on a strategic framework called the five forces model[3]:

1. *The market is large enough:* assuming the same penetration rate as in France, Librinova can break even in a reasonable period of time.
2. *The distribution channels are accessible:* Librinova can put books on sale in bookstores at a reasonable cost.
3. *Competition is not too intense:* the less numerous the competitors and the higher the prices, the better.
4. *Reliable suppliers (printers, editors, web consultants, etc.) are available at a reasonable price:* this is indispensable in making the Canadian platform able to develop a range of services for writers.
5. *Canadian publishers are open to dealing with a self-publishing platform:* it is crucial for Librinova to play its literary agent role vis-à-vis local publishers, as this is its main source of competitive advantage.

These are necessary conditions: proving any of them wrong would suggest that expanding into Canada is not a good option. They are mutually exclusive, as they don't overlap and can be right or wrong independently. But are they collectively exhaustive? Since we used a framework that provides a standard approach to evaluate industry attractiveness, we probably didn't miss anything crucial: as we'll discuss in the next chapter, this is the key advantage of using a framework. However, we can't be certain we haven't overlooked something. When a decomposition is complex, it can be difficult to guarantee the conditions we identify are collectively exhaustive.

Figure 5.3 provides a decomposition of the three other "pillars" of the pyramid. In this example, the elementary hypotheses are necessary conditions, making the rule of MECE particularly important. We let the reader gauge whether our hypothesis pyramid remains MECE at all levels. We know from experience there is always room for improvement. If you work in a team, making everyone challenge the MECEness of the hypotheses, it is an excellent practice. It can prevent huge mistakes.

Logic in a hypothesis pyramid is a means to an end, rather than an end in itself. The objective is not to confirm or disconfirm the "veracity" of the leading hypothesis in purely logical terms, such as in a math proof. Instead, it's to assess the extent to which the hypothesis holds and the relative business impact of the recommendations it suggests. In practice, you'll engage in an iterative process through which you'll revise and refine the leading hypothesis, based on the logic you're developing when you structure the problem and the results you get when you perform the analyses.

If you find support for the leading hypothesis in the Librinova example, this support will probably be partial and will vary across the various "bricks" in the pyramid. This is good news: the CEO of Librinova will learn little if you just confirm her candidate solution, but she'll learn a lot if you come up with convincing views on the expected costs and benefits of implementing it. The problem-solving process will produce interesting insights on sizing the Canadian market, assessing the competition, discovering which Canadian publishers might use the platform, shaping the agreements to propose to De Marque, and so on.

Hypothesis-Driven Problem Structuring: Pros and Cons

The Irresistible Appeal of the Hypothesis-Driven Approach

Hypothesis-driven problem solving is efficient when you start from a sound hypothesis. It saves time and energy by focusing your efforts on a candidate solution (or a range of consistent solutions). Experts and senior business people often structure problems in this way. They are frequently right, but as we'll discuss a little later, they're dramatically wrong sometimes.

Experts use hypotheses because their expertise provides them with a catalog of solutions to problems in their area of expertise. When experts face a problem, they start with a candidate solution that their expertise suggests—a hypothesis—and they try to validate it while adapting it to the peculiarities of the problem at hand. They recognize patterns and work from them.

Pattern recognition is a highly efficient way to solve problems. Once a pattern is recognized, the problem solver can focus on refining and quantifying the solution, to support it with a business case that makes it actionable. Like patients who want to be told how to cure their disorder, the average decision-maker is only interested in hearing about solutions and their likely impact on the problem.

The hypothesis-driven approach not only saves exploration efforts, but also anticipates solution selling. As we start with a candidate solution, the arguments we use to confirm it are also selling points we'll use to convince the problem owner of its relevance. We simultaneously generate the solution and the arguments to sell it. In the Librinova example, you can use the hypothesis pyramid to sell the solution to the CEO, who may use the same arguments to convince the investors. We'll explore this further in Chap. 10.

Finally, political and organizational circumstances also favor the hypothesis-driven approach. When a problem solver is under pressure, and admitting ignorance isn't an option, quickly identifying a candidate solution using this approach provides a shortcut between problem solving and solution selling. A CEO issuing a profit warning can't afford to say publicly he doesn't know how to address the problem. In such circumstances, you can't start from a blank sheet of paper. You must demonstrate you can think on your feet by identifying a candidate solution quickly.

For all these reasons, the problem solver's mandate is sometimes limited to confirming a pre-sold, good-enough solution that satisfies the problem owner, and to looking carefully into the conditions that will make the candidate solution work. In such contexts, it can be counterproductive to search for other options and prove you can find better ideas. For example, if Librinova's shareholders were convinced the company should go international quickly and the CEO was convinced the alliance with De Marque was the best option, would you waste your time fishing for other ideas? Investigating a pre-sold solution saves you both unsolicited investigations and solution-selling efforts. This doesn't mean you should dishonestly validate the leading hypothesis if you find it wrong, only that you can limit the scope of your work to challenging and refining it.

The Dangers of Hypothesis-Driven Problem Structuring

Hypothesis-driven problem structuring isn't without risks. It exposes you to at least five potential mistakes—the pitfalls we introduced in Chap. 2. First, hypothesis-driven thinking can creep in during the problem statement stage. You might be tempted to think like an expert in domains in which you don't have the expertise, or even in which no true expertise can be developed.[4] You may then mistakenly recognize patterns in problems, believing, incorrectly, you know what's going on, and use these patterns to quickly arrive at candidate solutions. As we learned from the story of the music industry in Chap. 2, while this is highly efficient, it can lead one to develop hypotheses about candidate solutions that are flawed. At best, this results in a waste of time. At worst, it can lead to severe errors, as we illustrated with the *flawed problem definition pitfall.*

Second, once the hypothesis is stated, it immediately narrows the problem frame. Hypothesis-driven problem structuring can lead you to fall prey to a self-inflicted *narrow framing pitfall.* You focus on the solution you have in mind and look for alternatives only if your candidate solution is proved inadequate. The WYSIATI syndrome we mentioned in the introductory chapter creates the delusion that the hypothesis addresses the whole problem: nothing needs to exist outside of it.

In the Librinova example, hypothesizing that Librinova teams up with De Marque to launch a platform in Canada hinders the examination of other moves that could also solve the stated problem—how to respond to investor pressure to expand internationally. While you can consider alternative moves, as we did in Fig. 5.3, many hypothesis-driven problem solvers might limit their attention to the first three sub-hypotheses that directly relate to the candidate solution, and overlook the fourth, limiting their understanding of the problem and their search for solutions.

Moreover, even though we include a fourth sub-hypothesis, we miss out on another question: whether international expansion is an attractive strategy, given the domestic nature of the publishing industry. There might be better ways to meet shareholders' growth aspirations—for instance, by acquiring local (French) competitors or expanding into related businesses. Considering these alternatives helps redefine the problem by broadening it beyond international expansion. This is precisely the point: starting with a hypothesis encourages a narrow definition of the problem. As a consequence, if your leading hypothesis is validated, you'll never know whether a better option was feasible: "What You See Is All There Is!".

Third, the tools you use to understand and analyze the problem may implicitly limit the hypotheses you develop. This can happen when the problem owner calls on experts. The choice of experts determines the hypothesis and implicitly rules out other relevant viewpoints. For example, the CEO of an automotive company accused of tampering with emissions tests can rely on different experts to address the problem. Should he call an automotive engineer? A lawyer? A management consultant? A communications guru? All four? Each expert will have a different approach, including different frameworks endemic to their respective area of expertise, to understand the problem and formulate hypotheses. The candidate solution proposed will depend on the expert chosen and the frameworks deployed. When you pick the wrong expert, you risk facing the *wrong framework pitfall.*

Fourth, hypothesis-driven thinking can lead you to communicate the solution before solving the problem. Part of the appeal of a hypothesis pyramid is that its logic is the same as the structure of a story that sells the candidate solution. But this confusion creates risks. Would you want to see the same thinking in the White House's situation room as in its press room? In the situation room, the focus is (or should be) on finding the best solution to deal with a crisis. In the press room, the press secretary sells the solution to the press corps and the world. Identifying candidate solutions based only on what can be sold to an audience is dangerous. This is a form of the *miscommunication pitfall* we discussed in Chap. 2.

Finally, hypothesis-driven problem structuring can lead to the *solution confirmation pitfall*. A hypothesis that looks sensible can lead problem solvers to be more inclined to search for and be receptive to information that confirms it rather than information that disconfirms their belief in its soundness. Even the most experienced problem solvers can fall into this trap—the more experienced and successful they are, the greater the repertoire of cases in their mental libraries, the more likely they are to trust their instincts, increasing the risk of confirmation bias.

Logical Challenges

Another hurdle with hypothesis-driven problem structuring is that it requires more rigorous logical reasoning than meets the eye. While the approach seems user-friendly and intuitive, it creates a complex web of hypotheses and supporting conditions that risk logical mistakes.

A typical error is to confuse sufficient and necessary conditions with causes and consequences, which creates ambiguities and logical flaws. While looking for potential causes of a problem can help state and structure it, taking possible causes for hypothetical conditions can be misleading. A frequent mistake is to think that a plausible cause is a necessary condition because it's "obvious." The saying "There's no smoke without fire" illustrates this error. As fire causes smoke, we infer fire when we can see smoke. However, smoke can come from things other than fire, such as an electric boiler or an internal combustion engine. In reality, fire is sufficient, but unnecessary, to produce smoke. Therefore, the saying "There's no smoke without fire" is logically wrong. It's inherently wrong even as a metaphor because rumors are often unfounded! In a business context, many announcements, such as profit warnings, acquisition projects, or layoff plans, can cause a drop in a company's stock price. While all are very plausible causes, none of them is a necessary condition for the stock to lose value.

In the Librinova case, a necessary condition for the Canadian market to be attractive is that it's large enough regarding the number of potential authors who would use the platform. You can check this condition by estimating the number of Canadian writers who are stuck with unpublished manuscripts. However, this necessary condition is only one reason why the Canadian market is attractive, not a cause or a consequence of its attractiveness. It is obviously not a consequence: stating that there are many unpublished writers in Canada *because* the market is attractive would be simply stupid. But, more interestingly, it is not a cause either: the statement that the number of unpublished writers *causes* the market to be more attractive is also wrong, even though it sounds more sensible. Even if Canada was packed with unpublished writers, the Canadian market could be unattractive—for example, if intense competition among existing Canadian self-publishing platforms made it structurally unprofitable.

Many strategic mistakes stem from such logical flaws in which we confuse causality and logic. How often have you heard companies announce they're entering a market *because* it's large and growing? The size and growth of a market aren't sufficient conditions for market attractiveness—limited competition is another necessary condition, plus many others.

Another enemy of logic is the misuse of correlation. Correlations can be misleading if you confuse them with logical links. Correlations aren't logical conditions. They can be spurious and illogical: while the number of drownings in swimming pools correlates with the consumption of ice cream (because both increase with summer temperature), an ice-cream prohibition will save no lives … at least from drowning! While you can't rely on correlations at the problem-structuring phase, you can use them (with caution) as empirical evidence later in the process, when you analyze data to validate hypotheses. We'll discuss how to deal with correlational evidence in Chap. 7.

Building a hypothesis pyramid can prove difficult. The potential confusion between necessary and sufficient conditions, logic and causality, or causality and correlation can make the pyramid's logic cumbersome and fuzzy, although its visual representation makes it look clean and rational. Under its disguise of simplicity and efficiency, the hypothesis-driven approach is riddled with logical traps. Our natural tendency is to follow our intuition and "think fast," which makes us prone to fall into such traps. We tend to overinterpret correlation and take it for causation, and take causation for logical links. We may think that a list of necessary conditions is MECE and coheres into a sufficient condition. We may see support for our hypotheses in the faintest clues, while overlooking more significant, yet disconfirming information.

Practitioners might object to our characterization of the hypothesis-driven path as risky because it's such a widely used tool in strategy consulting. When applied effectively, it's largely free of confirmation biases, logical flaws, and other pitfalls. In practice, however, when you choose a hypothesis-driven approach, you risk falling into these traps without even realizing it. A possible remedy is to proceed down the issue-driven path instead.

Issue-Driven Problem Structuring

In contrast to the hypothesis-driven approach, the issue-driven problem-structuring path might seem mundane. Its underpinning theory is much simpler. But it's less popular in business contexts, because it requires more time, thoroughness, imagination, and critical thinking.

The Cartesian Rules: MECE Strikes Again

Issue-driven problem structuring draws heavily from the Cartesian method for conducting a systematic search of the truth. We can essentially describe it by repeating the four rules that the French philosopher and mathematician René Descartes posited in his *Discourse on the Method*[5] at the beginning of the seventeenth century:

1. Accept nothing for true without questioning it thoroughly.
2. Divide each issue into parts until you find adequate solutions to each elementary issue.
3. Conduct analyses by starting with the simplest issues and ascending step by step to reach more complex issues, while keeping a sense of order and priority, especially when considering disconnected issues.
4. Make sure nothing is omitted.

The second rule tells us that the rational way to solve a problem is to disaggregate it into issues and sub-issues, taking nothing for granted until you reach elementary issues that are simple enough to receive reliable responses. Most problems are too complex to be solved directly. Intuitive, synthetic solutions are misleading. Descartes analyzes a problem like chemists analyze a chemical, by isolating its elementary components. His method is to split each question into more detailed questions until the simple questions are analytically searchable. Critical thinking (the first rule) is the key ingredient for the whole process.

The last two rules are what we described as the MECE principle. Elementary issues must be mutually exclusive so you can solve them one by one. You ensure nothing is omitted if all elementary points cohere into a combination that covers all the facets of the problem.

Issue-driven problem structuring consists of decomposing the problem into MECE issues and sub-issues that you can solve one by one. The practical tool to do so is the issue tree, as depicted in Fig. 5.4.

Issue Trees Versus Hypothesis Pyramids

The choice to represent hypotheses as a pyramid and issues as a tree is arbitrary. We distinguish the visual representations of the two approaches to emphasize their conceptual differences. While hypothesis pyramids consist of hypothetical statements, issue trees consist of questions. Each branch of a tree

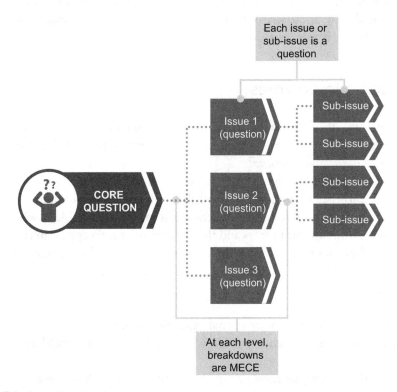

Fig. 5.4 Issue tree structure

bears a question divided into finer-grained questions on thinner branches. Thinner branches detail the broader questions posed on thicker branches to make them analytically searchable.

Although Descartes came up with his principles to guide the reasoning of individuals, consultants use issue trees as collaborative tools to organize problem-solving initiatives. They build the issue tree as a team, which fosters both critical thinking and a shared understanding of the problem structure.

In real-life situations, especially if you're under time pressure, building an issue tree may seem a waste of time. Starting with one question and ending up with more questions might seem counterproductive. You might think an issue tree is overkill because you'll never show it to the problem owner (who wants to hear about solutions, not problems). You might also believe that issue-driven structuring requires only common sense and critical thinking, as opposed to the hypothesis-driven path, which requires insight and business experience.

This is like saying issue trees are for beginners and hypothesis pyramids for advanced problem solvers, which is incorrect. Building a relevant issue tree requires insight and business sense. Experience helps a lot. An advantage of the issue-driven approach is that it's more thorough and avoids the traps induced by the hypothesis-driven approach.

Growing Issue Trees

Let's return to the Librinova example. We stated the problem as: *Which international expansion strategy—when, where, and how—should Librinova use to respond to shareholder pressure?*

To structure the problem using an issue tree, we must split this core question into sub-issues. Since we've stated the problem as a choice among possible options, one possible way to structure it is to think of a table in which the possible options appear in rows and the assessment criteria appear in columns. You could put a grade in each cell of the table to rank the different options based on the criteria. Thus, we can decompose the core question into two sub-issues:

- What are Librinova's international expansion options?
- What are the assessment criteria for Librinova and its shareholders?

Given the context, we must pay special attention to the De Marque option. A practical way to do so is to structure the first sub-issue around it. Figure 5.5 shows

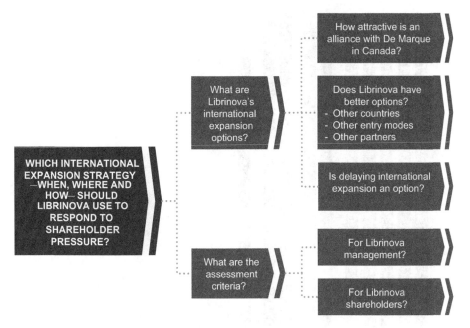

Fig. 5.5 Preliminary issue tree on the Librinova case

a preliminary issue tree. In it, we split the first sub-issue into two branches: (1) analyzing the De Marque option and (2) looking into alternatives, including other entry modes (in Canada or elsewhere), other countries, and other potential partners (in Canada or elsewhere).

For the breakdown to be MECE, we must consider the option to resist the shareholders' pressure and not to expand abroad for the moment. Librinova might have legitimate reasons to choose this route and, no matter our final recommendation, we had better examine these reasons. However, this line of investigation differs significantly from comparing international expansion options based on countries, entry modes, and potential partners. It entails analyzing Librinova's business model and the ability to replicate it in foreign countries. We think it makes sense to consider this stream of investigation as a sub-issue.

The De Marque option also deserves specific attention, so we can make it a sub-issue as well. Examining the De Marque option and discovering whether other options are available are different lines of work. For example, identifying other possible geographies draws on aggregated data on self-publishing in different countries, while analyzing the Canadian option requires more fine-grained information on local market circumstances. This leads us to the complete issue tree depicted in Fig. 5.6.[6]

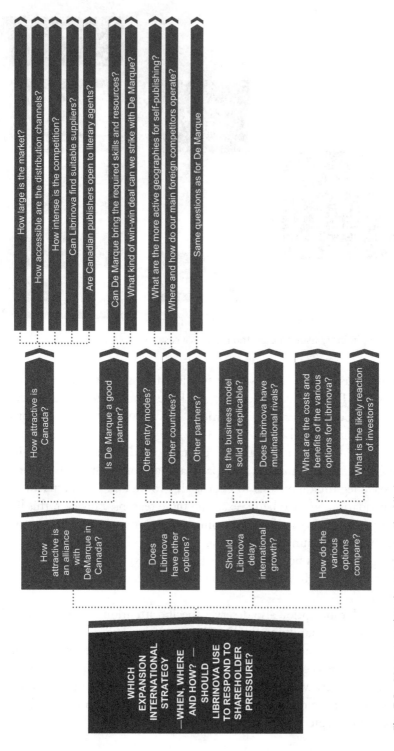

Fig. 5.6 More complete issue tree on the Librinova case

The 80/20 Rule

The challenge is to be thorough while keeping the issue tree manageable. Trying to make the issue tree exhaustive is beneficial at the beginning of the problem-solving process, but at some point, you must prune it by setting priorities and eliminating "dead-end" branches. A general rule of thumb is that 20 percent of the possible issues have the potential to generate 80 percent of the insights.

More than the percentage, which varies a lot, the message to remember is that, in most problems, a minority of key factors plays a major role. For example, in a company's business, 20 percent of key customers often generate 80 percent of sales, or 20 percent of product lines yield 80 percent of profits. Focusing on issues that entail maximum impact is more efficient. You can drop low-impact branches at early stages and keep others in standby mode while you are examining the most impactful issues. However, the tree must be trimmed based on likely impact, not because some areas are easier than others to search!

In the Librinova example, looking into the reasons Librinova could resist shareholder pressure and not go international might be a priority. It might reveal interesting insights about the company's strategy and shed a different light on the other sub-issues. When taking a hypothesis-driven approach, we were inclined to neglect this option (Figs. 5.2 and 5.3). Starting with an open issue and breaking it down in a MECE way can help you broaden the initial question by unearthing sub-issues you would have otherwise overlooked.

Growing a Tree or Building a Pyramid?

For narrowly defined problems, especially "yes or no" issues, the hypothesis-driven and the issue-driven approaches are equivalent. Consider, for example, a problem stated as whether or not to acquire a particular target company. An issue tree would ask the "yes or no" question, while a hypothesis pyramid would start by hypothesizing that the acquisition should be done. Both approaches would be essentially identical. The issue tree would look very much like the hypothesis pyramid, except all items would come as questions instead of hypothetical statements. The only benefit of the issue-driven approach would be to mitigate the risk of the solution confirmation pitfall, as the problem solver would be more likely to keep an open mind.

However, in most situations, you must choose between a hypothesis pyramid and an issue tree. Our recommendation here is simple: *the "default choice" should be to use an issue tree*, unless there are compelling reasons to be content with a hypothesis pyramid.

As we've seen, hypothesis-driven thinking is quicker and feels more natural. If you've never thought about how you solve problems, you probably follow the hypothesis-driven path. But the issue-driven structure can help you avoid common traps of hypothesis-driven thinking and reach more insightful conclusions, even when you have candidate solutions in mind. Whenever you have sufficient time and latitude to investigate the problem in depth, issue trees should be your first call.

Limit the use of hypothesis-driven thinking to two cases only:

1. *You have strong reasons to believe in your hypothesis.* This can be the case if you have deep expertise, or if the problem is trivially simple. In such contexts, an issue tree would be overkill. But reverse the burden of proof: before accepting any candidate solution as your leading hypothesis, put the onus on those who suggest this route and invite them to justify their belief in the hypothesis.
2. *You don't have the luxury of building an issue tree.* This may be the case because of time constraints, or because you're under pressure to show you have a solution in mind from the get-go (and you're also ready to accept the existing problem definition without challenging it). It's a risky route, but it is sometimes the only one.

Figure 5.7 summarizes the pros and cons of hypothesis pyramids and issue trees and the contexts in which you can use one or the other.

*   *   *

Overall, we recommend issue trees, rather than hypothesis pyramids, to structure problems. This helps mitigate confirmation biases and other problem-solving pitfalls. However, the main hurdle with issue trees is that decomposing issues and sub-issues into MECE components can be long and difficult, especially on unfamiliar problems, which are precisely the problems for which the issue-driven path is the most adequate. In the next chapter, we'll show you how to use frameworks to overcome this obstacle.

A limitation of the two problem-structuring approaches we've discussed is that they're analytical and rarely foster creativity. They tell us which analyses to conduct to find or confirm solutions based on logical reasoning, but they

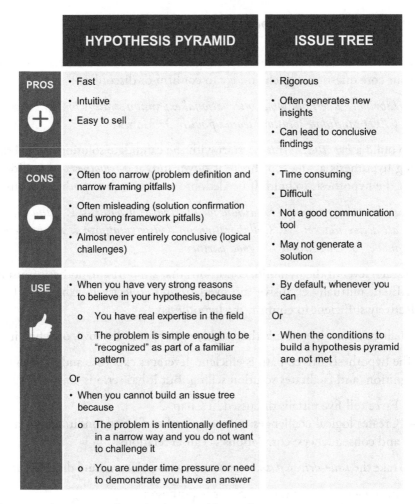

	HYPOTHESIS PYRAMID	**ISSUE TREE**
PROS +	• Fast • Intuitive • Easy to sell	• Rigorous • Often generates new insights • Can lead to conclusive findings
CONS −	• Often too narrow (problem definition and narrow framing pitfalls) • Often misleading (solution confirmation and wrong framework pitfalls) • Almost never entirely conclusive (logical challenges)	• Time consuming • Difficult • Not a good communication tool • May not generate a solution

USE 👍	• When you have very strong reasons to believe in your hypothesis, because
	  o You have real expertise in the field
	  o The problem is simple enough to be "recognized" as part of a familiar pattern
	Or
	• When you cannot build an issue tree because
	  o The problem is intentionally defined in a narrow way and you do not want to challenge it
	  o You are under time pressure or need to demonstrate you have an answer
		• By default, whenever you can
		Or
		• When the conditions to build a hypothesis pyramid are not met

Fig. 5.7 When to use a hypothesis pyramid or an issue tree

don't tell us how to come up with innovative solutions. If the problem requires thinking out of the box and inventing a new solution, they're both likely to fail. If you're looking to develop innovative solutions, you should turn to the design thinking approach we'll discuss in Chaps. 8 and 9.

* * *

Chapter 5 in One Page

- *Hypothesis-driven* problem structuring starts with a candidate solution to your core question, which you try to confirm or disconfirm:

  – *Librinova question: what international expansion strategy to implement?*
  – *CEO's candidate solution: team up with De Marque*

- To build a *hypothesis pyramid*, start with the candidate solution as the leading hypothesis at the top. Break it down into *sub-hypotheses*—conditions for the hypothesis to hold. If needed, break down sub-hypotheses again.

  – *At least three necessary conditions for Librinova's hypothesis:* 1. *Canada is an attractive market.* 2. *Collaboration on a sister platform is the best entry mode.* 3. *De Marque is a good partner.*

- At each level of the pyramid, conditions that support a hypothesis must be MECE: mutually exclusive (no overlap) and collectively exhaustive (collectively sufficient to confirm the hypothesis).

- Challenge each hypothesis thoroughly to confirm, disprove, or refine it.

- The hypothesis-driven path is efficient, leverages expertise and pattern recognition, and facilitates solution selling. But it has serious limitations:

  – Favors all five pitfalls discussed in Chap. 2
  – Creates logical challenges: necessary and sufficient conditions ≠ causes and consequences; correlations ≠ causal relations

- To take the *issue-driven path*, start with your *core question* and disaggregate it:

  – into questions, *not* statements or hypotheses;
  – in a MECE way: at each level, sub-issues must be both mutually exclusive and collectively exhaustive;
  – using the 80/20 rule (20 percent of issues = 80 percent of insights.)
  – *Librinova's core question can be disaggregated into four sub-questions:* 1. *How attractive is an alliance with De Marque in Canada?* 2. *Does Librinova have better options?* 3. *Should Librinova delay international expansion?* 4. *How do the options compare?*

- *By default, use issue trees.* Choose hypothesis pyramids only when you have strong trust in your hypothesis, or when you cannot build an issue tree.

Notes

1. Garrette, B. (2017). *Librinova: A Start-up for Digital Innovation in Publishing.* HEC Paris case study. Retrieved from https://www.thecasecentre.org/educators/search/results?s=CEAB419890C5284D1B09BE222FD036A3.
2. Eisenmann, T.R., Parker, G.G., & Van Alstyne, M.W. (2006). Strategies for Two-sided Markets. *Harvard Business Review, 84*(10), 92–101.
3. Porter, M.E. (1980). *Competitive Strategy.* New York: Free Press.
4. Kahneman, D., & Klein, G. (2010). Strategic Decisions: When Can You Trust Your Gut? *McKinsey Quarterly.* Retrieved from https://www.mckinsey.com/business-functions/strategy-and-corporate-finance/our-insights/strategic-decisions-when-can-you-trust-your-gut.
5. Descartes, R. (1637). *Discours de la Méthode.* Paris: Librio, 2013 reprint. English edition: *A Discourse on the Method.* Oxford: Oxford University Press, 2008.
6. As with all the examples provided in this book, this one is simply an illustration of how to handle an issue-driven structuring effort, not an "ideal" or "perfect" version of an issue tree. Our version might offer some room for improvement. For example, the split of the third sub-issue on delaying international expansion does not look very MECE to us. Do you have better ideas?

6

Structure the Problem: Analytical Frameworks

In the previous chapter, we discussed two ways to structure a problem: the hypothesis pyramid and the issue tree. Both approaches enable us to break down a big, complex problem (or a leading hypothesis) into smaller components, then smaller ones again until we can resolve the elementary issues. Each decomposition must be MECE—each problem (or hypothesis) must be divided into MECE sub-problems (or sub-hypotheses).

In principle, breaking down a problem into smaller problems is easy. If, for instance, someone asks you "Why did sales decrease?" you may quickly think of decomposing total sales by region, product family, customer type, or any other arithmetic breakdown readily available, and identifying which categories decreased. Using basic logic in this way is MECE and, usually, sensible.

Problem structuring gets much more difficult, however, whenever the problem is more complex, or when you face a broader question—for instance, "How successful will Company X be in the near future?" When you must address such a question, how do you break it down into MECE components?

Fortunately, there is a solution—or, rather, a toolbox full of solutions. That's because many problems are not genuinely unique; they belong to a *class* of similar problems. Company X is unique, but asking how well a company will perform in the near future is a problem many people address every day.

A stock analyst, for instance, might tackle this problem by saying, "Easy. I take the latest forecast that reflects the market's consensus, then adjust with company announcements, if there are any, and with the news flow that's relevant to the company's business. This gives me a new forecast" (Fig. 6.1).

© The Author(s) 2018
B. Garrette et al., *Cracked it!*, https://doi.org/10.1007/978-3-319-89375-4_6

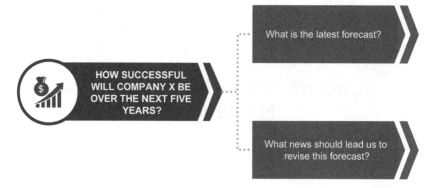

Fig. 6.1 A stock analyst's framework

This stock analyst may not be aware of it, but he is using an *analytical framework* (or simply "framework"). Analytical frameworks are prepackaged, MECE breakdowns of typical problems, such as the one we just described. They provide an invaluable shortcut to someone structuring a problem. We're applying a framework here to the top-level question, but frameworks can help break down questions at any level in an issue tree or hypothesis pyramid.

In this chapter, we'll discuss the power of frameworks, introduce frameworks you can use in your problem structuring, and provide a library of our "top" frameworks—our subjective, but informed, selection of the frameworks you should know and use. We'll also explain the limitations and dangers of frameworks so that you can use them appropriately.

Using Frameworks to Breakdown Problems

Frameworks are the building blocks of issue trees and hypothesis pyramids. Like a child assembling LEGO bricks, a skilled problem solver combines frameworks to structure problems in a MECE way.

Consider, for instance, the simple issue tree in Fig. 6.2, which addresses whether a private equity (PE) firm[1] should invest in Company X.

The figure shows a basic breakdown of the question along the time axis: there is the short-term question of how Company X will perform while the PE fund owns it, and the longer-term question of how much value the fund can realize when selling it. Note that the first branch of the tree is the question we saw in Fig. 6.1. In theory, you could arrive at this split knowing nothing about the PE business, except that it consists of buying, holding, and reselling companies. Whether you should buy logically depends on what you think about (1) what will happen while you hold, and (2) at what price you can sell.

But if you're doing this analysis for a PE firm, you do know something about the PE model. You don't need to start from a blank page and rely on pure logic every time you ask yourself whether to invest in a company. This is a problem you've encountered before, and you have a predefined way of dealing with it. A PE analyst, for instance, might break down the question as illustrated in Fig. 6.3.

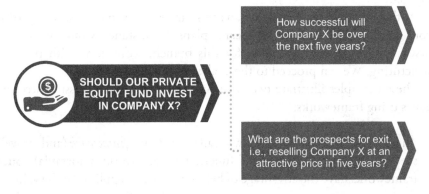

Fig. 6.2 A basic question breakdown for a private equity firm

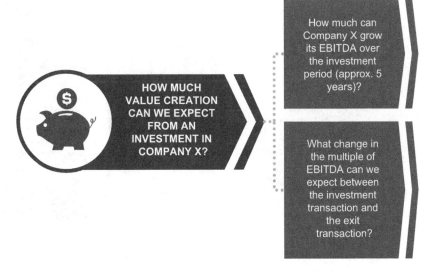

Fig. 6.3 Private equity firm issue tree

As you can see, these questions are similar to the ones in Fig. 6.2. In fact, they're the same questions, reformulated more precisely and quantitatively using financial concepts. To do this, the PE analyst is using an analytical framework, which is a simple corporate finance formula: EV = EBITDA x (EV/EBITDA).[2] The formula implies that value creation (change in EV) is driven by a change in one of the two terms in the equation—EBITDA and transaction multiple. The PE firm can now tackle each question by using other frameworks. For instance, what drives growth in EBITDA? A possible framework to break down this question into smaller ones might be the one in Fig. 6.4.

At this level, we see how direct analysis can resolve some questions: getting your hands on the management team's plans, for instance, would answer the first question. This means that, for this branch, we're done with problem structuring. We can proceed to the analysis stage.

These examples illustrate two ways we can break down an issue into sub-issues using frameworks:

- The split in Fig. 6.3 is what we will call a *functional framework* (and, as we'll see shortly, a specific style of functional framework: a formula). Such frameworks have the advantage of being universally applicable: the value of *any* company can be decomposed into a profit indicator and a multiple of that indicator. Functional frameworks are the core building blocks of

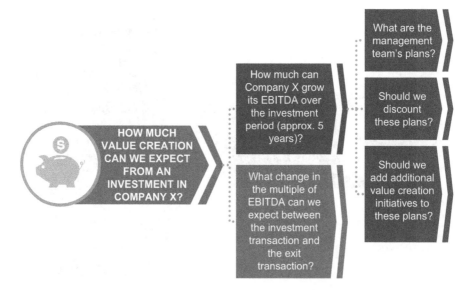

Fig. 6.4 Private equity firm issue tree (continued)

business reasoning. If you read textbooks in marketing, finance, or other disciplines, or if you attend a business degree program, you'll learn many functional frameworks.

- The second-level split of the first branch illustrated in Fig. 6.4 may have surprised you if you're not familiar with the PE industry. When you look at the resulting tree, it's a MECE split, and a practical way to think about this problem. But there is no way of knowing that, unless you know it. This is an example of an *industry framework*. Unlike functional frameworks, which we learn in classrooms and textbooks, businesspeople usually learn industry frameworks on the job. Every industry has its shortcuts to analyze the critical problems it routinely faces, and these frameworks are often embedded in the tools, methods, and decision rules it uses. In most PE firms, for instance, a much more sophisticated version of the framework we illustrated here is embedded in the templates and metrics used to evaluate investment opportunities.

The Danger of Frameworks: Frameworks as Mental Models

The convenience of frameworks—whether functional or industry specific—comes with a warning: because they assume the question to which they're applied is generic, they also assume it belongs to the class of questions for which the framework was designed. To use a framework is to adopt the mental model of the function or industry in question, with all the assumptions it takes for granted.

For instance, compare Figs. 6.1 and 6.4. The stock analyst and the PE investor are both trying to predict how successful Company X will be over the next five years. However, the different frameworks they use reflect different assumptions.

The stock analyst's framework is a model to evaluate stock prices. It relies on several significant assumptions. For instance, it assumes the stock price correctly reflects, at any point in time, the company's prospects and public information about the company.

The PE investor assumes management actions create value. She also assumes a new owner—such as her firm—can suggest and monitor additional actions to improve value creation.

These frameworks reflect different worldviews. Is the real worth of a company a price set by changes in the supply and demand for a company's stock? Or is it a value calculated by anticipating future cash flows? Perhaps, as you read this, you've already sided with the stock analyst or the PE investor. If your personal experience is in either field, you may be drawn to one framework (or shocked by the oversimplification we make here, and already thinking of a much more elaborate version of these models). Our point here, however, is not to discuss the merits of these views, but to emphasize that different frameworks reflect different worldviews and assumptions.

The danger is that when we apply frameworks routinely and unquestioningly, we lose sight of the assumptions embedded in them. As we mentioned in Chap. 2, "A way of seeing is also a way of not seeing."[3] This is dangerous when the assumptions underlying our frameworks aren't met. A stock analyst's way of seeing, for instance, makes several assumptions about the efficiency and liquidity of markets; without them, the pricing model does not apply. Conversely, the PE investor's worldview assumes that information asymmetries make it possible to capture opportunities others don't see. Both assumptions are usually sensible, but neither is guaranteed to hold true all the time. A good discipline is to break down complex problems using *multiple* frameworks. We'll return to this idea at the end of the chapter.

But first, we must build our mental library of frameworks. It's hard to use multiple frameworks if we don't know any. We'll start with industry frameworks. These are the most powerful and the first place to start. Functional frameworks are the next best thing. If all else fails and you still don't know how to break down a question into smaller parts, you must do without a framework and use elementary logic. Figure 6.5 compares the three main ways to break down questions.

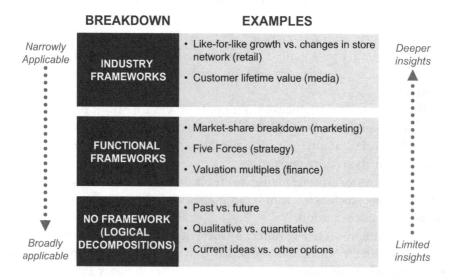

Fig. 6.5 Three ways to break down questions

Industry Frameworks: Value Drivers

To illustrate industry frameworks, let's imagine the CEO of Starbucks France has hired you as a consultant and asked you for advice on a classic, simple question: *How can we improve our profitability?*[4] If you ask yourself how to break down this question into components, the first answer that may come to mind is to decompose profits into revenues and costs, as in Fig. 6.6. This approach is easy, and it's popular—virtually all of our students propose it as a first approach. It also seems obviously MECE—it uses the same breakdown as the income statement, and you can trust accountants for their MECEness.

Unfortunately, this breakdown is practically useless. The reason is simple: while revenues and costs are a MECE decomposition of profit, *changes* in revenues and costs are not. Everything else being equal, price increases drive volumes down. Growing revenues without raising prices means increasing volumes, which almost always entails additional costs. Conversely, many ways to reduce costs will sooner or later impact revenues. Costs and revenues are independent and provide a MECE breakdown of the income statement when viewed statically. From a dynamic, managerial perspective, however, this decomposition isn't sensible.

If you have doubts about this, ask yourself what would come at the next level of the tree. On the revenue branch of the tree, you might ask, for instance: "Would increasing staff to reduce waiting times in stores increase revenues?" But on the cost side, you might ask questions such as: "How can Starbucks reduce personnel costs in stores?" Ideas you pursue on the cost side and the revenue side are intertwined. An issue tree that starts this way is not MECE: it is messy.

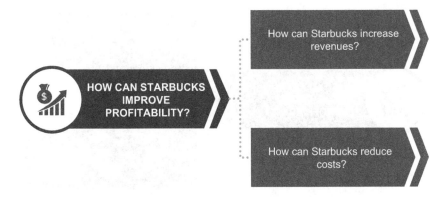

Fig. 6.6 Simple breakdown of Starbucks question

What we need here is a decomposition that doesn't blindly follow an accounting template, but reflects categories of things you can *do* to improve profitability. We need a framework that indicates how the *actions* of a retailer such as Starbucks create value—or fail to do so. Every industry has such frameworks: they reflect the industry's *value drivers,* the important levers of value creation in the business.[5]

A quick way to identify such value drivers is to look at the way companies in each industry analyze and explain their results. Don't look at their accounting statements, which are standardized across industries. Instead, examine the explanations of management actions in the financial reports they give to shareholders and financial analysts. For instance, Starbucks, like most retail chains, reports a critically important indicator: "comparable store sales growth," also called "same-store sales" or "like-for-like (LFL) sales growth." LFL growth measures the variation in sales for stores that were open the previous year and indicates the growth (or decline) that a chain would experience if there were no store openings or closures. This metric matters because it measures the intrinsic ability of a retail format to attract and serve consumers. It also captures a capital-efficient (and more profitable) source of growth, as same-store growth typically requires considerably less investment than new store openings. Businesses that operate chains of stores routinely break down revenues between LFL and other sources of growth.

Applying this framework to our problem suggests a different decomposition of the issue tree than the "revenues and costs" approach (Fig. 6.7).

There is, however, an obvious problem with this issue tree: the branches don't address the question! The decomposition we used is one of *growth*, not one of *profits*. If we want a useful breakdown of our problem, we can use the LFL versus new store split as inspiration, but we must customize it.

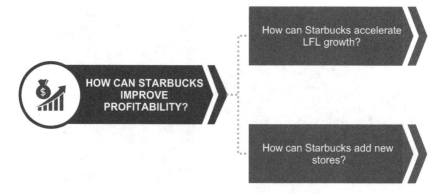

Fig. 6.7 Starbucks issue tree first attempt

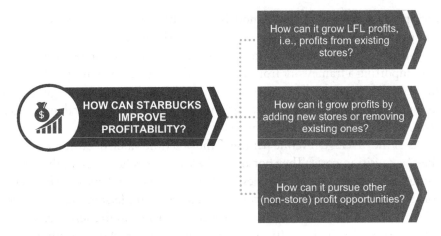

Fig. 6.8 Starbucks issue tree using industry framework

In Fig. 6.8, we have tailored the split to a profitability problem. We're now using the distinction between LFL performance and change in store portfolio to analyze profits, not just sales. To be exhaustive, we've added a third branch: the framework we're using is a retail framework, but our problem statement doesn't imply that we limit the pursuit of growth to the current retail business model. If we didn't add this branch, we'd exclude the possibility for Starbucks to pursue other avenues, such as selling Starbucks-branded products in super-markets or developing an online business.

Choosing the Right Industry Framework

Our three-branch approach feels like a promising first-level framework to think about value creation for a chain of retail coffee shops. But would it work for, say, an automotive company—replacing "stores" with "dealerships"? Technically, yes—the issue tree would still be MECE. But we would miss some of the key drivers of profitability in a car company—like which models to develop, how to price them, or the profitability of financing services. Value drivers in the automotive industry differ from those in restaurant chains. Moreover, if you were looking at an industry in which there are no physical points of sales to consumers (for instance, passenger aircrafts or investment banking), the framework we use here would be irrelevant.

This illustrates a fundamental principle of problem structuring: *to choose the right framework, you must know something about the industry*. Executives who move from one industry to another sometimes ignore this principle at their peril because their mental models—and the frameworks they use to analyze problems—are out of sync with their new situation.

This doesn't mean industry frameworks are eternal, immutable truths, and that importing a framework from another industry is always wrong. Changing frameworks is especially important when the industry is changing. For instance, when phone services transitioned from being a regulated utility to a competitive business, phone companies started to think of value creation in terms of the "average revenue per user," the "lifetime value of customers," and their "acquisition cost." They borrowed these concepts (and, often, the people using them) from other industries, such as insurance and travel, where customer loyalty is a crucial framework to analyze for understanding value creation. But this was not accidental: it reflected a change in the actual drivers of value creation in the industry. When consumers had a choice in phone services, phone companies needed to change the business levers they examined. The new frameworks were a purposeful reflection of these changes. Frameworks are mental representations of reality: changing them is justified when reality changes.

You might argue, however, that this is too narrow a view of how to choose frameworks. Even if reality doesn't change, isn't it a good idea to consider it anew? When we say it takes a "fresh pair of eyes" to solve a strategic problem, don't we mean that applying a different framework, learned in a different industry, can help us come up with fresh insights?

This objection is correct. A veteran from Procter & Gamble (P&G), for example, would look at our Starbucks question differently. Using a framework familiar to marketers of consumer products, she might ask, for instance, which brands and product lines drive existing stores' sales. This might lead her to notice that the tea product line is performing well and to consider a marketing campaign to increase the awareness of these products. Or perhaps she would analyze store sales by consumption occasions, and notice that sales are brisk in the morning but relatively slow in the afternoon. This would lead her to suggest testing further changes to the product lines. She would think about this problem differently than a veteran retail executive.

Or imagine Starbucks has just hired someone who had a long and successful career as an operations executive at Toyota. Looking at the long lines in the store, perhaps this person would immediately focus on ways to speed up service. Can the layout of the food preparation counters be optimized? Can parts of the production process be standardized without losing the customization of the finished product that is Starbucks's trademark? Can some orders be placed in advance and payments accelerated, perhaps by having consumers use a mobile app?

Some of these ideas could indeed be valuable. Such fresh thinking is useful as a *complement* to the core frameworks on which an industry relies. But these frameworks, and the mental models they reflect, are not industry-specific frameworks. What our hypothetical P&G and Toyota executives are applying to Starbucks is deep *functional* knowledge they've gained in their previous industries. It's not expertise in the fast-moving consumer goods industry the P&G executive brings. Instead, she uses brand management frameworks, which are part of the marketing toolkit familiar to consumer goods marketers. Likewise, the Toyota executive brings a "lean production" mindset that has served auto companies and other industries well. What these examples illustrate is the value of *functional frameworks*.

Functional Frameworks

Let's come back to the Starbucks case. Imagine you're not familiar with the retail industry and its value drivers, but you are an experienced businessperson familiar with core concepts in marketing, finance, and so on. How might you think about this issue?

One place you might start is with some basic breakdowns of revenues and costs—not the simplistic "increase revenues, reduce costs" approach we started with (and which we've seen is impractical), but a slightly more sophisticated and equally universal breakdown of profits, as shown in Fig. 6.9.

This approach is perhaps less elegant than the approach of Fig. 6.8, but it's a useful start. It tries to address the problem of overlaps between cost and

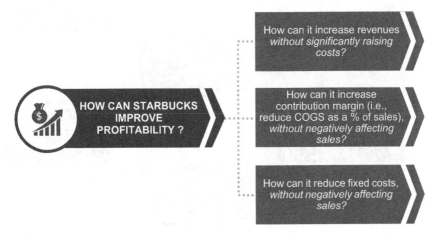

Fig. 6.9 Starbucks issue tree using functional framework

revenue levers by focusing on how to change the profit equation, "all other things being equal" (as the italicized phrases in Fig. 6.9 emphasize). The logic of this breakdown may be apparent if you're a management controller. Controllers are skilled at analyzing sources of change in past financial results. Their expertise lies precisely in disentangling the effects that contribute to financial results.

Let's further analyze the first branch—how to increase revenues without raising costs. One MECE way to make this first-level split is to distinguish between new and existing customers. This split may come naturally to those with a marketing background. So might the next-level split between frequency of purchase and spend per purchase, which is another classic way marketers break down revenues (Fig. 6.10).

These are examples of *core functional frameworks* from the areas of finance and marketing, respectively. These frameworks are second nature to experienced professionals in these specialties, but they're sufficiently important and universally applicable to be worth knowing, even if you don't work in these functions. Most issue trees will require you to use several functional frameworks at one level or another in the decomposition of the core issue. Being familiar with the main functional frameworks is, therefore, an essential skill for all problem solvers.

As with industry value drivers, however, some precautions are needed before using functional frameworks.

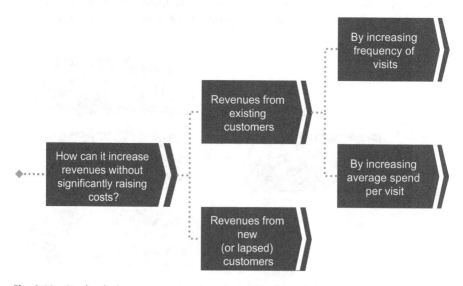

Fig. 6.10 Starbucks issue tree using functional framework (continued)

First, you can't use everything you learn in business school or elsewhere as a framework for problem structuring. The concept of competitive advantage, for instance, is vitally important (some might call it a "framework" for thinking about strategy), but it won't help you build an issue tree. It might be useful at an earlier stage (especially in your problem statement), but not in problem structuring. Many essential business concepts and tools aren't analytical frameworks: only those that provide a MECE decomposition of a generic problem qualify.

Second, since frameworks are decompositions of a *particular* generic problem, it's vital not to use them to decompose a *different* problem. Many people who master a business framework—whether it's a perennial favorite such as Porter's Five Forces model or a hot, trendy one—seem consumed with a desire to apply it to any question that crops up. Porter's Five Forces model, for instance, is useful to address only one question: "Is this industry attractive for investment?" If you face an issue that consists of determining the future of a brand or discussing the merits of an acquisition, trying to break down your question into five forces will only create confusion.[6] This principle may seem obvious, but it's violated in just about every issue tree we see.

Third, functional frameworks, like industry frameworks, reflect a functional mental model. Most business problems, however, aren't narrowly functional. Consider the Starbucks case: is this a finance problem? A strategy problem? A marketing problem? All three? Evidently, this question has no simple answer. Problems, in real life, don't come with a label attached to them that tells you to which subject they belong and in which textbook to look for the solution.

One of the most frequent sources of bad problem structuring is the tendency of people who know one framework well to want to apply it to all problems. Our Starbucks problem may look like a brand positioning problem to an advertising person, a cost management problem to an accountant, and a store location problem to a realtor. The desire to reuse (only) frameworks we know well can lead to the *wrong framework pitfall* we introduced in Chap. 2. As another version of the saying we mentioned in that chapter (this one attributed to Mark Twain) goes, "To a man with a hammer, everything looks like a nail."

Our Top Functional Frameworks

Having more than a hammer in your toolbox will help you become a better problem solver. In this spirit, we've assembled a catalog of functional frameworks in Tables 6.1, 6.2, 6.3, 6.4, and 6.5 at the end of this chapter. It's not an exhaustive list. On the contrary, it's an intentionally restricted selection of

Table 6.1 Selected marketing frameworks

Question addressed	Framework	Components	Style of framework
How to slice a market into groups that are homogeneous regarding a particular issue?	Market segmentation	Segments: e.g., demographic groups, geographic regions, attitudes to the category, past behavior regarding product, etc.	Typology
How to grow the market? (e.g., smoking, mobile phones, etc.)	Market size	Penetration (% of users in population) * consumption per user	Formula
Where do revenues come from?	Revenue breakdown (basic)	Market size * market share *(see also: market share breakdown)*	Formula
How to grow revenues?	Revenue breakdown (basic approach)	Number of transactions * transaction size, *or* number of purchasers * frequency of purchase * number of items per transaction * average price per item	Formula
How to grow market share?	Market share breakdown (advanced)	Market share = penetration share (%) * share of wallet (%) * heavy usage index (I)	Formula
How to reach end consumers?	Market channels	Channels to market	Typology
What levers can we use to change our marketing mix?	Marketing mix	Product, price, promotion, placement	Checklist
Is it worth investing in acquiring new clients for a recurring-revenue business?	Customer lifetime value	(recurring annual revenues * average years a customer remains)– customer acquisition cost	Formula

Marketing frameworks are discussed in various textbooks, including: Kotler, P.T., & Keller, K.L. (2015). *Marketing Management* (15th edition). Upper Saddle River, NJ: Prentice Hall

"must-know" frameworks. We handpicked these frameworks subjectively, with three principles in mind:

1. We looked for the "classics," not the trendy new ideas. For each classic question in strategy, for instance, there are many (often conflicting) schools of thought, each of which claims to offer the "correct" way to think about the problem, and often a framework to reflect it. We erred on the side of

Table 6.2 Selected strategy frameworks

Question addressed	Framework	Components	Style of framework
How to get a quick snapshot of a business?	3Cs	Company, customers, competitors	Checklist
Is this business model solid and viable?	Business model canvas	Key partners, key activities, key resources, value propositions, customer relationships, channels, customer segments, cost structure, revenue streams	Checklist
What external trends can affect this business?	PESTEL	Political, economic, social, technological, environmental, and legal	Typology
Is this industry attractive?	Porter's Five Forces	Internal rivalry, barriers to entry, substitutes, supplier power, buyer power	Checklist
What generic source of advantage do we pursue for a business unit?	Generic business unit strategies	Cost strategy, differentiation strategy, niche strategy	Typology
What resources is our advantage based on?	Strategic resources	Assets/skills/relationships	Typology
Is our competitive advantage based on defensible resources?	VRIO resources	Valuable, rare, hard to imitate, exploited by organization	Checklist
How can we grow?	Modes and directions for growth (corporate strategy)	*Modes:* organic growth, alliances, acquisitions *Directions:* same business, international expansion, vertical integration, diversification	Typology
What would be the benefits of growing?	Scale and scope benefits	Scale, scope, and learning	Typology

Strategy frameworks are discussed in various textbooks, including: Grant, R.M. (2016). *Contemporary Strategy Analysis* (9th edition). Chichester: Wiley

picking the tried-and-tested "oldies but goodies." (We excluded, however, classic "frameworks" that are now near-universally regarded as obsolete, such as the SWOT—Strengths, Weaknesses, Opportunities, and Threats—strategy framework.) We recognize that, in some domains, there is no clear consensus about what should be the "dominant" framework.

Table 6.3 Selected organization and change frameworks

Question addressed	Framework	Components	Style of framework
Are the components of this organization coherent?	7Ss	Strategy, structure, skills, staff, systems, style, shared values	Checklist
How can we structure an organization?	Types of organization structures	Functional, divisional, matrix, horizontal/networked/flat	Typology
How to make change happen in an organization?	Kotter's eight-step process for leading change	Urgency, coalition, vision, army, barriers, quick wins, acceleration, institutionalization	Checklist
How to get individuals to change their behavior?	McKinsey influence model	Role modeling, understanding and conviction, talent and skill development, formal mechanisms	Checklist

Organization frameworks are discussed in various textbooks, including Robbins, S.P., & Judge, T.A. (2017). *Organizational Behavior* (17th edition). Harlow: Pearson

Table 6.4 Selected operations frameworks

Question addressed	Framework	Components	Style of framework
How to optimize production capacity based on trade-off between utilization and waiting time (or inventory)?	Operations management triangle (based on queuing theory models)	Waiting time/ inventory level, capacity utilization, variability of process and demand	Formula
What is the optimal purchase frequency of a recurrent supply? ("How often should I fill my gas tank?")	Economic order, quantity	Purchase frequency, transaction cost, financial cost of inventory	Formula
How to match uncertain demand profitably? ("How many copies should a newspaper vendor carry each morning?")	News vendor model	Production capacity, future demand, idle capacity cost	Formula

Operations frameworks are discussed in various textbooks, including: Chase, R.B., Jacobs, F.R., & Aquilano, N. (2005). *Operations Management for Competitive Advantage* (11th edition). New York: McGraw-Hill

Table 6.5 Selected finance frameworks

Question addressed	Framework	Components	Style of framework
Does this business generate a profit?	P&L (profit and loss statement)	(Net) profit = revenue−COGS−Unallocated expenses (− taxes)	Formula
Which costs depend on volume and which don't?	Cost breakdown	Fixed vs. variable costs	Typology
From what volume (or price) does this business cover its fixed costs and generate a profit?	Breakeven	Breakeven number of units = fixed cost/contribution margin per unit (Note: can also calculate breakeven price given several units)	Formula
What return is an investment (or the aggregate set of investments made by a firm) generating?	Return on investment ratios	Some return/some investment (e.g., ROCE, ROIC, ROI for a specific investment, etc.)	Formula
What is the minimum return on investment to achieve economic profitability?	WACC (weighted average cost of capital)	Share of equity in capital structure * cost of equity + share of debt * cost of debt	Formula
How much is this project (or company) worth in present money?	NPV (net present value)	Present value + value of predicted cash flows + terminal value	Formula
How much is this company worth, based on the cash it generates and the valuation of comparable companies?	Valuation based on multiples	EV = EBITDA x (EBITDA/EV multiple) *or* formula based on multiples of other result (EBIT, net income, etc.)	Formula
What levers can increase the total value of this business?	Valuation hexagon	Perception gap, operating improvements, new owner, growth opportunities, financial engineering	Checklist

Corporate finance frameworks are discussed in various textbooks, including: Berk, J., & DeMarzo, P. (2016). *Corporate Finance* (4th edition). Harlow: Pearson; and: Koller, T., Goedhart, M., & Wessels, D. (2015). *Valuation: Measuring and Managing the Value of Companies* (6th edition). Hoboken, NJ: Wiley

Note: COGS is Cost of Goods Sold. ROCE is Return on Capital Employed. ROIC is Return on Invested Capital. ROI is Return on Investment. For other abbreviations, please see endnote 2.

2. These frameworks are the workhorses of issue trees and hypothesis pyramids: they break down problems you are likely to encounter frequently. There are a multitude of specialized frameworks immensely useful to solve highly targeted questions. For example, if your problem is to engineer "nudges" that will modify people's behaviors, the EAST framework will remind you that the behaviors you are encouraging should be Easy, Attractive, Social, and Timely.[7] While this is a fascinating problem, you are likely to deal with it less often than quantifying the size of a market. We picked frameworks that address the questions we believe—subjectively and based on our own experience—to be the most frequently asked.

3. Finally, the list overrepresents strategy frameworks. We know this reflects our own mental models as strategy professors ... but it also reflects a choice to focus on "general management" topics, in which the questions are more difficult to frame. These are the questions, we anticipate, that prompted many readers to pick up this book. Had you readily identified your problem as a marketing issue, you would probably be reading a marketing book now.

We don't discuss each framework in detail—if we did, this would be a much longer book. But we try to be specific about what question the framework addresses to help you avoid the "hammer-in-search-of-a-nail" problem. Intentionally, the entry point into this table of frameworks is the problem to which the framework applies, not the framework: the nail, not the hammer. This is not how these frameworks are usually taught in their respective functional disciplines. Our perspective on these tools may be restrictive, as many of them have other applications besides being useful analytical frameworks to decompose problems. In a problem-structuring effort, however, this simplification is useful.

We also specify which "style" each framework adopts. We distinguish between three styles of functional frameworks:

- *Formula* frameworks, which connect a result and its components. Formulas are useful whenever you define the problem as computing a number and thus requiring a calculation.
- *Typology* frameworks, which list different categories of things. Typologies are useful whenever the problem you deal with calls for a MECE list of things—options, reasons, factors, whatever—and you want to make sure you don't forget one.
- *Checklist* frameworks, finally, are similar to typologies, but are lists in which *all* elements must be present simultaneously for a condition to be true.

When All Else Fails, Try Good Old Logic

If you master enough industry and functional frameworks, you'll be in good shape to deal with many "classic" problems you routinely encounter. That is what experience should bring you: not having the answers, but knowing which questions to ask—which frameworks to use.

But when a problem is complex, the issue tree used to tackle it isn't just a juxtaposition of two or three ready-made analytical frameworks. In your problem-structuring approach, you'll need a "cement" to hold these blocks together. You'll also need a basic material to fill the holes when no handy framework is available. This is when you'll need *logical decompositions*.

Logical decompositions, as the name implies, include all the ways to break down a problem that are MECE in a purely logical sense. Suppose, for instance, you are drilling down one branch in Fig. 6.10: you ask how Starbucks might increase average spend per visit. To do so, you're investigating several possible new product ideas—teas, soft drinks, food, and so on. How can you make sure your list of ideas is MECE? There's no limit to your creativity. Fortunately, a logical framework can help you, as Fig. 6.11 illustrates.

That's right: the magic "other." "These/others" is a basic logical distinction you'll use all the time to make an issue tree MECE. There are many equally handy (and similarly commonsensical) logical splits you can use: "old/new," "past/present/future," "inside/outside," "intended/unintended," and so on. We can't list all the ways logic can help you divide problems into their components, but with practice, you'll discover that many splits become natural.

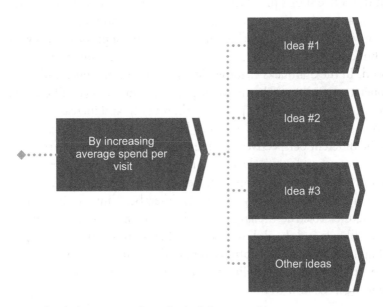

Fig. 6.11 Starbucks issue tree using a logical decomposition

Logical decompositions are MECE and nearly universal in their applicability. Their analytical effectiveness—the insight they bring—is no match for the power of analytical frameworks. But they'll help you when you're stuck.

*   *   *

Charlie Munger, vice chairman of Berkshire Hathaway, once advised aspiring businesspeople to "have models in [their] heads …, multiple models, because if you just have one or two that you're using, the nature of human psychology is such that you'll torture reality so that it fits your models …, and the models have to come from multiple disciplines—because all the wisdom of the world is not to be found in one little academic department."[8] What Munger says of models is true of the subset of models we call analytical frameworks. Good problem solving requires the ability to mobilize, combine, and contrast many frameworks. As Munger suggests, you must constantly strive to broaden your personal "library" of frameworks.

Multiple frameworks are also the reason solving problems is often more effective—and sometimes more difficult—when you work in teams. It's more effective than working solo because different team members have different mental models and different frameworks to leverage. Sometimes it's more difficult, however, because these different frameworks can make it difficult to communicate. If all you have is your single lens on the problem, another person's view may strike you as irrelevant or uninformed. Recall our Starbucks example: the marketing and operations experts had different perspectives about the coffee shop's profitability, which could lead to conflict rather than a broader, and more accurate, consensus view of the problem.

Frameworks are rarely "the" method to structure a problem. They are, however, building blocks of the method—an integrative issue tree or hypothesis pyramid. In the Starbucks example, ideas about product lines and in-store service operations are both relevant to the problem and belong in different branches of the issue tree. To structure problems thoroughly, and increase our chances of developing valuable solutions, we must be willing and able to leverage and integrate the different perspectives and frameworks of different contributors.

An effective problem solver is not only someone who masters multiple frameworks, but also someone who excels at combining these frameworks (and the ones contributed by other team members) into an integrative problem structure. To structure large, complex problems, you need frameworks as building blocks and the skill to assemble them—this is the art and practice of building issue trees and hypothesis pyramids. Your ability to develop an integrative problem structure will enhance your ability to solve it. In the next chapter, we'll see how to do it.

Chapter 6 in One Page

- Analytical frameworks = MECE breakdowns of generic problems
- Frameworks reflect mental models and the assumptions underlying them:
  - *A stock analyst and a PE investor use different frameworks to value a company.*
- You must be aware of the assumptions underlying the frameworks you use.
- Industry frameworks are most powerful to address value drivers in an industry:
  - *Retail: LFL versus new stores, <u>not</u> revenues versus costs*
- Functional frameworks are the most versatile:
  - Build your mental library of formulas, typologies, and checklists in the main disciplines (see Tables 6.1, 6.2, 6.3, 6.4 and 6.5).
  - *Don't be a "hammer in search of nails."*
- Use logical decompositions to break down problems when frameworks aren't available.
- Issue trees and hypothesis pyramids integrate multiple frameworks and logics.

Notes

1. PE usually refers to investment funds that are not publicly traded and whose investors are typically large institutional investors, university endowments, or wealthy individuals. PE firms typically use extensive debt financing to purchase companies, which they restructure and attempt to resell for a higher value.

2. EV (enterprise value) is a measure of a company's total economic value. EBITDA (earnings before interest, tax, depreciation, and amortization) is an often-used proxy for the earning potential of a business. There are many other valuation approaches that could be used. In this example, there are also other ways a PE firm could help create value in the target company, including using financial leverage. Also, an evaluation of this investment would not be complete without an assessment of risk. Our aim here is not to offer a complete approach to company valuation, but merely to illustrate the process of problem decomposition using analytical frameworks.

3. Burke, K. (1935). *Permanence and Change: An Anatomy of Purpose.* Reprint, Berkeley: University of California Press, 1984: 70.

4. We assume here that a complete TOSCA problem statement has been written, but it is not necessary for our purposes to go over all its elements.

5. We assume here that the problem you are trying to solve is one of strategy, or value creation, in the industry in question. You may be pursuing a more specific goal—for instance, trying to increase customer satisfaction, reduce employee turnover, or increase on-time deliveries. If that is the case, you have a functional question, and functional frameworks will give you a better starting point.

6. On each of these questions, industry attractiveness may appear as one of the branches on your issue tree. For instance, if you're considering an acquisition, evaluating whether the target company plays in an attractive industry may be one of the first-level *sub*-issues. Once you get to that level (and only then), Porter's Five Forces model might be the right framework.

7. Service, O., et al. (2014). *EAST, Four Simple Ways to Apply Behavioural Insights.* UK Cabinet Office and NESTA.

8. Munger, C. (1994). *A Lesson on Elementary, Worldly Wisdom As It Relates To Investment Management & Business.* Speech to USC Business School students. Retrieved from https://old.ycombinator.com/munger.html.

7

Solve the Problem: Eight Degrees of Analysis

Remember Tracy, the CEO we met in Chap. 3? As you'll recall, Tracy is trying to determine the fate of Pluto and Uranus, the two money-losing units of Solar.

Tracy has been busy since we last met her. Based on extensive discussions with her team, she formulated two hypotheses. First, she believes Pluto is an essential component of Solar's portfolio and its performance problems can be addressed. She has entrusted this task to the newly appointed head of that division. Second, she believes Uranus should be sold—and she's asked you, an analyst on the Chief Financial Officer's team, to identify and conduct the required analyses to determine whether this leading hypothesis is correct. Having stated and structured the problem, it's finally time to solve it, and you're the lucky one who gets to do it. How will you proceed?

From Structuring to Analyses

Your starting point is Tracy's leading hypothesis: Solar should sell Uranus. Tracy believes that Uranus is a non-core unit in Solar's business portfolio and that it can be sold at an attractive price. These two reasons comprise Tracy's hypothesis pyramid.

Since Tracy is the boss and the problem owner, and since she has devoted considerable thought to this problem, your mission is not to broaden the problem scope, but to look into her hypothesis. A hypothesis pyramid, rather than an issue tree, is appropriate (refer to Fig. 5.7 on the pros and cons of the two approaches, if necessary). Because the hypothesis-driven path increases

© The Author(s) 2018
B. Garrette et al., *Cracked it!*, https://doi.org/10.1007/978-3-319-89375-4_7

the solution confirmation risk, you must be watchful and challenge Tracy's reasoning (and your own) at each step in the problem-solving process. First, ensure that the hypothesis pyramid is logically sound (see Chap. 5). As you listen to Tracy, you realize it isn't: the two sub-hypotheses Tracy has given you are necessary conditions for her leading hypothesis to hold, but they're not sufficient. In an effort to make the hypothesis breakdown MECE, you immediately add a third necessary condition: "The sale of Uranus will not create other problems for Solar." (Well done: Tracy is already impressed with your problem-structuring skills.) This first level of the hypothesis pyramid appears in Fig. 7.1.

Each of the three sub-hypotheses breaks down into elementary hypotheses (numbered in the following paragraphs in reference to Fig. 7.2).

The first sub-hypothesis states Uranus is a "non-core" component of Solar's portfolio, which means it's not an essential part of the business portfolio from a corporate strategy standpoint. Tracy's assessment relies on a few elementary hypotheses. First, Solar's corporate strategy, as Tracy has defined it, doesn't require the technologies Uranus uses (elementary hypothesis 1.1). Second, although Uranus's products were historically sold to the same corporate customers as those of Earth and Mars (Solar's core business units), and this commercial synergy had been the reason for Solar to acquire Uranus, technological changes have made Uranus's products less and less relevant to this core customer group (1.2), and this trend is expected to continue (1.3). Uranus has no other meaningful synergies with Earth and Mars (1.4) and can easily be carved

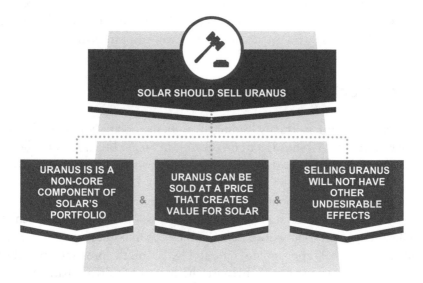

Fig. 7.1 First level of hypothesis pyramid on Solar case

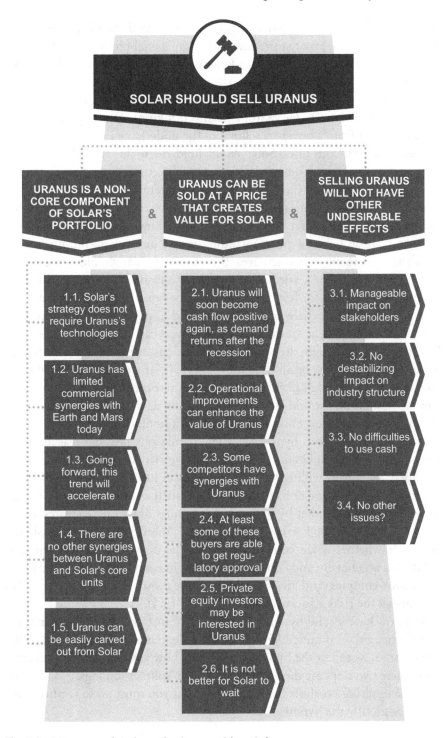

Fig. 7.2 More complete hypothesis pyramid on Solar case

out from Solar, implying that its operations can be decoupled from Solar's without creating major organizational and managerial problems (1.5).

The second sub-hypothesis states Uranus can be sold at a price that creates value for Solar. This reasoning uses a corporate finance framework we mentioned in Chap. 6, the valuation hexagon: it compares the net present value of the cash flows Solar can derive from Uranus if it keeps the company with the price it can get from a buyer by selling it. The underlying logic is that, even if Uranus is a non-core unit, Solar could hold on to it. Tracy believes that Uranus's losses are temporary and the unit will return to profitability when the economy improves (2.1). Uranus management has told her of several manufacturing effectiveness programs that aim to restore profitability within two years (2.2). Solar should therefore calculate how much Uranus is worth under a realistic business plan, including the value of these improvements, which it's confident it can achieve. This value to Solar should represent its "reservation price" for a sale: Solar doesn't face cash constraints and has no reason to sell Uranus for less than the value the business would generate if it kept it. Tracy believes there are buyers prepared to pay more for Uranus than this reservation price. Some other industry players can generate synergies with Uranus (2.3), although they would need to get approval from anti-trust authorities, which may be an issue for some (2.4). There may also be financial buyers, such as PE funds (2.5). Finally, a legitimate question to ask is whether any of these buyers would pay a good price for Uranus *now*, when it's not showing a profit. If not, Solar should wait until results improve (2.6).

Finally, the third sub-hypothesis tries to rule out possible reasons Solar might not want to sell Uranus, even if it's appropriate to regard it as non-core and there are buyers willing to pay a good price. Reasons might include, for instance, unwanted reactions by stakeholders such as labor unions or regulators (3.1), or the risk that by selling Uranus, Solar unwittingly creates a dangerous competitor for Earth and Mars (3.2). Another question you should explore is whether Solar knows how to use the cash generated by the sale. While this is generally not a difficult question, in a family-owned company, it can prove complex and divisive (3.3). There's also no guarantee this list includes all the risks associated with this move (3.4).

You now have a solid hypothesis pyramid. Your task as a problem solver is straightforward. You must identify, for each elementary hypothesis: (1) what you must know to test the hypothesis, and (2) how you will get that information. These two steps are the "analyses" and the "sources" on Figs. 7.3, 7.4 and 7.5. The resulting "analysis plan" tells you what you must do to confirm, disprove, or modify the hypotheses.

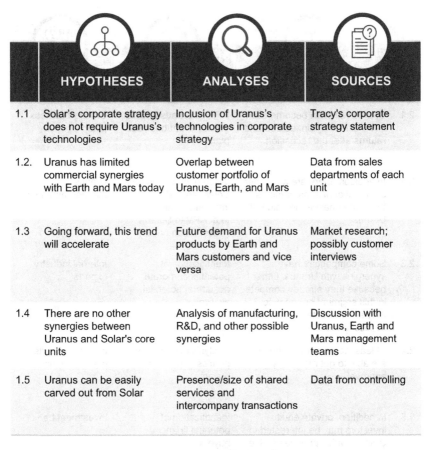

HYPOTHESES	ANALYSES	SOURCES
1.1 Solar's corporate strategy does not require Uranus's technologies	Inclusion of Uranus's technologies in corporate strategy	Tracy's corporate strategy statement
1.2. Uranus has limited commercial synergies with Earth and Mars today	Overlap between customer portfolio of Uranus, Earth, and Mars	Data from sales departments of each unit
1.3 Going forward, this trend will accelerate	Future demand for Uranus products by Earth and Mars customers and vice versa	Market research; possibly customer interviews
1.4 There are no other synergies between Uranus and Solar's core units	Analysis of manufacturing, R&D, and other possible synergies	Discussion with Uranus, Earth and Mars management teams
1.5 Uranus can be easily carved out from Solar	Presence/size of shared services and intercompany transactions	Data from controlling

Fig. 7.3 Analysis plan for Solar case (sub-hypothesis 1)

Eight Degrees of Analysis

The word "analysis," with its connotation of fact-based, quantitative processing, can be misleading. In reality, as we'll show by reviewing this analysis plan, "analyses" can be thought of as a continuum that starts with accepted or indisputable facts, and ends with subtle judgments. On this continuum, we can identify eight degrees of analysis, which increase in complexity:

1. *Hypotheses that can be taken as a given without further analysis.* This is true of the hypothesis that Uranus is not a core business in Solar's corporate strategy statement (1.1). In principle, you could challenge this hypothesis—perhaps a viable alternative corporate strategy could be built around Uranus. But since the brief comes from Tracy, it seems acceptable to take this corporate strategy statement as a given.[1]

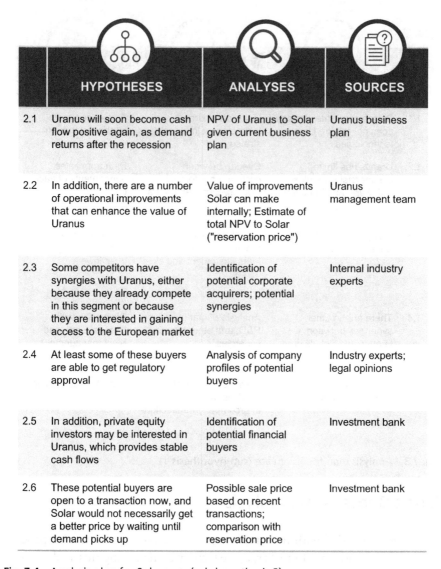

	HYPOTHESES	ANALYSES	SOURCES
2.1	Uranus will soon become cash flow positive again, as demand returns after the recession	NPV of Uranus to Solar given current business plan	Uranus business plan
2.2	In addition, there are a number of operational improvements that can enhance the value of Uranus	Value of improvements Solar can make internally; Estimate of total NPV to Solar ("reservation price")	Uranus management team
2.3	Some competitors have synergies with Uranus, either because they already compete in this segment or because they are interested in gaining access to the European market	Identification of potential corporate acquirers; potential synergies	Internal industry experts
2.4	At least some of these buyers are able to get regulatory approval	Analysis of company profiles of potential buyers	Industry experts; legal opinions
2.5	In addition, private equity investors may be interested in Uranus, which provides stable cash flows	Identification of potential financial buyers	Investment bank
2.6	These potential buyers are open to a transaction now, and Solar would not necessarily get a better price by waiting until demand picks up	Possible sale price based on recent transactions; comparison with reservation price	Investment bank

Fig. 7.4 Analysis plan for Solar case (sub-hypothesis 2)

2. *Analyses requiring hard numbers that are easy to identify*, if not always to obtain. Tracy asserts, for instance, that there are limited commercial synergies between core businesses (Earth and Mars) and Uranus (1.2). Verifying this hypothesis involves quantifying how much of their respective business comes from shared customers. This may prove challenging—for instance, if you discover that the divisions use different codes for the same customers or treat units of the same customer corporations differently. But this is a question of fact and you possess all the information, even if it's not easily accessible.

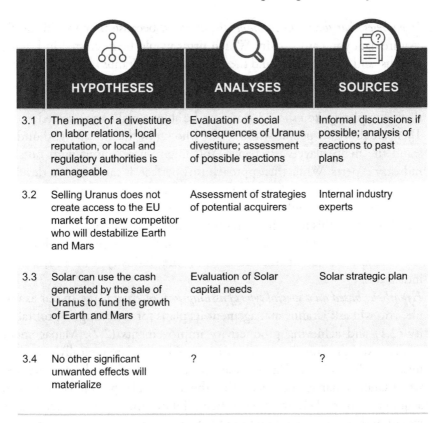

 HYPOTHESES	ANALYSES	SOURCES
3.1 The impact of a divestiture on labor relations, local reputation, or local and regulatory authorities is manageable	Evaluation of social consequences of Uranus divestiture; assessment of possible reactions	Informal discussions if possible; analysis of reactions to past plans
3.2 Selling Uranus does not create access to the EU market for a new competitor who will destabilize Earth and Mars	Assessment of strategies of potential acquirers	Internal industry experts
3.3 Solar can use the cash generated by the sale of Uranus to fund the growth of Earth and Mars	Evaluation of Solar capital needs	Solar strategic plan
3.4 No other significant unwanted effects will materialize	?	?

Fig. 7.5 Analysis plan for Solar case (sub-hypothesis 3)

3. *Assessments based on facts that are not numbers.* Technological changes in the industry and their impact on customer demand (1.3) are an important question. Depending on what information is available, you may, for instance, need to collect it through interviews with a selection of customers (or employ a market research firm to do so more discreetly). Your customers' views on their future needs are not easily summarized in a few numbers, but have a crucial impact on your conclusion. Qualitative facts are still facts.

4. *Hypotheses that can be settled by simple analysis beyond the facts.* Assessing whether a disposal of Uranus would be complex or costly for your shared services (1.5) is largely a question of fact, but calls for some analysis: if Uranus accounts for 20 percent of personnel, will you reduce headcount in the HR department by 20 percent to compensate? And if you don't, how much of a burden does that place on the remaining units?

5. *Hypotheses that force you to make assumptions,* because they would ideally require data you can't obtain. Which firms would be interested in buying Uranus, and how much would the synergies with Uranus be worth to them (2.3)? These are questions of fact, but without deep knowledge of these companies' strategies and of their manufacturing assets, you can't answer them completely. You should, however, be able to make an educated guess. There are probably people within Solar who know the industry and understand the main players' strategies. You might also consult with outside industry experts. While this approach isn't perfect, it can help you develop sound assumptions. If, for instance, credible sources confirm that three players would be highly interested in acquiring Uranus, this will sufficiently confirm this hypothesis. It's impossible to know with certainty how much a buyer would pay for Uranus (2.6) until you attempt to sell it, but the analysis of recent transactions in the industry can provide an indication.

6. *Hypotheses based on a special type of assumption: internal plans.* In our example, you will ask Uranus management its plans for returning to profitability (2.1) and achieving productivity improvements (2.2). Management teams under pressure to improve their profitability are typically overoptimistic in their plans.[2] This natural optimism is likely to be accentuated when Uranus management fears that the unit will be put up for sale to an acquirer who is likely to replace them. Taking these plans at face value would probably lead you to set too high a reservation price. Deciding how much to discount the plans is a matter of judgment, which you must make explicit in your discussions with Tracy.

7. *Assumptions that call for technical expertise.* Unless you're an expert in antitrust law, your assessment of whether a competitor would get regulatory approval for the purchase of Uranus (2.4) may not be relevant. You'll need to get a professional opinion. Likewise, some of your colleagues may suggest names of potential buyers from the industry, but you should use an investment bank or other financial advisor if you want to identify PE buyers (2.5). A good financial advisor may also identify trade buyers you didn't think of, such as foreign competitors in adjacent industries.

8. *Assumptions that are, irreducibly, a matter of judgment.* The reactions of stakeholders to a divestiture can be emotional and unpredictable. They are inherently hard to evaluate, as it may be impossible to "sound them out" at an early stage (3.1). Likewise, to assume you haven't omitted any unwanted consequences (3.4) is essentially a gamble that there are no residual "unknown unknowns." While tools such as scenario planning can reduce the potential for such surprises[3] and a focus on uncovering them can reduce

our tendency to be overconfident in our judgments in the face of uncertainty,[4] no amount of analysis will eliminate the uncertainty in a major business decision. When a hypothesis relies on educated judgment (assuming we've been rigorous and exhaustive in our analytical efforts), the best we can do is recognize that it's a matter of judgment and make sure the problem owner is aware of the importance of that judgment. The alternative (which too many problem solvers adopt) is to use judgments, but let the audience believe, implicitly, that those judgments are based on facts, even though no facts are available. This can lead to unpleasant surprises.

Planning the Work

Once you've identified which type of analysis can settle each elementary hypothesis, you can plan the work and conduct the analysis. Work planning is beyond the scope of this book, as it depends on the context and type of analysis you're doing. Faced with the analysis plan we just described, a whole team of consultants would not organize the work in the same way as the lone financial analyst to whom Tracy turns. Two considerations, however, are universal.

First, start with the critical, "make or break" hypotheses, especially when they're relatively easy to test. In our example, verifying that there are no customer synergies between Uranus and Solar's core units is crucial. If that hypothesis is proven wrong, the entire hypothesis pyramid collapses. Good work planning should give priority to the analyses that can change the overall answer or solution to the problem.

Second, some analyses you identify may be too difficult, or even impossible, to conduct. This can be because you don't have the required skills and can't access them (e.g., if highly specialized technical expertise is required). More often, the concern will be that by conducting the analysis, you change the answer. In our example, confidentiality is obviously an issue, and you'll want to consider it when deciding what analyses to conduct. For example, if you're analyzing a plant productivity problem and your analysis calls for time and motion studies in which you stand by workers on the shop floor with a stopwatch, your presence would probably affect their performance. Social scientists refer to this confounding influence as the Hawthorne effect.[5] It's only when you identify the sources—and realize the challenge of accessing them—that you can complete your list of analyses.

With these principles in mind, you can build an analysis plan and turn it into a work plan for any hypothesis pyramid. The same is true if you've chosen an issue tree: instead of identifying the analyses to confirm or disprove a hypothesis, you'll list the analyses needed to answer the questions in your issue tree. Many analyses will be the same for the two approaches. The main difference will be that an issue tree, as it is more open ended, will require more analyses.

Conducting the Analysis

Once you've defined and structured the problem, established the analysis plan, and planned the work, it's time to perform the analyses. This is where the number crunching (and the other forms of analysis) starts. Your solution will only be as good as the analysis it's based upon. Even the most carefully stated and skillfully structured problem won't yield a satisfactory solution if the analysis is flawed.

As any experienced analyst in any field will tell you, there's no foolproof way to avoid all analytical errors. But *common* errors tend to creep into the work of even very good analysts. What follows is a short, subjective list of these analytical pitfalls, and some suggestions on how to avoid them. It's based on our experience as consultants and professors who have checked the analytical work of thousands of colleagues and students and made our own share of mistakes.

Because we focus solely on analytical work, we assume the problem is defined and structured correctly. At this point, you're concerned with finding the right data, making sound assumptions when necessary, analyzing the data accurately, and drawing correct conclusions from each piece of analysis. Let's review each step in sequence.

Picking the Right Data

Good analysis starts with good data:

1. *Get the right numbers.* How do we know we're looking at the right numbers? Tim Harford's weekly BBC show *More or Less* examines, week after week, examples in which seemingly reliable statistics are deeply misleading.

Here's a recent example[6]: official 2016 figures citing the number of homicides recorded by police in England and Wales showed a 21-percent increase in the number of homicides, to 697. Such a sharp rise in crime figures is unsettling.

It doesn't seem unreasonable to assume that if you're looking for crime statistics, police data is a good place to start. But not in this case. Most (80 percent) of the increase is attributable to a single event: the 1989 Hillsborough football stadium disaster in which 96 people died. Twenty-seven years later, the deaths were reclassified as "unlawful killing." This isn't the sort of event people typically have in mind when they think about homicides, and it didn't take place in 2016.

Mistakes of this sort are frequent in business analysis. Perhaps you're looking for data on the consumption of a commodity—say, sugar—and you think production data—which is easier to find—is a good-enough proxy? Think again. Supply and demand are equal over long periods of time and large areas of space, but they're unlikely to move in sync if you consider them within a geographic area and time period. There's too much trading and inventory variation for that. Another common example is the assumption that a company's stock price reflects the value it creates for shareholders. When reporting on a CEO's performance, for instance, observers often comment on the change in stock price since the CEO's appointment. Yet, this is an oversimplification: an analysis of total shareholder returns (TSR) must factor in dividends, share repurchases, and stock splits.

2. *Adjust the right time frame of time series.* Think of unemployment data, new car sales, or house prices: all these types of data are time series. Usually, you'll want the most recent data available, up to the present—or as close to it as is possible. But when should the time series start and end? Your choice could change the conclusion you draw.

Consider Jeff Immelt, who took the helm at General Electric on September 7, 2001, and left his CEO position on October 2, 2017. Between these two dates, GE's stock price sank by 39 percent. On that basis, Immelt's 16-year tenure would seem to have been an unmitigated disaster for GE shareholders.[7] However, the Friday before September 11, 2001, the day of the murderous terrorist attacks against the World Trade Center and Pentagon, was arguably an unfortunate date to become CEO of a large American company: Immelt can't be blamed for GE's stock losing one-quarter of its value in his first two weeks as CEO. If you consider the change between that low point and the end of 2016, the last full year Immelt oversaw, GE's stock price went *up* by 4.1 percent. This still isn't an impressive performance if you compare it with the S&P 500 over the same time frame, but it tells a very different story. What a difference a few days make. Not all cases are this extreme, but the period you pick is always a choice you must be able to justify. A sure way to select a "wrong" time frame is to unthinkingly pick the one that is most easily available.

3. *Get the right qualitative data.* Qualitative data is no less treacherous. Suppose, for instance, that your analysis entails interviewing customers to determine how satisfied they are with your company's products. Which customers will you talk to? If, as is often the case, you select them based on how easy they are to find, your sample will probably be biased. Relying on the sales force to organize interviews, for example, is likely to produce meetings with the salespeople's best friends—not a tough crowd. Another tactic would be to call customers who expressed a willingness to be interviewed as part of filling out a survey or a complaint, but this, too, can bias the sample (albeit in the opposite direction). Such sampling biases are frequent in qualitative analysis, and often go unnoticed.

One frequent type of sampling bias deserves special attention. Suppose the reason you're interviewing customers is because you've been losing business. Is dissatisfaction with your product the reason? You ask customers, and their answer is "no." In fact, they like the product, although there are other areas in which they'd like you to improve. Unfortunately, it's misleading to conclude anything from this analysis: your sample includes only current customers, and tells you nothing about the ones who actually left. Lapsed customers may have very different tastes and preferences, which you must understand. When we hope to understand the reasons for a change (the loss of customers) by focusing on what is still here after that change (the remaining customers), we are guilty of *survivor bias.*[8]

In most examples, the reason for choosing the "wrong" data is simple: it's readily available, while the more relevant data is harder to find. One way to limit the risk of dangerous shortcuts is to label the data with precision. "Consumption" and "production" of sugar are different. But sometimes even an accurate label can be grossly misleading, as the example of "Homicides recorded by police in 2016" demonstrates.

There is no substitute for two basic disciplines of rigorous analysis. The first is to read the fine print patiently. In the Office of National Statistics report on crime in England and Wales for 2016, you'd have had to read down to page 25 of a 58-page report to find an explanation about the Hillsborough deaths. The other is simply to ask. Back in the day when gathering numbers meant—mostly—interviewing people with access to them, it was natural enough to ask them questions that put numbers in context. Now that the world's information is available at our fingertips, it has become all too easy to skip that step.

Making Sound Assumptions

You will conduct much of the analysis not only by using hard data, but also by making assumptions. If you're building a business plan, computing the cost of a future project, or simply estimating something for which no perfect data is available, you're in assumption territory.

The cardinal rule of assumptions is that they must be explicit. Suppose you're making a forecast that depends, in part, on currencies. No one will expect you to know for sure what the dollar–euro exchange rate will be a year from now, but it's well worth mentioning what specific value you picked. Remember, the assumptions you make may seem obvious to you, but they're probably not obvious to your audience.

Making assumptions explicit has another benefit: it facilitates dialogue with your audience. It's reasonable for the problem owner to want to know your assumptions. This isn't an attack on your analysis, but a necessary step toward accepting your conclusions. The best way for you to establish this dialogue is to proactively offer a list of your key assumptions whenever your conclusions depend on them. It's much better to start this dialogue on your own terms, not defensively and under questioning.

This raises the difficult question of how to make realistic assumptions—or how to get your audience to accept them as realistic, which is your immediate concern. There's no magic answer to such a broad question, but four tips can help avoid frequent pitfalls.

1. *Get physical to be realistic.* Many assumptions are expressed as abstract numbers such as percentages, ratios, or indices. These are useful as reference points (as we'll discuss below), but a sound discipline in making assumptions and in sharing them with others is to translate them into tangible quantities. A forecast that anticipates a 15-percent month-on-month increase in your new store's sales, for instance, may seem sensible—until you calculate how this translates into the number of people visiting your store one year from now and find that the number is implausible. It's easier to discuss tangible, physical quantities than abstractions.

2. *Check that all your assumptions are consistent with one another.* It's not uncommon (especially when proposals are assembled from the work of several contributors) to see different parts of the same presentation include inconsistent assumptions on the timing of outside events, the behavior of competitors, or even basic inputs such as commodity prices or exchange rates. More frequently, assumptions that seem realistic in isolation become hard to believe when considered together. In a business plan, for example, your audience may believe either in your bold revenue projections or in your plans for aggressive cost reductions, but not in both.

3. *Benchmark your assumptions.* The best way to bolster an assumption's credibility is to provide relevant comparables. Suppose you're forecasting revenues for your new product, based on an estimate of how much of your product consumers will use (an application of the "get physical" principle outlined above). Your audience may have no intuitive reaction to this number (do you know how many grams of toothpaste, sugar, or flour you consume every year?). Without context, people may question the plausibility of the assumption. If your assumption is, however, calibrated on the market average or a relevant competitor, your estimate becomes more plausible. This assumes the competitors you choose as benchmarks are not "extreme" examples (e.g., don't use Facebook as a benchmark for the growth of your user base).

4. *Test sensitivities.* It's natural to be confident in our assumptions, but it's also natural to be *overconfident* about the precision with which we can estimate unknowns or forecast the future (this brand of overconfidence is known as "overprecision" or "miscalibration"[9]). When you're 90 percent certain that a number you estimate lies within a certain range, you'll typically be wrong at least 50 percent of the time.[10] Even when you're very confident in your assumptions, you must ask yourself, "If I'm wrong, will my conclusions change?" That's the purpose of a sensitivity analysis. Would your conclusion still hold if an assumption (i.e., forecast, estimate) about a key input changed by 20 percent? Or 50 percent? Even better, reverse the question and ask: *by how much* would your assumptions need to change, either individually or collectively, for your conclusion to be wrong? It's even more important to test sensitivities when you have reason to doubt the reliability or the objectivity of your sources. In the Solar example from earlier in this chapter, Uranus's business plan contains its assumptions. Since Uranus's management is more likely to be overoptimistic than the average management team, it would be critical to test the sensitivity of your conclusions by varying these assumptions.

Detailing, benchmarking, and testing your assumptions with your audience may seem unnatural. You might think that you're expected to project confidence in your calculations, and fear that by sharing your hypotheses, you're exposing weaknesses. Or maybe you're simply concerned about wasting your audience's time with details. Isn't that the reason the problem owner entrusted you with the analysis? These fears are misplaced. Pretending we can be certain of things that are difficult to predict isn't confidence—it's foolishness. And sharing the boundary conditions under which your recommendations hold true doesn't make them less compelling, but more credible. A good problem solver makes good assumptions—but most of all, she's not shy about explaining and sharing them.

Getting the Numbers Right

Now that you have the data and have made the assumptions explicit, you must run the numbers. This is not the stage at which most errors occur, because calculations typically aren't done by hand. In our experience as consultants and educators, however, we still occasionally see old-fashioned calculation errors. The following tips can help you minimize that risk:

1. *Beware of percentages—they're treacherous.* As you may have learned years ago, if your costs shot up by 50 percent, getting them back where they started requires a reduction of 33 percent, not 50 percent. And if a €100 price includes 20-percent value-added tax (VAT), the pre-tax price is not €80, but €83.33. This simple arithmetic causes a surprising number of mistakes—usually when we reason directly with percentages. Imagine a case interview, for instance, in which you hear that your sales are down by 10 percent versus last year. You propose to regain lost ground with two ideas that add 5 percent each to your revenues: you're close, but not quite right.[11]
2. *Orders of magnitude are your friends.* With results, like with assumptions, "get physical" and ask if the result is in the right ballpark. Business calculations are not particle physics or astronomy—it's usually possible to get a feel for the answer.
3. *If it looks wrong, it probably is.* If you calculate that your (legitimate) business generates a 99.9 percent return on sales or grows 5000 percent a year, redo the numbers. There will be surprises in your analysis, but surprises are rare (that's why they *surprise*). At a minimum, get someone with a fresh pair of eyes to review any surprising results.

4. *If it looks right, it may still be wrong.* Even in this age of automation, plain old calculation errors, accidental mistakes in Excel spreadsheets, and other lapses of attention remain frequent.[12] Star economists Reinhart and Rogoff, authors of the bestseller *This Time Is Different*, admitted that an oversight in an Excel formula led them to an incorrect conclusion in their analysis of the effect of debt levels on economic growth.[13] In the wake of the Lehman Brothers bankruptcy, as Barclays Bank was rushing to send an offer to acquire some of the troubled bank's assets, an analyst at its law firm neglected to delete "hidden" rows in an Excel spreadsheet before converting them to a PDF format, unwittingly including on Barclays's bid several toxic assets it had not intended to acquire. Such human errors are inevitable—*errare humanum est.* The only antidote to plain old slips and lapses is plain old double checking, preferably by a second pair of eyes. This is easier said than done, especially when working under pressure and tight deadlines.

Making Sense of the Numbers

Now that you have your data, assumptions, and calculations, it's time to look at the analysis and ask "So what?" to draw conclusions. As we'll see in Chap. 10, these "so whats" will support the key messages of the storyline you'll create to sell your solution to the problem owner. And as we'll see in Chap. 11, they'll also determine the main headlines on the slides you'll prepare when you put together a presentation. So it's critically important not to draw the wrong conclusions.

Analytical results are sometimes clear-cut, leading to obvious, unassailable conclusions. More often, there is more than one way to look at the data, more than one "spin" to put on it. As with every step in the problem-solving process, the danger here is that we immediately jump to the conclusion that supports our ingoing hypotheses and the storyline we have in mind, failing to consider an alternative interpretation. This problem—confirmation bias—is so deep-seated that the only way to overcome it is to have someone else challenge your analysis. Have colleagues look at the same data and ask them if they come to a different conclusion. The results will often surprise you.

One type of evidence that requires especially careful challenge is *correlation data*. For simplicity, and because it's beyond the scope of this book to discuss the statistical tests that determine a "significant" correlation, we'll assume that correlations have been properly calculated and are statistically significant. It's useful, however, to remember that a test of statistical significance doesn't *guarantee* that a correlation is meaningful in the ordinary sense that lay people understand. When we're told a result, like correlation, is "statistically significant," it doesn't mean this result reflects a causal link between the examined variables. It simply means you can be confident, to the level specified by the test (e.g., 99 percent), that the correlation actually exists in reality (i.e., in the population you are studying). Statistical significance measures the extent to which the correlation you observe is a reliable piece of evidence, but it doesn't tell you why the two variables are correlated, and the reason may have nothing to do with a cause–effect relationship.

Consider for instance this passage gleaned from a recent report on the rise of artificial intelligence (AI): "Only 20 percent of 3,000 companies we surveyed use AI extensively. However, those that report using it have margins that are three to fifteen points higher than the average of their industry." Or this conclusion from a study on gender diversity: "We found a strong correlation between the presence of women in company top management and better financial results."

In both cases, the analysts observe a correlation between two variables—the adoption of a practice (AI or female board members) and firm financial performance. But do these correlations mean that the practices *cause* the superior performance? There are several possible interpretations of this evidence.

First, it may be true that using AI and women board members, respectively, cause better results. Sometimes, correlation reflects causation. There is a significant correlation between heat waves and deaths by dehydration, or between smoking and lung cancer, and in each case, carefully designed studies show that the former causes the latter (although, in the second example, the tobacco industry claimed for decades that the causation was dubious).

Second, it's possible that companies with higher profitability are more prone to be early adopters of new technologies and more active proponents of gender diversity. If that is true, then profitability is the cause, not the effect, of the practices. This error is called "reverse causation." A practical way to mitigate it is to look into the chronology of events: if you observe that the considered companies already enjoyed higher profitability levels *before* they adopted the new practices, you must suspect reverse causation. If you confirm that profitability increased *after* the introduction of the practices, you can take it as a clue that supports the hypothesized causal impact of the practices on firm profitability.

A third possibility that accounts for an observed correlation between two variables is that a third, unobserved factor drives both, making the observed correlation spurious. We already mentioned in Chap. 5 the classic example of spurious correlation between the number of people who drown in swimming pools and the consumption of ice cream: neither causes the other, but a common factor—hot weather—contributes to both. In our examples, the use of AI and the selection of female board members reflect choices made by companies and are not randomly assigned like they would be in an experimental study. For instance, firms focused on innovation, as reflected by the intensity of their R&D expenditures, may make these choices disproportionately, because innovative firms are more likely to adopt novel practices.[14] Innovation is also a driver of firm financial performance.[15] In such a situation, even if the new practices had no real impact on firm performance, their adoption would appear as correlated with higher performance levels.

Finally, these correlations may be mere juxtapositions of unrelated facts—coincidences, which occur frequently in time series data. There is, for instance, a near-perfect correlation between the rate of divorce in Maine and the consumption of margarine, or between the number of people who die strangled by their bedsheets and the per capita consumption of cheese.[16] This may strike you as absurd, and it is. But when the observed phenomena are not as laughably unrelated as these are, we are far too prone to infer causality from correlation.

How should we use correlations? Two words: *very carefully*. We don't suggest you ignore correlations. But they should be considered in light of the discussion of "necessary" and "sufficient" conditions we introduced in Chap. 5. While a correlation between two variables is not a sufficient condition for causation, a statistical association is a necessary condition.[17]

Logic dictates that before we conclude that causation is present, we formulate hypotheses about the mechanisms by which one factor causes the other and identify and measure all potential confounding variables in addition to those specified in our hypotheses. In the examples mentioned above, the analysts formulate such hypotheses, explaining *how* AI and gender diversity contribute to financial performance, control for the influence of potentially confounding effects in their analysis, and provide evidence to back up their causal claims.

Remember Librinova, the company whose international expansion strategy we discussed in Chap. 5? Suppose it discovers a study conducted on a sample of 100 small French companies that expanded into Canada, and reads that 75 percent of them had closed their subsidiary within three years. It would be tempting to conclude that this strong correlation between expansion into Canada and failure is reason enough to give up the plan and look for another country. But Librinova shouldn't draw this implication from the correlation. Instead, it should ask *why* these companies failed. Could it be because the timing of the study coincided with a brutal recession in Canada or with a sudden change in exchange rates? Also, did these companies adopt a direct expansion strategy, as opposed to the partnership approach Librinova is considering? The correlation is a clue that Librinova should notice and try to make sense of, but, on its own, it's inconclusive.

*   *   *

Good analysis is the heart of good problem solving. But while brilliant insights in problem definition and structuring sometimes occur, they're rare in the analytical work. Good analysis means proceeding with rigor and avoiding mistakes. The "Solve" stage of the 4S process, when it entails a hypothesis pyramid or an issue tree, is all about disciplined execution.

As we'll see in the next two chapters, the way in which problems are solved in the design thinking approach requires just as much rigor and discipline, but leverages the analysis and synthesis of qualitative data to develop innovative solutions to complex business problems.

Chapter 7 in One Page

- From the hypothesis pyramid or issue tree, build an *analysis plan*: the requisite analyses to address elementary hypotheses or issues and the *source* for each.

- "Analyses" are not entirely fact based and numerical. Recognize eight types of analysis, in increasing order of complexity:

  - Facts: (1) existing data, (2) easy-to-find numbers, and (3) non-numerical facts
  - (4) Fact-based analyses (e.g., *how much can you reduce overheads?*)
  - (5) Analyses based on assumptions, which should be stated (e.g., *synergies*)
  - (6) Internal plans and forecasts, also based on assumptions (e.g., *sales plan*)
  - (7) Expert input (e.g., *legal opinion*)
  - (8) Judgment calls (e.g., *anticipation of stakeholder response*)

- To plan your work, prioritize analyses that can change the overall answer.

- Common analytical mistakes include:

  - Misleading data (*did homicides in the UK really increase by 21 percent?*)
  - Disputable time frames (*what time period to evaluate Jeff Immelt?*)
  - Biased samples (*only dissatisfied customers? only remaining customers?*)
  - Assumptions that are unrealistic, inconsistent, untested, or hidden:

    - *Check: physical plausibility, internal consistency, benchmarks, sensitivities*

  - Numerical errors:

    - *Check: percentages, orders of magnitude, "surprises"*

  - Data interpretation errors, especially with correlation data:

    - *Does correlation reflect causation? Reverse causation? Common cause? Coincidence?*

Notes

1. Alternatively, such "givens" could be included in the problem statement and wouldn't need to be repeated in the hypothesis pyramid (or issue tree). In practice, however, hypothesis pyramids often include "given" components that are necessary for the logic to hold, and that have not been expressly formulated in the problem statement.

2. Kahnemann, D., & Lovallo, D. (1993). Timid Choices and Bold Forecasts: A Cognitive Perspective on Risk Taking. *Management Science, 39*(1), 17–31.

3. Ramanesh, R.V., & Browning, T.R. (2014). A Conceptual Framework for Tackling Unknown Unknowns in Project Management. *Journal of Operations Management, 32*, 190–204.

4. Walters, D.J., Fernbach, P.M., Fox, C.R., & Sloman, S.A. (2017). Known Unknowns: A Critical Determinant of Confidence and Calibration. *Management Science, 63*(12), 4298–4307.

5. Landsberger, H.A. (1958). *Hawthorne Revisited.* Ithaca: Cornell University Press.

6. Harford, T. (2017). Where the Truth Really Lies with Statistics. In *Tim Harford, The Undercover Economist* (blog). Retrieved from http://timharford.com/2017/06/where-the-truth-really-lies-with-statistics/.

7. Notwithstanding the dividends paid by GE during that period, which, as mentioned above, are part of the return to shareholders.

8. Survivor bias is also frequent in quantitative analysis, for instance, when analyzing a sample of "surviving" companies and neglecting the ones that disappeared over the period of study.

9. Ben-David, I., Graham, J.R., & Harvey, C.R. (2013). Managerial Miscalibration. *Quarterly Journal of Economics, 128*(4), 1547—1584.

10. Russo, E., & Shoemaker, P. (1992). Managing Overconfidence. *Sloan Management Review, 33*(2), 7–17.

11. Here's why: if sales are down 10 percent from, say, $1 million the previous year, then current year sales are $900,000. Increasing this amount by 10 percent (i.e., 2 × 5 percent) results in sales of $990,000 ($10,000 short of the goal). While this may seem a trivial difference, the case interviewer will not be inviting you back for the next round.

12. Gandel, S. (2013, April 17). Damn Excel! How the 'Most Important Software Application of All Time' is Ruining the World. *Fortune.* Retrieved from http://fortune.com/2013/04/17/damn-excel-how-the-most-important-software-application-of-all-time-is-ruining-the-world/.

13. Reinhart, C.M., & Rogoff, K.S. (2009). *This Time Is Different: Eight Centuries of Financial Folly.* Princeton, NJ: Princeton University Press.

14. Wejnert, B. 2002. Integrating Models of Diffusion of Innovations: A Conceptual Framework. *Annual Review of Sociology, 28*, 297–326.
15. Calantone, R.J., Cavusgil, S.T., & Zhao, Y. (2002). Learning Orientation, Firm Innovation Capability, and Firm Performance. *Industrial Marketing Management, 31*(6), 515–524.
16. *Spurious Correlations.* Retrieved from http://tylervigen.com/view_correlation?id=1703.
17. A statistical association, but not a bivariate, linear correlation. Conventional correlations are linear, while many causal relationships are non-linear. Trying to fit a straight line between two non-linearly related variables will often result in zero correlation. Additionally, a causal relationship may exist between two variables, but detecting it may depend on knowledge of a third variable. This is a confounding effect like the cause of spurious correlations, but works in the opposite way: by explicitly controlling for the influence of the third variable, the *partial* correlation between the two other variables can be detected.

8

Redefine the Problem: The Design Thinking Path

Doug Dietz is the prototypical Midwestern American—he's earnest and soft-spoken, with an easy smile and a big heart. Doug has spent the past 27 years working in Waukesha, Wisconsin, as an industrial designer of medical imaging systems for GE Healthcare, an $18 billion division of one of the world's biggest companies.

In a 2012 TEDx talk, Doug describes an epiphany that forever changed his perspective on designing medical scanners. A few years earlier, after spending over two years working on a new magnetic resonance imaging (MRI) machine, he visited a hospital to see it in action. As Doug tells the story, he felt like a proud papa to finally see his new baby at work. He even told the MRI technician that the scanner had been nominated for an International Design Excellence Award.

During their conversation, the MRI tech asked Doug to step out in the hall because a patient was coming in for a scan. As he did, he saw a young girl walking toward him clutching the hands of her parents. He could see the parents looked worried and the little girl was scared. As the family got closer, the girl began to weep. The father leaned down and said, "Remember, we've talked about this, you can be brave." When the family entered the MRI suite, Doug followed them in and saw that the girl, when confronted with his new MRI scanner, froze in fear and sobbed. The parents looked at each other grimly. Doug knew they were worried about getting their child through the ordeal. During his talk, Doug's eyes well up and his voice breaks with emotion as he recalls that moment.

For Doug, witnessing the fear and anxiety his MRI machine evoked in the little girl and her parents triggered a crisis that profoundly and permanently

© The Author(s) 2018
B. Garrette et al., *Cracked it!*, https://doi.org/10.1007/978-3-319-89375-4_8

changed his perspective. He no longer viewed these devices from the vantage point of a designer as sleek, artistic high-tech artifacts worthy of awards and pride. Instead, by seeing them through the eyes of a young child, he understood them to be big scary monsters. As Doug recalls, "That was a huge awakening for me."

A new, state-of-the-art MRI scanner produced by GE Healthcare can cost a hospital more than $1 million. Installation and construction of the MRI suite and patient support area can bring the total investment to $3–$5 million. To justify the expenditure, hospital administrators seek to maximize the number of patient scans performed each day. More scans mean more money to cover the large investment.

If you've ever had an MRI scan, you know the challenge is to keep the body part being scanned still for 15–90 minutes, all the while listening to strange, loud noises emanating from the scanner. If you move too much, the scan must be redone, reducing the number of patient scans performed that day. The good news for hospital administrators is that adults are good at following instructions and fighting the urge to fidget.

The story is very different for young children, who often find it difficult to stay still even for a few minutes. To make matters worse, as Dietz discovered, going to a hospital for an MRI scan can be scary—hospitals are big, sterile places full of doctors with needles and lots of sick strangers. To compound matters, MRI machines make loud, strange noises and have big holes that can swallow up little children, who often can't see and be comforted by their parents during the scan. These anxiety-producing aspects of an MRI help explain why around 80 percent of all young patients are sedated or anesthetized before being scanned. A sedative administered by an anesthesiologist increases the cost and risk of a scan, so hospital administrators often define the economic problem they face in operating pediatric MRI suites as: "How can we maximize the number of child patient scans per day while reducing the cost of anesthetizing?"

This problem statement contains two challenges—maximizing patient scans and minimizing sedation costs. In fact, sedation is a solution to the challenge of increasing patient scans and the medical community recommends this solution. Given the status and authority medical doctors have, the assumption that sedation is necessary for young children could easily go unquestioned.

Witnessing the fear and anxiety his MRI machine caused a little girl led Dietz to question this assumption and search for the root cause. While anesthesia solves the immediate problem of children moving during MRI scans, it does not address the underlying cause of the fear and anxiety that leads them to squirm. By understanding why children are anxious and scared,

Doug reckoned he might find a way to redesign MRI scanners to alleviate these feelings, eliminating the need for anesthesia.

Doug and a small team of GE volunteers embarked on a process of discovery. They observed young children at a local daycare center, consulted with child development specialists, doctors, and staffs from two local hospitals to better understand pediatric patients. They also worked with experts from a local children's museum to learn how to engage young children in lengthy activities. Through this discovery process, Doug and his team developed a critical insight: sick children want to feel like normal, healthy kids and one of the best ways to accomplish this is through play. The team learned that if you can capture children's imaginations by involving them in an adventure, they will play along as directed. This insight led Doug and his team to redefine the problem by asking: "How might we turn MRI scans for children (who fear medical treatment) into an adventure?"

Because of this insight and reframing, the GE Healthcare team developed a unique solution that transformed a typical sterile and scary MRI suite into a real-life adventure, with the young patient in the starring role and the healthcare staff as supporting characters. Making no changes to the internal MRI technology, Doug and his team applied large decals to the exterior of the scanner, the floor, walls, ceilings, cabinets, and other equipment in the room to convey a particular adventure theme, such as a pirate ship or rocket ship. They also developed scripts for the scanner technicians to lead their patients through the adventure, and soundtracks and aromatherapy to reinforce the themes. In the pirate ship installation, a giant decal of a wooden captain's wheel surrounds the scanner chamber, which makes the hole seem larger and less claustrophobic. In the rocket ship theme, ground controllers (MRI operators) inform rocket ship captains (patients) to listen carefully to the sound of the engines as the ship goes into hyperdrive, incorporating the typically scary noise of the scanner into the adventure. GE Healthcare has branded these themed installations as the GE Adventure Series.

The impact of Doug's GE Adventure Series installations has been dramatic. Hospitals have drastically reduced the need for anesthesia or sedation—at Pittsburgh Children's Hospital, it fell from 80 percent to 27 percent, while other locations have dropped as low as 10 percent. Kate Kapsin, director of Radiology at Pittsburgh Children's Hospital, concluded, "The best way to keep a child motionless during an MRI scan is to keep them engaged and entertained." Patient satisfaction scores increased by up to 90 percent. As a result, the number of scans per day increased significantly. While these outcomes improved the ROI for hospitals that purchased GE Adventure Series scanners and increased GE Healthcare scanner sales, they aren't what Doug Dietz is most proud of. Toward the end of his TEDx talk, Doug tells the story of a little girl who just finished her scan in a pirate ship-themed MRI scanner. The girl pulled at her mother's shirt, looked up and asked, "Can we come back tomorrow?" His voice quivering with emotion, Doug humbly says, "That's a pretty powerful thing."

Neither the hypothesis-driven nor the issue-driven problem-solving path would have led Dietz to his solution. His epiphany led him to take a different route to address the MRI-for-kids problem. He realized he lacked an understanding of how young children experience an MRI scan. So he immersed himself in their world to learn how they think and feel about it. Dietz's immersion efforts paid off. They helped him develop new and valuable insights about young users, leading him to redefine the problem from their perspective. By stepping into the shoes of young children and seeing the emotional journey of an MRI scan through their eyes, Doug was able to imagine a novel solution that reduced fear for children and costs for hospitals, while also leveraging existing GE technology. Doug's investment in empathizing with young users complemented his technical expertise in developing MRI solutions.

Dietz's approach to problem solving reflects the *design thinking path* we introduced in Chap. 3. He revisited his understanding of the problem he was solving by deeply engaging with the audience that would use his solution. He used his new knowledge of the challenge young children face in receiving an MRI scan to redefine the problem and search for innovative solutions. Using the TOSCA problem statement framework from Chap. 4, Doug started the problem-solving process by empathizing with the *Actors* who experienced the *Trouble*, and treated them as the real problem *Owners*. By engaging with young users, he generated new insights into their *Constraints* and what they considered a *Successful* experience. A principal advantage of design thinking is that it helps problem solvers reframe problem statements and open up new opportunities for innovative solutions like it did for Doug Dietz at GE.

In this chapter, we'll introduce the design thinking approach, explain when to use it, and describe activities and tools you can use to empathize with users and redefine problems accordingly. In the next chapter, we'll explain the rest of the process by focusing on how to generate ideas for solutions and then prototype and test them.

Design Thinking and When to Use it

Design thinking is a disciplined process for solving human-centered, complex problems that are poorly understood by solution developers. This approach puts the observation and discovery of human needs at the core of the problem-solving process. Design thinking has a bias for action by promoting iterative testing of assumptions about potential solutions. It requires solution developers, known as *designers*, to translate their insights about the people experiencing the problem, known as *users*, into explicit assumptions about what users want and don't want in a solution. This is done by developing concepts of possible solutions and then translating them into prototypes that can be iteratively tested using feedback from the actors who are expected to implement the solution.

When should you set aside the hypothesis-driven and issue-driven approaches we described in the preceding chapters and use the design thinking method? Here's a quick test that will help you decide:

1. *Is the problem human centered? Will the solution be designed for and used by people?* This is a leading reason why analytically generated solutions may not work.
2. *Is the problem complex? Are there likely to be multiple explanations of the problem that are somehow interlinked?* When this is the case, attempting to write a problem statement too quickly may ignore essential dimensions of the problem.
3. *Are you uncertain about the causes of the problem?* Answering "yes" to this question and question 2 implies that structuring the problem using the analytical methods of hypothesis pyramids and issues trees might be ineffective.
4. *Are you struggling with precisely stating the problem?* Answering "yes" to this question also suggests the design thinking approach.

When you answer "yes" to the majority of these questions, you don't know enough to effectively state the problem. In this situation, as the 4S method flowchart in Fig. 3.1 shows, you should choose the design thinking path and begin by empathizing with the users of your solution (box 2).

The flowchart also shows two other conditions for choosing the design thinking path. One is when you think you've defined the problem, but struggle to structure it, either with an issue tree or with a hypothesis pyramid. The other condition is when you've defined and structured the problem using the conventional approaches, but you can't find a satisfactory solution. In either case, you should enter the design thinking path at the Ideate phase (box 5). As the flowchart shows, you can use some design thinking tools without adopting the entire approach.

Although you may not need to follow the entire design thinking process for each problem you tackle, we explain all five phases of the approach together because they build on one another and require a common mindset.

Five Phases, One Mindset

In practice, design thinking consists of five iterative phases, illustrated in Fig. 8.1. The five phases—Empathize, Define, Ideate, Prototype, and Test—also appear in the design thinking path in Fig. 3.1 (boxes 2, 1, 5, and 8). They are as follows:

1. When addressing a complex and uncertain problem faced by a group of users, designers *empathize* with them by discovering how they think and feel about the problem, the context in which they experience it, and the constraints they face. During this phase, designers develop rich insights about users and the problem they face.
2. Armed with these insights, designers *define the problem* and reframe how they understand it by viewing it from different users' perspectives.
3. This altered definition and framing of the problem inform the *ideation* phase in which designers generate and examine many potential solutions.
4. In the *prototyping* phase, designers choose promising potential solutions to represent in tangible form for users to interact with. Prototypes embody designers' hypotheses about desirable solution characteristics.
5. Prototypes are *tested* by users in the final phase. User feedback about prototypes helps designers choose the final solution for implementation.

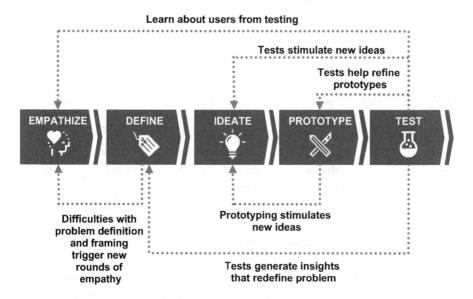

Fig. 8.1 Process of design thinking

Before examining each step, we'll highlight the core features of design thinking, beginning with the tension between divergence and convergence.

Divergence and Convergence Alternating between divergence and convergence is at the heart of design thinking. Decades of research show these are the engines of creative problem solving.[1] Although divergence is often associated with generating diverse ideas for solutions and convergence with selecting among these ideas, the two modes of thinking are essential in every phase of the design thinking process.

In his book *Change by Design,* Tim Brown, CEO of design firm IDEO, explains that divergence creates options for choices at each phase of the design thinking process, while convergence is about making choices.[2] Variation in the users you engage with creates more opportunities for converging on valuable insights. Variation in insights increases the potential for converging on a useful problem definition and framing. Divergence in the ideas generated increases the likelihood that a high-quality solution will be discovered and chosen. Finally, variation in the concepts and prototypes developed can increase iterative learning and convergence to a valuable solution. By cycling through divergent and convergent thinking across each phase of design thinking, you increase the chances of developing an effective solution to a difficult problem.

Concrete and Abstract The design thinking process requires problem solvers to move between the concrete world of real people, artifacts, and experiences, and the abstract world of models, theories, and ideas.[3] It also requires designers to alternate between analysis of data from the concrete world and synthesis of these data for the creation of future solutions.

The process begins with designers empathizing with diverse, real-world users to observe and learn what their reality is as it relates to the problem. Designers then move from the concrete to the abstract realm as they analyze and distill their observations into conceptual models of users, the problem they face, and why it exists. This analytical process leads to a better understanding and typically a reframing of the problem from the user's perspective. The first two phases of design thinking help designers synthesize a better abstract representation of the problem space as well as a set of design imperatives. These imperatives represent the benefits a solution must provide users and serve as a guiding vision for the ideation, prototyping, and testing phases. Once designers establish imperatives, they continue in the abstract world by generating different ideas for solutions. The process returns to the concrete realm to translate ideas into tangible prototypes that are tested with real people to converge to a final solution. In using the design thinking process, problem solvers use insights and evidence from users—rather than their own opinions—to develop and choose solutions.

Iterative and Collaborative Like the other problem-solving paths illustrated in the 4S flowchart (Fig. 3.1), we present the design thinking process as linear for simplicity. In reality, the process is highly iterative—probably more so than traditional approaches. As Fig. 8.1 shows, there are many feedback loops between the design thinking phases. The process is also iterative within phases. Problem statements are iteratively refined, as are ideas for solutions and prototypes, which improve their quality. Prototyping is a highly iterative phase to allow assumptions about solutions to be tested and validated, reducing the potential for the costly implementation of ineffective solutions. The focus on experimentation via prototyping reflects design thinking's bias for feedback from users based on their interaction with tangible artifacts—an inherently iterative process.

Design thinking is collaborative because it involves frequent and intense interaction between users, designers, and other stakeholders during all five phases. Design thinking is also collaborative because it is interdisciplinary. Complex problems require useful knowledge from different domains to be integrated and the diversity of perspective this provides helps to discover innovative solutions. Problems amenable to design thinking need teams composed of diverse problem solvers.

Creative and Tolerant Finally, because of the nature of the activities it entails, design thinking requires a different mindset than conventional problem-solving approaches. Specifically, it needs:

- Creative confidence: the belief that everyone (including you) is creative; a belief that you can and will discover creative solutions to challenging problems if you have a disciplined process to follow.
- Tolerance of failure: a willingness to look at opportunities for feedback from users on your ideas and prototypes as experiments, and negative feedback about them as learning opportunities rather than as failures.
- Empathy: a desire to deeply engage with and understand people different from yourself in order to see the world from their perspective.

- Comfort with ambiguity: a willingness to tackle a problem when you have no inkling of the solution, coupled with the belief that the design thinking process will help you discover one.
- Begin like a beginner: a willingness to suppress your assumptions and beliefs, enter the process with fresh eyes, and learn from users.

If you can adopt this mindset, then you can use design thinking as a powerful approach to solve challenging, human-centered problems. In this chapter and the next, we'll take you deeper into each phase of the design thinking process. We'll address what each phase is, why and when you do it, and how you do it, including practical activities, tools, and deliverables.

We won't attempt to be exhaustive. The toolkit for design thinking is incredibly large, diverse, and growing. To explain it all would require a multi-volume encyclopedia. We will, however, equip you with the primary tools design thinkers use. Along the way, we'll provide stories that illustrate their use for each phase of the process.

Phase 1: Empathize

Empathy is the foundation of design thinking. The results from this phase inform and influence the steps that follow. Your success in the following phases, and indeed the success of the entire design thinking process, depends on what you learn during the Empathize phase.

At this point, your task is to understand the people for whom you are designing—those who face the problem you are attempting to solve. You must understand the physical and emotional needs users are trying to satisfy, the constraints they face in doing so, the way(s) they are trying to satisfy these needs, the aspects of the existing solution with which they are happy or disappointed, the context in which they encounter their current solution, and how meaningful they find the overall experience. Your goal is to put yourself in the shoes of the users and understand how they experience the problem.

Empathizing consists of three broad activities: observation, engagement, and immersion. Each represents an "in-the-field" research orientation designed to get close to and understand people in their natural settings. Observation involves watching and listening to users in the actual setting in which they encounter the problem and experience the artifacts they use to solve it. Observation is focused on learning about how users actually behave. Engagement is about interacting with users and capturing how they say they behave and what they think and feel. Immersion involves becoming a user and experiencing the artifact for yourself. We'll examine each empathic activity below.

Empathizing with users is no small feat—it requires substantial effort. But the effort is worth it when you face a complex problem you understand poorly. Without the deep insight into the problem space that comes from empathizing with users, you'll have limited opportunity for developing new and useful solutions. Research shows that the ability to view problems from the perspective of others, such as users, increases the odds of developing novel and relevant solutions.[4]

Empathizing can help you develop novel insights about users that traditional research tools can't. Traditional approaches such as surveys can provide reliable information about users' beliefs, attitudes, and behaviors—such as how frequently they use an artifact (like a product or service) or what feature of it they like. But they don't help you understand why a behavior is exhibited (such as why people are using the service infrequently) or why an attitude exists (such as why a feature of the service is attractive or not). Empathy can provide such insight. It can also help you identify unexpected uses of artifacts, user-led customization efforts or workarounds, intangible emotional associations, as well as unarticulated user needs, all of which provide valuable insights that traditional research doesn't.[5]

Starting to Empathize: The Design Brief

To begin the *Empathy* phase, you'll need to initially define and frame the problem you're trying to solve and scope the project. In the language of design thinking, this is known as a *design brief*. It's similar to the TOSCA problem statement we discussed in Chap. 4, but with two critical tweaks.

The first tweak is the point of view (POV) you adopt. Like Doug Dietz, you need to view the problem from the perspective of the users of your future solution. This means that you'll treat the users as the problem *Owners*. Sometimes, this will be straightforward because there will be a single group of users. In other cases, you may face multiple groups of *Actors* with a stake in the problem. In these situations, you must identify the stakeholders who'll be affected by your solution and assess their interest in your problem-solving effort and their ability to influence its success. While focusing on young children as users, Dietz and his design team had to consider a mix of stakeholders: MRI technicians who would operate the equipment and participate in the adventure, other healthcare providers (such as nurses) who would accompany children for scans, hospital administrators who would make the purchase decision, and insurers who would pay for the scans. Once you've identified the relevant users and other actors, you'll need to state the problem from their perspective (the *Trouble* they face), and the design goal as they perceive it (the *Success criteria*). You'll also need to identify project *Constraints*.

The second significant difference between a conventional problem statement and a design brief is that the latter is probably wrong—and that's fine. The purpose of the Empathy phase is to help you reframe your initial problem statement in the following *Define* phase. At this early stage, you merely want to use whatever information you have about users, whether it's from your initial research or some other source, to write a design brief and start the learning process.

Once you've completed the initial design brief, you're ready to develop empathy with the relevant users and stakeholders.

Activities for Empathy

To empathize, you'll act as a cultural anthropologist, using ethnographic research methods to collect data on users and other relevant actors in their natural, everyday contexts. From this, you'll understand, from their perspective, their experiences and the meaning they make of them. You'll focus on how people act, what they say, what they think, and how they feel.

Ethnographic methods generate qualitative data and are exploratory. As an ethnographic researcher, you won't enter the field with specific hypotheses to test or assumptions to validate. Instead, you'll focus on building a systematic understanding from the bottom up, through the analysis and synthesis of qualitative observations. These methods will help you interpret the meaning and purpose of the behaviors you observe and how they relate to the context in which they take place.[6]

Participant Observation This is the original ethnographic research method. It requires you to participate in the lives of the people you're studying while maintaining a professional distance to observe and record. The challenge is to become sufficiently immersed so that you can understand the experience as an insider while being able to describe it to outsiders.

Before beginning your observation efforts, there are a few things to do. You'll need to identify who to observe (users) and where to observe them, and define what you want to learn about them. You may need to obtain consent from users and others for your observation efforts. Once you gain access, you must build rapport, credibility, and trust with the people you're observing to minimize your impact on their behavior. You'll also need to decide how to record your observations: while the original ethnographer toolkit consisted of the five senses, a pen, and paper notebooks, audio recorders, still and video cameras, and tablet computers are now part of the arsenal. Just having the tools and knowing why you are using them isn't enough, however. Table 8.1 provides guidelines to follow to be a good observer.

There are three fundamental approaches to conducting observations. The most common is to *participate in the activities of the users and disclose* that you're observing them. In this approach, you embed yourself in the lives of your users to observe and record what they say and do. This may involve living with or working alongside the people you observe.

In some situations, you may choose to *observe activities overtly without participating* in them. Shadowing is a widely used example. In shadowing, the researcher closely follows an individual or a small group over time and records their behavior, particularly as they interact with an artifact of interest (such as performing a process or using a product). Shop-alongs, where a researcher accompanies and observes a person shopping, are a type of shadowing research. Shadowing often involves questions that prompt users to comment on what they are doing and experiencing (e.g., "What are you doing now and why?" or "You seem frustrated, what's going on?"). Young children are experts at shadowing their older siblings to learn from (and annoy) them.

Finally, in some cases, you may choose *covert participant observation*. This allows you to see and hear how people behave without being influenced by your presence as a researcher. Mystery shopping, in which a researcher plays the role of the customer to observe various aspects of the retail experience, is a form of covert observation. Another example is observing people in public

Table 8.1 How to be a good observer

Don't be conspicuously detached from those you're observing. Remember, participate appropriately to build rapport. Having informal conversations is part of the process.

When taking notes, be concrete and descriptive about what you observe. Avoid summarizing and drawing conclusions. Record what happened, when it happened, to whom it happened, and what the immediate context was where it happened. Preserve the sequence of the events.

Write notes or dictate using a recorder soon after the observation to maximize your recall of the events. However, be discrete to minimize your impact on people's behavior.

Record your own interpretations and emotional reactions separate from your concrete, descriptive observations. These are valuable data, too.

spaces, such as waiting lines at airports, without disclosing your research role. A primary drawback of this approach is that it restricts data collection—note-taking and audio or video recording may be impossible.

Covert research raises ethical and legal concerns. If you pursue covert observation, limit it to public places where people have no reasonable expectation of privacy. Don't record individual identities and don't reveal them in any way (e.g., in text, photographs, or video). Avoid the potential for your research to create any risk or hardship for individuals you observe. Ethnographic research is often highly personal and sometimes sensitive. Always be careful to protect the privacy of the people you observe to prevent any risk to them. If you're concerned with the legality of covert research, check with a knowledgeable attorney.

Engagement Directly engaging with people provides you substantial access to their internal world: their thoughts, feelings, needs, goals, and values. Engagement allows you to ask "why?" to get at the motives and reasons behind their behaviors and thinking. Understanding why users think and act as they do can provide valuable insights for designers. Although the stories people tell and what they say they do don't necessarily coincide with how they actually behave, what they say they do is indicative of their beliefs and values,[7] which can be useful insights for designers. Deep engagement can also reveal thoughts and values that users are only vaguely aware of, providing both designers and users with unanticipated insights.

Semi-structured interviews are one of the most widely used approaches for engaging with users. Unlike structured interviews (which are essentially surveys and not very useful during the Empathy phase) and unstructured interviews (such as spontaneous conversations that occur during observations), semi-structured interviews rely on a predefined set of open-ended questions that guide the conversation. The strength of semi-structured interviews lies in their flexibility: the open-ended nature of the questions allows subjects the opportunity to influence where the conversation goes and allows you to probe for greater detail on specific topics to understand what they think and feel.

In designing the interview protocol that you'll use to structure your conversation, remember that the purpose is not to validate assumptions or test hypotheses, but to explore. This will help you avoid leading questions. The questions you ask should be based on your research goals—what you want to learn. Good questions are brief, simple to understand, and open ended. Ask for concrete descriptions of particular experiences. You might ask, for instance,

"Can you give me an example?" You can then use the journalist's approach of the "Five Ws and an H" to get the whole story: *who, what, where, when, how,* and *why.* Note that "why" is at the end of the list: asking people for explanations of their behaviors, thoughts, and feelings is critical to empathizing with them, but can make them defensive and guarded. By asking "why" after people have described their concrete experiences, you minimize these risks and encourage richer, more insightful conversations.

Once you've developed your interview guide, get feedback on it from an accomplished interviewer. After you've finalized your guide, you're ready to interview. Just like participant observation, *how* you engage users in semi-structured interviews determines how much you'll learn. Table 8.2 provides additional guidelines.

Immersion An extreme approach to participant observation is *immersion*—when you simulate being a participant and record observations about your own experience. You live like a user and reflect on your own experiences to better understand users.

Table 8.2 How to conduct semi-structured interviews

An overarching objective is to develop a trusting and comfortable environment that encourages the person to be open and forthcoming about their experiences.
Conduct the interview in a place where the person will be comfortable, focused, and unconcerned about confidentiality. Consider hosting the interview where the person can demonstrate or use the artifact you're studying. For example, if you're trying to understand how people experience a kitchen utensil, you could conduct the interviews in their kitchens.
Dress neutrally and unobtrusively. You want to be viewed as legitimate, but not be a distraction.
Provide context. Briefly explain the project, its purpose, and why you're conducting interviews. Assure the person of confidentiality and ask for consent to interview.
With permission, record the interview using an audio recorder and have the recording transcribed to text. Alternatively, interview with a partner, who focuses on taking notes.
Set the stage by describing the subject matter of the questions you'll ask. Explain that they will be open ended, and that you may often ask "why" to understand the person's intent, logic, or beliefs.
To build rapport, start with broad questions, unrelated to the experience you're trying to learn about, such as questions about the person's background.
Listen attentively. Make eye contact. Use reflective listening and asking follow-up questions based on what was just said.
Be careful to observe and record facial expressions and body language you think is important and when it occurred in the interview so you can link it to the interview transcript.
Be respectful. Follow the Golden Rule.

This approach is often called "a day in the life." For example, if you were trying to address the challenge healthcare providers face in monitoring chronic conditions such as diabetes, you could simulate living like a person with diabetes for a day or more. This would mean altering your diet to remove simple sugars and reduce carbs, following an exercise regime, strictly monitoring your blood sugar levels multiple times per day by pricking your fingers for blood samples and then adjusting your diet and exercise. By living with the constraints of a person with diabetes, you'd be able to empathize with them, helping you generate useful insights for your problem-solving efforts.

Immersion allows you to develop a deeper personal understanding of the user experience by participating in it. When you embed yourself in the context of users and interact with existing solutions as they do, you can compare your own experience with what you have learned from observation and engagement. This can result in new insights to inform your solution efforts.

With Whom to Empathize?

Interviewing and observation are a powerful combination for empathizing with users. But what type of users should you observe and engage with? The tendency for most problem solvers is to focus on the average user. But as IDEO's Tim Brown warns, "By concentrating solely on the bulge at the center of the bell curve … we are more likely to confirm what we already know than learn something new and surprising."[8] To create divergence at the Empathy phase and expand your understanding of the problem space, increasing your opportunities for an innovative solution,[9] consider focusing on extreme users. These are people who fall in the tails of the distributions of users—those whose needs, behaviors, attitudes, and emotions are atypical. Observing and engaging with extreme users can help you identify otherwise unanticipated (and unimaginable) workarounds, hacks, and uses. Without understanding users at the edges of an existing solution, it's unlikely you'll arrive at a new solution that works for them. And yet, a solution that works for them will also likely work for mainstream users. Rather than ignore extreme users because they're an atypical minority, you should seek to learn from them.

Harvard Business School professors Jill Avery and Michael Norton suggest identifying extreme users in the following ways[10]:

- People who are experts with the artifact you are studying and those who have never used it
- People who suffer from constraints that make it difficult to use the artifact and those who use it in ways you never imagined

- Rabid fans who love the artifacts and those who talk trash about it
- People who use the artifact excessively and those who reject it (as a matter of principle or necessity)

A great example of learning from extreme users is the development of OXO Good Grips kitchen tools. After retiring from the cookware company he founded, Sam Farber and his wife Betsey were vacationing in a rented house in the south of France. Sam noticed his wife was having difficulty using a vegetable peeler because of her mild arthritis, leading him to wonder why ordinary kitchen tools had to be uncomfortable and difficult to use. Sam saw an opportunity to create more comfortable and easy-to-use cooking tools that would benefit all users, not just those with mild arthritis.

Soon after, Sam teamed up with his son John and hired Smart Design, a New York City industrial design firm, to research and develop a new line of kitchen tools. In 1990, after extensive research, hundreds of models, and dozens of design iterations, the first 15 OXO Good Grips kitchen tools, including the now-iconic peeler, were introduced to the US market. These ergonomically designed, transgenerational tools were fitted with soft, black plastic handles, which made them easier to hold and use. OXO Good Grips have inspired fierce brand loyalty from the whole spectrum of kitchen utensil users.

There is no hard-and-fast rule for ending the Empathy phase. While academic ethnographers may spend months or years immersing themselves in research sites, you'll spend far less time, from a few days to a few weeks. Project time and budget constraints as well as the willingness of those you're observing and interviewing will greatly determine the duration of the Empathy phase. Short-duration observations are usually sufficient to develop new insights that will inform your problem-solving effort.

The Power of Empathy: The LEGO Turnaround

The remarkable turnaround of the LEGO Group is, in part, a story of the power of user empathy through ethnographic research.[11] By the middle of the 2000s, LEGO had lost touch with its core customers and was losing about $1 million a day. CEO Jørgen Vig Knudstorp attributed this death spiral to LEGO's misadventures in leveraging its brand to move into adjacent markets. Knudstorp believed that children—LEGO's historical core customers—had lost connection to the LEGO brand, and that LEGO had lost sight of them. He realized that LEGO needed to understand kids and play better. The opportunity to do so arose in 2005.

That year, Søren Holm, the head of LEGO's Concept Lab, a group tasked with creating revolutionary play experiences grounded in the LEGO brick, attended a lecture by Mikkel Rasmussen, a partner at Copenhagen-based innovation consultancy ReD Associates. Rasmussen discussed using anthropological research methods to explore consumers' lives and use the resulting insights to drive innovation. One slide, in particular, made a lasting impression on Holm and other leaders of the Concept Lab: "If you want to know how a lion hunts, don't go to a zoo. Go to the jungle." Shortly after that, LEGO and the Concept Lab teamed up with ReD to launch an ambitious project named "Find the Fun." The project would explore twenty-first-century childhood and reveal the needs and desires of kids that LEGO wasn't addressing.

LEGO Concept Lab designers and ReD ethnographers then embarked on lengthy in-home visits with families in the UK, USA, and Germany. A designer and an ethnographer would arrive at a home early in the morning to watch the family get ready for the day. They would interview one or both parents during the day and play with or just observe the kids in the evening. LEGO designers had never stepped so directly into the lives of its customers. The teams spent months visiting families, shopping with them and visiting toy stores, amassing a vast amount of qualitative data in the process.

As the LEGO and ReD team methodically sifted through the data, three key insights emerged. First, they realized that, although they'd thought of LEGO mainly as a solitary activity, childhood play involves a significant social dimension. Second, while LEGO viewed competition among children and the status hierarchy it produces as a negative, ethnographic research showed that self-ranking relative to others is a natural, instinctive part of childhood. Finally, the team learned that kids have an innate desire to master skills, and they demonstrate their mastery to their peers in competition for social status and social connections. The LEGO team realized that LEGO products poorly addressed social play, skills mastery, and competition for status. The identification of these unmet needs opened up opportunities for LEGO to develop new suites of play concepts and better position its core brick products for young customers. Intensive ethnographic research also served as the foundation for the development and launch of LEGO Friends in 2012, a wildly successful line of LEGO mini-dolls targeted at young girls.

As the LEGO story demonstrates, using ethnographic research to observe and engage directly with users can provide unexpected (and possibly otherwise unknowable) insights about users. The LEGO example also shows that these insights don't materialize instantly from research—they must be identified through a systematic distillation process. This is the purpose of the Define phase of design thinking, which we turn to next.

Phase 2: Define

Once you believe you've observed and interviewed a sufficiently diverse group of people, it's time to turn your attention to making sense of the data you've collected. The Define stage is where you transition from the concrete to the abstract, from observing how and why people act, think, and feel to developing abstract representations of them and their experiences. This involves identifying patterns in your data, extracting valuable insights, and ultimately identifying what is most important to users in solving their problem. To do so, you'll need to process and make sense of a large amount of qualitative information. You'll use analytical tools to synthesize your observations into a coherent understanding of the problem, which you'll reflect in the form of models: empathy maps, journey maps, and user personas. The purpose of the Define phase is to crystallize your understanding of the problem from the perspective of users and, in doing so, reframe how you see it. Changing your POV can open up otherwise unimaginable possibilities for new and useful solutions.[12]

The POV Statement

The objective of the Define phase is to develop an actionable and meaningful problem definition, which is identical to the purpose of the problem statement we discussed in Chaps. 3 and 4. What is specific to the design thinking approach is that you define the problem from the perspective of users. This is often called a POV statement.[13]

A POV statement identifies a particular type of user, a fundamental need the user is trying to fulfill, and insights about why the need exists and what is important to the user in fulfilling the need. Needs are emotional or physical necessities or desires, expressed as verbs—something with which users need help. Solutions are nouns and are developed to satisfy needs. Insights are unexpected findings about how users act, think, or feel that you can leverage in your problem-solving effort. Here is the POV statement in stripped-down, template form:

_____ need(s)to _____ because _____.
[user]   [user's need]   [insight]

Using the example of Doug Dietz and MRI scanners, we can fill in these blanks as follows:

- User: Young kids with a medical condition (requiring an MRI scan)
- Need: Play and have fun to feel like a normal kid
- Insight: Kids participate when they perceive it as an adventure

POV statements represent an explicit expression of the user-relevant problem you'll address. They also capture insights that help you understand and define the problem in ways you couldn't otherwise while opening up new possibilities for solutions. POV statements focus and energize your search for solutions.

To develop a POV statement, you'll use the qualitative data you collected during the Empathize stage. You'll build from the bottom up, by analyzing and synthesizing your raw observations, models of how people act, think, and feel about the problem you're addressing. You'll use these models to develop a meaningful and actionable problem statement to guide the remainder of the problem-solving process. We'll walk you through how to do this next.

How to Define: Activities, Tools, and Deliverables

Before you analyze and synthesize, prepare your data. It may be tempting to move quickly and avoid this step, but this can cause delays later. Convert handwritten notes to typed summaries that all team members can understand. Taking the time to do this, ideally just after your observations or interviews, will help you recall information you didn't record initially. Audio recordings should be transcribed, preferably by a professional transcriptionist who can copyedit for readability. Photographs and videos should be edited to remove extraneous images. Consider using a qualitative data analysis software package such as NVivo or ATLAS.ti. These programs allow you to store and organize your text, audio, and image data as a single project and enable you to annotate, search, and visualize the data.

Once you've prepared the data, you're ready to analyze and synthesize. This may seem overwhelming at first if you've collected a lot of data. To avoid the paralysis of analyzing such a mass of qualitative data, you need ways to structure the information. This is where tools and models are useful.

Empathy Maps A widely used tool for organizing and synthesizing observations of individual users is an empathy map. A user empathy map is a template laid out on a single large page, table, or whiteboard and divided into six sections, often with a headshot of the observed user at the center accompanied by basic descriptive info (such as first name, age, gender, family situation, etc.). See Fig. 8.2 for an example of an empathy map. The six sections reflect summary observations about the user along these dimensions:

- *Think and feel*: What really matters to the user? What does she think about the experience? How does she feel about it?
- *Say and do*: What did the user say about her experience? What actions and behaviors did you observe related to the experience?
- *Hear*: What has the user heard from her friends, family, and other influencers that impacts her experience?
- *See*: What does the user see in her environment that influences her? Who is she observing to inform her experience?
- *Pains*: What frustrations and challenges does the user face?
- *Gains*: What is the user hoping to get out of the experience? What does success look like for her?

To complete an empathy map, you'll need to review and synthesize all of your observations about a particular user and make inferences about the person's thoughts, beliefs, and feelings. After you complete an empathy map, focus on identifying the need the person is trying to satisfy and unexpected insights that could help you develop a better solution. To help with this, look for tensions, contradictions, or disconnects within categories, such as what the person says and does, or across categories, such as what they think and feel

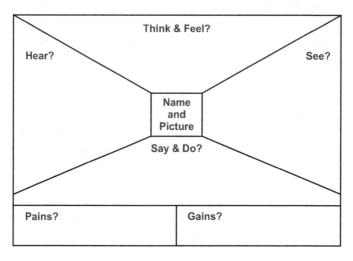

Fig. 8.2 Template for user empathy map

versus what they say and do. Record these needs and insights on the side of the empathy map. You'll use your completed empathy maps as a foundation for identifying patterns and themes across the users you observed.

Journey Maps Another useful tool for organizing data about each person you observed is a user journey map (also known as an experience map). A journey map is a time-ordered model of the activities a person performs and experiences in using a particular artifact, such as a service or product, and what they think and feel about each activity. For example, the user journey for an adult undergoing an MRI scan would begin when she learns of her need to have a scan and include a sequence of many activities: searching for an appropriate scan provider, scheduling an appointment, traveling to the clinic, parking, entering the clinic, locating the reception area, checking in for the appointment, completing the appropriate paperwork, waiting to be scanned, being called, changing clothes, waiting, receiving instructions, positioning for the scan, receiving the scan, exiting the scanner, returning to the changing area and redressing, returning to the waiting area, paying, waiting, discussing scan results with the physician, exiting the clinic, and driving away. The experience wouldn't end until the patient consulted her own physician about the results of the scan. At each point in the overall process, she would need to perform certain actions and may experience positive or negative feelings in response.

A journey map captures each element of the overall user experience. A generic way to frame the phases of any experience is the 5Es model[14]:

- *Entice*: the things that trigger users' interest in and make them aware of and attracted to a particular experience
- *Enter*: the signposts and cues that guide and orient the user to begin the experience
- *Engage*: the specific tasks and interactions that involve the user with the artifact
- *Exit*: the signposts and cues that guide and orient the user to end the experience
- *Extend*: the post-exit reminders and follow-ups that keep the user connected to the experience

Like empathy maps, user journey maps help you structure your observations about individual users and identify needs and insights. To help identify needs and insights, look for bright spots, hot spots, and gaps. A bright spot is a point in the experience that the user truly enjoys. A hot spot is the opposite—

a point in the experience where the user is uncomfortable, frustrated, anxious, or upset. Once you identify a bright spot or hot spot, try to understand why they occurred—what was going on that helped make that part of the experience great or poor? For hot spots, look for workarounds—things the user does to compensate for deficiencies or problems they encounter. Finally, look for gaps, transitions between different activity phases that create challenges or confusion for the user. This can help you zero in on the user's needs and also develop insights. Record these needs and insights on the side of the journey map. You can then compare and contrast the maps to synthesize needs and insights to inform your solution development.

Journey maps can even be used during the Empathize phase of the problem-solving process to structure and guide how you collect data about users. Table 8.3 provides guidance on how to construct journey maps.

Insight Cards Another tool for structuring observations is the insight card. An insight card summarizes an unexpected finding about how a user acts, thinks, or feels. A typical format for an insight card includes a title that summarizes the finding, a snippet of the original text from the research that is the foundation for the insight, and the source of the insight. You can generate insight cards during the Empathize phase—just after an interview or observation session, for instance—or during the Define phase, as you are reviewing your qualitative data or constructing empathy and journey maps.

Synthesizing the Findings Once you've organized your observations about individual users using empathy maps, journey maps, and insight cards, you can move on to searching for patterns and themes in your data. The goal is to distill your structured data into a coherent understanding of the problem

Table 8.3 How to build a journey map

Determine the experience you want to map. Use the initial problem definition from the Empathize stage to set your focus.
Scope the experience. Identify the beginning and end of the experience. This will establish what you will observe and what you won't.
Lay out your hypothesized view of the journey from beginning to end. Identify the discrete activities involved and their sequence, regardless of whether you or your client is involved in the activities.
Conduct one or two pilot interviews or shadowing sessions to be sure you are capturing all the activities in the journey and can collect the data you need.
Develop a template of the journey to guide data collection and capture observations. Include fields that designate the specific activity phases, user touchpoints, actions, thoughts, and feelings. Be prepared to update and modify this as you observe more users.
Conduct the remaining observations using interviewing and/or shadowing.
Use the journey map to summarize the data for each person you observed.

faced by users. You'll reflect this knowledge in models that identify important needs of users and insights about them. These models will help you and your team see the problem from a different POV, opening up opportunities for innovative solutions.

Although the method for synthesizing structured qualitative data across cases of individual users goes by different names in the design thinking world (such as *affinity diagramming, mind mapping,* and *saturate and group*), it consists of a few core steps: search for patterns in the observations across users, cluster similar observations together into themes, and identify how the themes are related to each other. There are at least two types of themes you'll need to identify—those related to user needs and those related to user insights. In other words, you should search for similar needs across users and cluster them into themes and do the same for user insights.

A goal of this synthesis exercise is to define *design imperatives*, the equivalent in the design thinking approach of the "Success Criteria" in the TOSCA problem statement. Imperatives are statements of what the solution must do and how users should experience the solution, phrased in such a way that they are independent of the actual form and implementation of the solution. For example, a child's need to "play and have fun to feel like a normal kid" is a user need, but it is not yet a design imperative. The design imperative that emerged from the research by Dietz and his team stated that the solution should "involve the child in an adventure" while receiving a scan. Imperatives serve as a guiding vision for solution development and an important point of convergence in the design thinking process.

Table 8.4 provides specific instructions on how to synthesize observations.

User Personas The user persona is a powerful way to convey the results of your data synthesis that will guide your solution development. A persona is a vivid and realistic description of a fictional character that represents a composite of real users. It represents the needs, values, aspirations, limitations, lifestyle, attitudes, and background of a hypothetical group of users synthesized from observations of actual users.[15] A persona is a meaningful archetype that combines the needs of real users and insights about them.

Personas are powerful because they put a human face and story to otherwise complex and impersonal data. These realistic, composite characters help overcome the tendency to view the problem from your own perspective and impose your own implicit assumptions on developing a solution. Personas are also easy to communicate, helping develop a shared understanding among your problem-solving team.[16]

Table 8.4 Synthesizing user needs, user insights, and design imperatives

---

Work as a team. The synthesis of qualitative data about users is best done collaboratively with a team consisting of members with diverse perspectives.

Make observations mobile. To leverage and engage your team, make observations visible and portable. Print and post your empathy and journey maps and insight cards. Use pictures from your research and link to structured observations to convey additional information. Making data visual and portable facilitates discussion and sense-making, allows for easy reorganization, and provides opportunities for team members to reflect and build on each other's ideas.

Display your data. Lay out all of your data on a wall or whiteboard. Saturate the space with the observations to make inspection quick and facilitate pattern recognition. Vertically stack your empathy and journey maps and insight cards so you can easily scan them up and down and look for similarities.

Walk through. Once you have all of your data laid out, treat the layout as an art gallery—walk around and review all of the observations to get a holistic sense of the data.

Prepare for clustering. Have the team focus on one set of structured observations at a time. For example, you might begin with the customer journey maps. Write each entry in each component of each journey map onto individual Post-its (e.g., each negative feeling a person had about a particular step in the journey). In effect, you would explode each journey map into its components onto individual Post-its. You could then cluster these observations into themes.

Think about how to cluster. A simple approach is to look for similarities in the content of observations. For example, many MRI patients' feelings about getting a scan can be grouped into a theme of "health worries about MRI scan." Other approaches include clustering observations based on the similarities of users, empathy or journey map component, or proximity between observations. Experiment with different clustering approaches, as there is typically no one best way.

Cluster the data. One approach is for each team member to develop their own clusters for a particular tool (e.g., empathy or journey map) and then come together to share and integrate these efforts. An alternative is to move straight to the team-based approach, working together to cluster observations into themes. Regardless of the approach, some observations may not be assigned to a cluster. Don't ignore these outliers; they may be important.

Summarize themes. Once the clusters are complete, the team should capture the essence of the clustered observations into a thematic description, written on large Post-its and placed on the clusters. Flag each theme as related to user needs or user insights.

Look for connections. Once you've identified the themes, look for relationships between them to help tease out additional insights.

Develop imperatives. After identifying themes and relationships among them, your team should step back and translate what you've learned into design imperatives. To do this, answer the question, "What must our solution address and accomplish for users?"

To develop personas, return to your structured data. Use the empathy maps to search across users to identify dimensions of commonality, whether demographic, behavioral (what users do and say), emotional, or based on the needs and insights you developed. What you're looking for are subsets of users that are similar to one another on one or more of these dimensions. You may find there are two or three such groups, where users are internally similar but different across groups. Develop a persona for each group. Shoot for no more than three personas to keep the solution development process focused. Each persona represents a potentially different segment for your solution.

After you've identified the basis for your personas, flesh out their descriptions. Use the foundational dimensions as a starting point. Use your other data from the empathy maps, journey maps, and insight cards. Most important, summarize the needs and insights you identified for each group of users and include them in the personas, describing them in a way that helps your team to empathize with the (fictitious) person. To aid in this effort, use one or two pages to provide additional details for each persona: the user's education, lifestyle, interests, values, goals, desires, limitations, and patterns of behavior; a few fictional details, such as their age, gender, salary, occupation, and marital status; and a fictional name and stock photograph to help refer to the persona in later phases.

Define the POV Statement and "How Might We" Design Goal Once you've completed your personas, you're ready to close the Define phase by developing a POV statement for each persona. As we explained at the beginning of this section, a POV statement identifies a type of user (such as one represented in a persona), a fundamental need the user is trying to fulfill, insights about why the need exists, and what is important to the user about fulfilling the need. The purpose of a POV statement is to reorient how you see the problem to help you see new ways to solve it. This is precisely what happened to Doug Dietz at GE.

The POV statement Dietz came up with after his empathetic insight into the needs of young patients could be stated in the following way:

A young child with cancer needs to play and have fun to feel like a normal kid when receiving an MRI because kids participate when they perceive it as an adventure.

Dietz and his team used this POV statement to pose a question that would lead to the development of the highly innovative GE Adventure Series scanners:

How might we turn MRI scans for children who fear medical treatment into an adventure?

This type of question is called a "how might we" design goal. "How might we" questions energize and direct the search for potential solutions. They flow from your POV statements and design imperatives. A good "how might we" question is broad enough to stimulate many ideas for solutions, but narrow enough to provoke you and your team to think of specific, novel ideas.[17] Research shows that when problem-solving questions are framed in an exploratory, open-ended way, we imagine more options and identify better solutions than when we think in terms of what we should or must do.[18]

Generating "how might we" questions is a great way to cap the Define phase. Once you've zeroed in on a powerful "how might we" question, building on what you learned during the Empathize phase, you understand enough about the problem to begin solving it. In other words, you've overcome the challenge that led you to embark on the design thinking path, and completed the State stage of the 4S problem-solving method using the tools of design thinking.

You're now able to transition from the Define to the Ideate phase of the design thinking path, which corresponds to the transition between the State and Structure stages of the 4S method shown in Fig. 3.1. In making this transition, you're departing from your examination of the problem space and beginning your exploration of the solution space. You're also moving from a focus on investigating the present situation facing users to imagining and creating the future for them. The Empathize and Define phases were concerned with learning as much as possible about an existing problem. The purpose of the Ideate, Prototype, and Test phases is to use what you learned from the first two stages to identify what could be, and ultimately what should be, the solution. We discuss the final three phases of design thinking in the next chapter.

Chapter 8 in One Page

- Use design thinking for complex, ill-understood, human-centered problems.

  - *Doug Dietz reimagined MRI scanners by seeing them through the eyes of young children who feared them.*

- Design thinking phases: Empathize, Define, Ideate, Prototype, and Test.

- Empathize = understand the problem from the perspective of users.

- Tools of empathy:

  - Participant observation: observe and record how users behave
  - Semi-structured interviews: explore how users think and feel
  - Immersion: live like a user

- Empathize with extreme users—learn from the outliers:

  - *Sam Farber's wife had difficulty using a peeler because of arthritis, inspiring Sam to develop easy-to-use OXO Good Grips kitchen tools.*

- Empathy is the engine of design thinking:

  - *LEGO's ethnographic research into childhood play identified significant unmet needs, resulting in new offerings that helped turnaround the firm.*

- Define = understand and frame the problem from the perspective of users.

- Define phase activities and tools:

  - Empathy map: what user thinks, feels, says, does, hears and sees
  - Journey map: sequence of activities a user experiences pains and gains
  - Insight card: new insights about how user acts, thinks, or feels
  - Synthesis: cluster data into themes and identify how they're related
  - Design imperatives: what solution must do for users
  - User persona: archetype of needs and insights of group of users observed

- Define phase ends with POV statements and "how might we" questions:

  - POV statement: summary of needs and insights about archetypal user
  - "How might we?": use POV to pose question to guide solution search

Notes

1. Sawyer, R. (2006). *Explaining Creativity: The Science of Human Innovation.* Oxford: Oxford University Press.
2. Brown, T. (2009). *Change by Design.* New York: HarperCollins Publishers.
3. Beckman, S.L., & Barry, M. (2007). Innovation as a Learning Process: Embedding Design Thinking, *California Management Review, 50*(1), 25–56.
4. Grant, A.M., & Berry, J.W. (2011). The Necessity of Others Is the Mother of Invention: Intrinsic and Prosocial Motivations, Perspective Taking, and Creativity. *Academy of Management Journal, 54*(10), 73–96.
5. Leonard, D., & Rayport, J.F. (1997). Spark Innovation Through Empathic Design. *Harvard Business Review*, November–December issue, 102–113.
6. Hammersley, M. (2007). Ethnography. In G. Ritzer (Ed.), *The Blackwell Encyclopedia of Sociology.* Malden, MA: Blackwell Publishing.
7. Nisbett, R.E., & Wilson, T.D. (1977). Telling More Than We Can Know: Verbal Reports on Mental Processes. *Psychological Review, 84*, 231–259.
8. Brown, T. (2009). *Change by Design.* New York: HarperCollins Publishers. p. 44.
9. Csazar, F.A., & Levinthal, D.A. (2016). Mental Representation and the Discovery of New Strategies. *Strategic Management Journal, 37*(10), 2031–2049.
10. Avery, J., & Norton, M.I. (2014). *Learning from Extreme Consumers.* Harvard Business School Industry and Background Note. Harvard Business School Publishing.
11. Robertson, D.C., & Breen, B. (2013). *Brick by Brick: How LEGO Rewrote the Rules of Innovation and Conquered the Global Toy Industry.* New York: Crown Business.
    Madberg, C., & Rasmussen, M.B. (2014). An Anthropologist Walks into a Bar … *Harvard Business Review, 92*(3), 80–88.
12. Lipshtitz, R., & Waingortan, M. (1995). Getting out of Ruts: A Laboratory Study of Cognitive Model Reframing. *Journal of Creative Behavior, 29*(3), 151–172.
    Ohlsson, S. (2011). *Deep Learning: How the Mind Overrides Experience.* New York: Cambridge University Press.
13. Hasso Plattner Institute of Design, Stanford University (2009). *An Introduction to Design Thinking Process Guide.*
14. Conifer Research. (2002). *How to Find Buried Treasure Using Experience Maps.*
15. Nielsen, L. (2013). Personas. In M. Soegaard, & R.F. Dam (Eds.). *The Encyclopedia of Human-Computer Interaction* (2nd Ed). Aarhus, Denmark: The Interaction Design Foundation.

16. Pruitt, J., & Adlin, T. (2006). *The Persona Lifecycle: Keeping People in Mind Throughout Product Design*. Burlington: Morgan Kaufmann.

17. Hasso Plattner Institute of Design at Stanford University. (2017). Bootleg Bootcamp. (pp. 26). Retrieved from https://dschool.stanford.edu/resources/the-bootcamp-bootleg.

18. Zhang, T., Gino, F., & Margolis, J. (2014). *Does "Could" Lead to Good? Toward a Theory of Moral Insight*. Harvard Business School Working Paper 14–118.

9

Structure and Solve the Problem Using Design Thinking

Walt Disney World in Orlando, Florida, isn't just a highly successful amusement park; it's a sprawling metropolis spread across some 25,000 acres. It includes four theme parks, about 140 attractions, over 300 dining locations, and 36 resort hotels. Disney theme parks play a crucial role in Disney's corporate strategy by helping cement its characters into the lives of families around the world. In the mid-2000s, however, Disney World, the engine of Disney's theme parks division, was sputtering. Key customer metrics, such as intent to return, were dropping because of long lines, high ticket prices, and numerous other park pain points. Simultaneously, the rapid rise of social media and smartphones threatened the park's relevance. Inside the company, Disney World became known as a "burning platform."

In 2008, at the request of Disney World President Meg Crofton and with the backing of Jay Rasulo, chairman of Disney's Parks and Resorts division, the division kicked off the Next Generation Experience (NGE) project. The project began with a small team tasked with reinventing the vacation experience and keeping Disney World relevant. In mid-2009, the by-then larger NGE team partnered with the San Francisco design consultancy Frog. The NGE team and Frog designers studied what customers did in the park, using ethnographic observation and interviewing. They also mapped family journeys throughout the park.

An early idea that the team developed to address numerous customer pain points became known as the MagicBand. The MagicBand concept was an electronic bracelet that could act as a digital ticket, a key, money, coupons, and photo storage. It would allow guests to seamlessly and effortlessly interact

© The Author(s) 2018
B. Garrette et al., *Cracked it!*, https://doi.org/10.1007/978-3-319-89375-4_9

with Disney during their vacation. The team selected the MagicBand idea from others it generated about digital access devices, including lanyards and even a Mickey Mouse hat. In a dedicated NGE design lab, team members developed and tested over 40 MagicBand prototypes, the first of which they made from materials bought at a local Home Depot. The MagicBand concept became the centerpiece of the NGE project.

As the NGE team swelled and focused on reimagining the entire customer experience around the MagicBand, it moved into a 12,000-square-foot sound-stage at Disney World's Hollywood Studios. There, it developed a sophisticated living blueprint of its vision of the redesigned customer journey. The detailed mock-up included a full-scale living room, complete with an iMac, where an archetypal family would book their Disney World vacation. The family's set of MagicBands would arrive by mail, in packaging designed by Frog to feel like a special gift. The next mock-up was of the flight arrival area of Orlando International Airport, complete with actual seats from the airport. This would be the first place family members would touch their MagicBands to a Disney digital access point. Then came the hotel mock-up, with actual front-desk counters, to simulate the new check-in process using the MagicBands. There were also mock-ups of the main entrance of the park, a mini-version of an attraction, a new restaurant concept that would know what you ordered and be able to deliver it to your table by using MagicBand sensors, and mock-ups of retail shops.

The living blueprint allowed the NGE team to prototype and test multiple aspects of the redesigned experience with Disney World employees and actual customers. It also helped the team sell their vision to CEO Bob Iger and other senior executives and board members. The leadership team committed to the project, called the MyMagic+ initiative, in 2011 with a $1 billion investment.

In 2014, Disney World rolled out the MagicBands and other elements of the MyMagic+ project across the park. Customer satisfaction soared, as digitally monitored wait times fell, and preordered food materialized as if by magic as guests entered restaurants. As a sign of its impact, *Fast Company* magazine bestowed its 2014 "Innovation by Design" award on the MyMagic+ system.[1]

In this chapter, we'll continue our examination of the design thinking process by focusing on idea generation, prototyping, and testing. As the Disney World story illustrates, these aspects of design thinking are powerful tools for helping to solve challenging user problems. They are the continuation on the design thinking path of the 4S method: having *Stated* the problem during the Define phase, designers use the Ideate phase to *Structure* it, and the Prototype and Test phases to *Solve* it.

Phase 3: Ideate

Once you've defined the problem from the user's perspective and synthesized a set of design imperatives, you're ready to generate ideas for solutions, known as *concepts*. A concept is an approximate and concise description of the solution artifact (e.g., a new service, business model, or organizational structure), how it will work, the form it will take, and how it will address user needs. Concepts are typically two-dimensional representations in graphic and/or text form. A great way to jumpstart the transition from the Define to the Ideate phase is by developing "how might we" questions, which we introduced at the end of the Define phase.

In the Ideate phase, you'll continue to operate in the abstract realm, but you'll shift your focus from analyzing and synthesizing *what is* to imagining *what could be* for your users. You'll use your understanding of the problem space and the people for whom you're designing to inform and inspire your thinking. The work you did in the Define stage, especially the development of design imperatives and user personas, will help you and your team stay connected to users and guide your search for solutions.

The Ideate phase consists of two steps. In the first, you'll diverge by generating as many concepts as possible. The goal is to go big, regarding both the volume and the variety of ideas you develop. You'll need to resist the temptation to evaluate others' ideas and censor your own. Instead, encourage wild ideas—the impractical, infeasible, and outlandish. This will help you explore the solution space and expand your universe of concepts, which represents the pool of possible solutions from which you'll choose. In the second step, you'll make choices. You'll refine and evaluate your concepts and select a few promising ones to prototype and test to converge on the final solution.

How to Generate Concepts: Principles and Methods

Linus Pauling, the only person to win two solo Nobel Prizes, quipped, "The best way to have good ideas is to have lots of ideas and throw away the bad ones."[2] Pauling was pointing out something profound yet straightforward: the success of idea generation depends on the quality of the (single) *best* concept developed. Developing one outstanding idea and 99 duds is better than 100 good ideas. In innovative problem solving, the extremes of the distribution matter, not the average.

Maximizing variation with no concern for the average contradicts what we typically want and expect. Most of the time we're trying to maximize average performance and minimize variation. We want consistency and reliability, not variability. We'd prefer 100 of our customers to have a good experience instead of one customer having an excellent experience and the other 99 a mediocre one. Organizations reflect this preference by using hierarchies, performance metrics, incentives, rules, and procedures intended to drive up average performance and drive out deviations.[3]

To increase the odds of finding innovative solutions to complex problems, you must abandon a convergent mindset—the temptation to critically evaluate ideas as they are generated—and adopt a divergent mindset that promotes volume and variety. Research has consistently found that divergent thinking is one of the strongest predictors of creative problem solving.[4] Below are guidelines and methods that research has shown can help with idea generation.

Guidelines for Ideation

Diversify the Team If you want to increase the volume and variation of ideas generated, then you need access to diverse problem solvers, including users. Teams typically outperform individuals in solving complex problems; and teams composed of individuals with different, but relevant expertise usually do better than homogenous groups, as they generate a greater variety and volume of ideas.[5] The downside of diversity is that it can lead to increased conflict and diminished cohesion and communication among team members.[6] To overcome these challenges and harness the benefits of diversity, you'll need to invest in building trust, respect, and acceptance among your team members.[7]

Defer Judgment Being critical kills creativity. Resist the temptation to critically evaluate your team members' ideas and censor your own. While you'll eventually do this in the selection phase, you should decouple idea evaluation from generation. Research shows that problem solvers are more creative when they withhold judgment of their initial ideas until they're more developed.[8] This is critically important when you're generating ideas as a team: judging ideas as they're generated leads to self-censoring, which reduces the number and variety of ideas produced.[9] Rather than dismissing ideas as too wild or infeasible, you should encourage them.

Go for Quantity Generating more ideas can increase the chances of finding new and valuable solutions.[10] By focusing on volume, you can reduce the temptation to judge and self-censor. Pushing for more ideas can energize idea generation and create a positive feedback effect as the generation of one idea triggers others. Setting specific goals (and rewards) for the number of desired concepts can reinforce this focus.

Be Visual As we explained in the Define phase, always seek to make your thinking visible and mobile. This is especially important during the Ideate phase. Visualizing your ideas by sketching them encourages you to clarify them and helps your team members build on them.

Stay Focused In the pursuit of generating greater volume and variety of ideas, it's easy to lose focus on the problem and the users. Use the problem definition, design imperatives, and user personas from the Define stage to inform and guide your ideation. One way to do this is to enlarge them and mount them on the walls of your workspace to serve as reminders.

Methods for Ideation

Now that you have a set of principles to follow, we can focus on some practices that will help you ideate. The toolkit for creative idea generation is vast. In his book *Thinkertoys*, author Michael Michalko describes 33 techniques to aid in the production of innovative ideas.[11] We'll explore a few methods that research has shown to aid in ideation.

Analogical Thinking Analogies are comparisons of the similar features of two things. Our minds seek to make sense of new situations by comparing the unfamiliar with things we've experienced before. Reasoning by analogy is a primary way people solve problems. Research has consistently shown that analogical reasoning can benefit idea generation and creative problem solving.[12] One reason a diverse team of problem solvers generates more (and more diverse) concepts is that it has access to a greater variety of analogies.[13]

The primary challenge of analogical thinking is that we often don't see the similarity between two domains and can't make the analogical leap, or we develop analogies based on superficial similarities, resulting in poor-quality ideas. We need a method to help us create analogies. Here's how to do it:

1. *Identify the critical aspects of your problem.* Use the design imperatives, problem definition, and any other outcomes of the Define phase to establish what you believe are the essential attributes of the target problem.
2. *Search for problems in different settings that share characteristics of your problem and identify their solutions.* Solutions to source problems represent

candidate solutions for your problem. To inspire genuinely novel ideas, search for distant problems and solutions—ones that, on the surface, don't appear to have much in common with your problem.[14] For example, Ford Motor Company's creation of the automobile assembly line resulted from an analogy to industrial food preparation.[15] In its early days, Ford used an inefficient production process where workers fetched parts from multiple bins and moved around what they were working on, such as engines or car bodies, on hand trucks. In 1913, Ford employee Bill Kann visited a Chicago slaughterhouse and observed a model of industrial butchering efficiency: animal carcasses moved on overhead trolleys, while a series of butchers performed specialized tasks in sequence as the carcasses advanced. After convincing founder Henry Ford of the applicability of the approach to producing automobiles, the moving assembly line became the signature of Model T production. This led to an explosion in productivity, which allowed Ford to reduce the price of a car from $575 to $280.

One way to identify distant analogies is to look to nature for source problems and solutions. Solving problems by analogy to biology, often called biomimicry, uses biological forms, processes, patterns, and systems as source solutions for target problems.[16] Biomimicry allows problem solvers to exploit solutions in nature, optimized over millions of generations through the process of natural selection. While designers are increasingly using biomimicry in developing innovative tangible artifacts, it's also being used to inspire novel solutions for the design of services, organizations, and strategies.[17] An additional way to create distant analogies is to search for source problems and solutions outside the industry of your challenge, as Bill Kann did in the early days of Ford Motor Company.

3. *Evaluate the extent to which your problem resembles the source problem.* The similarities you notice between your problem and the source problem are what bring to mind an analogy. However, focusing only on similarities, especially if they're superficial, can lead to bad ideas. To counter this possibility, consider what's different about the source problem and the solution that may make them irrelevant or misleading for your idea generation efforts. This can also help you assess whether the similarities you see are primarily superficial or more deeply connected to the underlying causes of the problems. As we saw in the story of Ron Johnson and J.C. Penney in Chap. 2, using superficial similarities between two situations without acknowledging their substantive differences can lead to disastrous solutions.

4. *Evaluate if the candidate solution might help solve your problem.* You need to translate the solution from the source domain to the domain of your problem. You'll need to adjust it for the differences you identified between

the two domains in the previous step. Once you've translated the solution, you can assess whether you think it will work in solving your problem. At this step in the idea generation process, you don't need to perform a thorough evaluation of the solution concept—you'll do this in the second step—you only need to evaluate whether you want to keep it in the set of potential solutions.

An inspiring example of the power of analogy in problem solving that reflects this four-step process comes from the world of pediatric cardiac intensive care. The handover of infants after complicated heart surgery from the operating theater team to the intensive care unit (ICU) team is a critical period in the recovery of these small, vulnerable patients. During this period, all the technology and support equipment—drug supply, ventilation, and monitoring equipment—are transferred twice, from theater systems to portable equipment and then to ICU equipment, all within 15 minutes. Simultaneously, valuable information about the patient gleaned from the four- to eight-hour procedure is transferred from the surgical team to the ICU team. The combination of these complex tasks in such a short amount of time makes the process susceptible to error when the patients are most vulnerable.

The staff at the Great Ormond Street Hospital for Children in London performs this process daily. Professor Martin Elliott and Dr. Allan Goldman are colleagues at Great Ormond Street. After a difficult day at work, Professor Elliot, the head of cardiac surgery, and Dr. Goldman, the head of the pediatric cardiac intensive care unit, slumped into chairs to unwind by watching TV. On the screen was a Formula 1 Grand Prix racing event. As the two men watched, they noticed the similarities between the pit stops of the F1 racing teams and the handover process from operating theater to ICU teams. This realization led to a collaboration between the leaders of Great Ormond Street's surgical and ICU teams, first with the McLaren F1 racing team and then with members of the Ferrari F1 team. They worked together at Ferrari's home base in Modena, Italy, in the pits of the British Grand Prix and in the Great Ormond Street surgical theater and ICU. This collaboration led to a complete redesign of the handover protocol, which resulted in significant improvements in all aspects of the handover process.[18]

Brainstorming   Brainstorming is probably the most well-known, widely used, and extensively researched idea generation method. Made famous in Alex Osborn's 1953 book, *Applied Imagination*,[19] brainstorming is a largely unstructured free-association approach to idea generation. You focus on the problem at hand and then imagine—using an unconstrained free-association process—

as many ideas as possible to solve it. You've likely participated in many brain-storming sessions. Although experimental research shows brainstorming groups produce fewer and less diverse ideas compared to similar groups of individuals working alone,[20] other studies show that brainstorming aids idea generation when the principles of good idea generation, which we discussed above, are followed.[21] The design firm IDEO has codified these principles into the following brainstorming rules, which its members follow diligently:

- Defer judgment
- Encourage wild ideas
- Build on the ideas of others
- Stay focused on the topic
- One conversation at a time
- Be visual
- Go for quantity

Using an experienced facilitator can also improve the idea generation per-formance of brainstorming groups.[22] This is standard practice at IDEO and other design firms. Besides helping with idea generation, brainstorming can also help problem solvers challenge their assumptions about the problem and potential solutions, and minimize their potential to jump to poor solutions.[23]

Brainwriting This is a variation on group brainstorming and was developed to overcome some of its challenges.[24] In brainwriting, participants indepen-dently generate a targeted number of ideas (e.g., three or four), or as many ideas as they can, without interacting with each other. Participants then share ideas with one another. This can happen in two ways. The simplest is to share them aloud, one person at a time, with someone recording all ideas on a flip-chart or whiteboard. An alternative approach promotes building on the ideas of others. In this approach, each team member shares their recorded ideas with another and then a second round of independent idea generation begins with the focus of generating additional ideas based on those of your team-mate. This process can continue for a specified period, after which all ideas generated are recorded and shared with the team for further discussion.[25]

Brainwriting addresses some challenges of brainstorming. Generating ideas on your own instead of in an interactive discussion eliminates the potential of a single group member dominating the conversation. It can also reduce the temptation for people to self-censor their ideas out of concern they'll be judged negatively, provides more time for reflection and incubation of ideas, and reduces the temptation for some participants to "freeride" on the contributions of others.[26] In a carefully designed experimental study, professors Karan Girotra of INSEAD and Christian Terwiesch and Karl Ulrich of the Wharton School found that groups that conducted an initial round of brainwriting before they brainstormed generated more and better ideas (regarding their business value and customer desirability) than similar groups that only brainstormed.[27]

Morphological Analysis Fritz Zwicky, the brilliant Swiss astrophysicist who discovered dark matter while at Caltech, developed this method for structuring complex problem solving.[28] Morphological analysis reflects a well-established insight from research on creativity, invention, and innovation: new and useful solutions to problems typically result from combining existing artifacts (e.g., ideas, concepts, technologies) in novel ways.[29] For example, the spork resulted from the combination of the spoon and fork. The iconic Reebok Pump introduced in 1989 was an athletic shoe combined with an air bladder borrowed from intravenous bag technology. Similarly, Waze, the app on which millions of drivers depend to minimize commute times, is a combination of existing technologies—GPS location sensor, smartphone, GPS system, and social network platform.

Morphological analysis treats artifacts as bundles of different attributes. To use this idea generation method, you first must identify the different *attributes* of the solution, such as its various performance dimensions, functions it must perform, physical characteristics, and so on. The purpose is to break down the artifact (product, process, system, or strategy) you're designing into its essential aspects. Once you've identified the attributes, you then determine the different possible *states* in which each attribute can exist. For example, in designing a physical product, one attribute could be the shape of the artifact, while the various shapes it could take on (e.g., spherical, cube, etc.) represent different states. Once you've identified the attributes and states, you can arrange them in a morphological matrix by listing the attributes as the column headings and the possible states for each underneath in the rows.

Michael Michalko provides a simple example of morphological analysis in his book *Thinkertoys*. Michalko offers the challenge of generating ideas for an improved laundry hamper. He identifies four attributes of laundry hampers: *material, shape, finish,* and *position.* For each attribute, he defines the followings states:

- Material: wicker, plastic, paper, metal, netting
- Shape: square, cylindrical, rectangle, hexagonal, cube
- Finish: natural, painted, clear, luminous, neon
- Position: sits on floor, on ceiling, on wall, chute to basement, on door

Once you've structured the morphological matrix, you can generate ideas for new solutions by searching it for combinations of states of different attributes that don't yet exist. You can do this randomly or by choosing particular combinations. You can eliminate combinations that are impossible or obviously inappropriate and keep the rest as possible innovative solutions. Research shows that morphological analysis can improve the number and novelty of ideas generated.[30]

In Michalko's hamper example, he used the matrix to create a laundry hamper fashioned into a basketball net, about 40 inches long, attached to a cylindrical hoop, and hung on a backboard attached to the back of a door. This design encourages kids to play basketball with their dirty laundry. When the hamper is full, a pull on a drawstring releases the clothes.

SCAMPER[31] A variation on the insight that innovative solutions are often novel combinations of existing ideas is that novel solutions often result from additions or modifications to existing solutions. SCAMPER builds on this insight by offering a checklist of idea-spurring questions. The acronym SCAMPER stands for Substitute, Combine, Adapt, Modify, Put to some other use, Eliminate, and Reverse. Table 9.1 illustrates how each of these themes, used in any order or combination, can trigger idea generation.[32] Using SCAMPER has been found to help in developing more novel, useful, and feasible solutions.[33]

For example, consider the challenge Southwest Airlines (SWA) faced in the US airline industry in the 1970s when it competed with much larger and richer domestic hub-and-spoke network carriers such as American Airlines. The problem SWA faced was: "How might we redesign the conventional value proposition (benefits for price) of network carriers to profitably attract people who would normally drive or take the bus (because flying is too expensive)?"

In effect, SWA executives asked and answered a series of SCAMPER questions, leading them to develop an innovative customer value proposition. For instance, SWA *substituted* the use of uncongested airports for the larger (more congested) and sometimes more convenient airports used by network carriers. It *eliminated* many of the customer benefits of network carriers, including full meals on its flights, long-haul flights, the provision of business

Table 9.1 Using SCAMPER to ideate

SCAMPER theme	Typical questions
Substitute *Think about substituting part of the product or process for something else*	What else instead? Who else instead? What other materials, ingredients, processes, power, sounds, approaches, or forces might I substitute? Which other place?
Combine *Think about combining two or more parts of the product or process to make something new or to enhance synergy*	What mix, assortment, alloy, or ensemble might I blend? What ideas, purposes, units, or appeals might I combine?
Adapt *Think about which parts of the product or process could be adapted or how you might change the nature of the product or process*	Does the past offer a parallel? What else is like this? What other idea does this suggest? What might I adapt for use as a solution? What might I copy? Who might I emulate?
Magnify, **M**odify *Think about changing part or all of the product or process, or distorting it in an unusual way*	What other meaning, color, motion, sound, smell, form, or shape might I adopt? What might I add?
Put to other uses *Think of how you might put the product or process to another use or how you might reuse something from somewhere else*	What new ways are there to use this? Might this be used in other places? Which other people might I reach? To what other uses might this be put if it is modified?
Eliminate *Think of what might happen if you eliminated parts of the product or process, and consider what you might do in that situation*	What might I understate? What might I eliminate? What might I streamline? What might I make smaller, lower, shorter, or lighter?
Rearrange, **R**everse *Think of what you might do if parts of the product or process worked in reverse or were sequenced differently*	What might be rearranged? What other pattern, layout, or sequence might I adopt? Can components be interchanged? Should I change pace or schedule? Can positives and negatives be swapped? Could roles be reversed?

lounges, business class, and seat choice. And it *magnified* many other benefits: it increased the number of daily departures on its routes, and the friendliness and reliability of its customer service. It got customers to their destinations faster by avoiding the use of hubs. Most important, it achieved a much-lower cost structure than the network carriers, allowing it to offer a substantially reduced price. This redesigned and innovative value proposition helped SWA become the most consistently profitable airline in history.

How to Evaluate and Select Concepts: Principles and Methods

After diverging by generating many solution concepts, the second step in the Ideate phase is to converge by determining which ones to carry forward into prototyping and testing. This raises two crucial questions: *how* should concepts be evaluated and selected, and *who* should do the evaluation and selection? We'll address both issues in this section.

Concept evaluation is best done using a structured approach. You start the process by defining criteria you'll use to evaluate your pool of concepts. These criteria will allow you to compare the relative strengths and weaknesses of the ideas in a disciplined way and select one or more for prototyping.

The objectives and criteria you develop should address three broad areas: user *desirability*, technological and organizational *feasibility*, and financial *viability*. The purpose of the Define phase was to help you understand what users desire from a solution. You must now translate these design imperatives into detailed evaluation criteria. The final solution must also be feasible to implement. The technology must exist and the organization should have the requisite resources and capabilities to implement it. Finally, you'll need to assess the extent to which the solution can be developed and implemented in an economically sustainable way.

A structured approach has many advantages over ad hoc, unstructured ones.[34] Because you'll evaluate concepts against criteria related to users and the problem owner, you're more likely to select ideas that fit with both constituents. Reflecting the design imperatives in your evaluation criteria pushes you to choose potential solutions that users may find more attractive than existing ones. A structured approach also reduces the influence of cognitive biases on concept selection by promoting the use of objective criteria and provides a record of the reasoning behind your choices.

Although concept selection is a convergent process, it's unlikely you'll identify a dominant concept to prototype immediately. Concept evaluation and selection is usually iterative. The process is likely to trigger essential conversations within your team that help refine your concepts further, by combining some into new ideas and modifying others. This will lead to additional rounds of evaluation.

To evaluate and select concepts, follow this six-step process[35]:

1. *Construct the selection matrix.* Enter your evaluation criteria in the rows and the title of the concepts at the top of the columns. You may weight the criteria (in percentages) to reflect differences in importance. You'll need a benchmark or reference concept to evaluate your ideas against. This could be a conventional or best-in-class solution or any concept in your set.

2. *Rate the concepts.* You can use a simple scoring system consisting of three levels: "better than" (+), "similar" (0), and "worse than" (−) a benchmark "reference concept"; or use a 1–5 scale. You can rate by row (i.e., focus on one criterion and rate each concept before moving to the next criterion) or by column (i.e., focus on a concept and rate it for each criterion before moving on to the next concept). When doing this as a team, you can rate the ideas by consensus or use the average of individual secret ballots.

3. *Rank the concepts.* After rating the concepts, sum the scores for each concept and record each at the bottom of the selection matrix. Rank-order the concepts by score from best to worst.

4. *Combine and improve the concepts.* After you've rank-ordered the concepts, discuss with the team whether the ranking makes sense. Assuming it does, look for ways to combine or improve concepts. If a well-scored concept is hurt by a low score on one or two criteria, try to identify how it could be improved on those dimensions without degrading its performance on the other criteria. Also look for concepts that are mirror images in their good and bad scores. Identify how you might combine the highly rated aspects of one concept to compensate for the low ratings of another.

5. *Select one or more concepts.* Once you and your team have completed additional evaluation rounds to account for modified concepts and are satisfied with the results, you can decide on which concept(s) to move forward into prototyping. If you have the time and resources, consider bringing two or three concepts into the prototyping stage.

6. *Reflect on the results and process.* At the end of the process, take time to discuss with your team their satisfaction and comfort with the evaluation and selection process. If someone is not in agreement, identify the source of concern. This may cause the team to review the criteria for completeness and clarity, and to revise the ratings assigned. Taking time to reflect on the process and identify issues can reduce the likelihood that mistakes are made and increase the commitment of the team to the next stage of the design thinking process.

Although a structured approach to concept evaluation improves your chances of selecting a desirable and value-creating solution, *who* performs this critical activity is also important.[36] When we're deeply involved in generating ideas, even when using a user-oriented approach such as design thinking, we risk falling in love with our ideas and overestimating their chances of success, resulting in "false positives" (i.e., approving poor concepts). In contrast, outsiders who are not involved in the idea generation process, such as managers who evaluate project proposals, are more likely to underestimate the value of novel solutions and overvalue conventional, familiar ones, increasing the risk of "false negatives" (i.e., rejecting winning concepts).

One way to overcome these challenges is to involve *creative peers:* people from outside the project team actively working on creating solutions to similar problems. Your creative peers will be less risk averse than uninvolved managers and more open to novel ideas, reducing the possibility of false negatives. They also aren't invested in your ideas, helping them provide a more objective appraisal and protecting against false positives. These outsiders can help improve your chances of selecting value-creating ideas to prototype and test, which we examine next.

Phase 4: Prototype

The Prototype phase is where you transition back from the abstract realm to the concrete. The core idea of prototyping is to make your abstract concepts tangible so that users can meaningfully interact with them and you can learn from these interactions. The point is to get ideas out of your head and off the page and into the world of your users.

A prototype is an approximation of your solution artifact (product, process, service, etc.). It is a tangible representation of at least one aspect or attribute of the solution you think will help solve your users' problem. Prototypes are experiments—they allow you to test hypotheses about what you believe are the appropriate attributes of the solution. IDEO CEO Tim Brown says, "Anything tangible that lets us explore an idea, evaluate it, and push it forward is a prototype."[37]

Prototypes come in many forms. They can be a storyboard that illustrates a process or service, a mock-up using foamcore of a physical space such as a hotel lobby or guest room, paper-based schematics of screenshots of a mobile app, or a three-dimensional (3D) printed artifact that approximates the final form of a physical product. Prototypes can be rough, such as the early one IDEO developed for the first Apple Computer mouse, which consisted of a roller ball from a tube of Ban Roll-On deodorant affixed to the base of a plastic butter dish, or more highly refined. Prototypes can focus on only one or a few attributes of a concept, or they can be comprehensive and fully integrated such as a preproduction concept car.

Prototyping is a highly iterative process. Because prototypes allow you to learn from feedback, you'll use what you learn from one prototype to refine successive ones as you converge toward a solution. As you do, your prototypes will become more realistic and comprehensive.

Early prototypes, however, should be fast, rough, and cheap. This allows you to learn rapidly and explore multiple solution possibilities. IDEO encourages its designers to "fail often to succeed sooner." Research shows that getting physical fast by building and testing tangible prototypes early improves the quality of the final solution.[38]

An example of fast, cheap, and highly informative prototyping comes from the world of fast food. In 1948, Richard ("Dick") and Maurice ("Mac") McDonald owned and operated a highly successful drive-in restaurant in San Bernardino, California. Despite their success, the McDonald brothers believed they could be more profitable if they could serve customers faster by streamlining their menu and improving the efficiency of food preparation. That year, besides slashing their menu to just nine items and developing standardized recipes and processes, the brothers boldly decided to close their doors to explore how to reinvent their kitchen operations.

Dick McDonald believed the kitchen layout affected order preparation speed, and that by changing the configuration of the kitchen equipment and stations, he could reduce interruptions, bottlenecks, and collisions among staff, decreasing preparation time and waste. To test this hypothesis quickly and cheaply, Dick and Mac retreated to the tennis court behind their home. Using thick chunks of red chalk, they drew the exact dimensions of their restaurant kitchen on the court.

This prototyping exercise was wonderfully captured in the film *The Founder*. Using their kitchen staff, the brothers simulated order preparation: grilling the burgers, frying the fries, and so on. Dick observed the action from the top of a ladder to monitor the flow. After changing the layout of the kitchen on the tennis court multiple times, Dick found a highly efficient production process. The McDonald brothers were then sufficiently confident to hire a contractor to build a kitchen customized to their specifications for their renovated restaurant. The new "Speedee Service System" allowed

McDonald's to prepare and deliver a meal to a customer in just 30 seconds.[39] This approach revolutionized the restaurant industry, helping to create the "fast food" category and a global behemoth.

Benefits of Prototyping

Prototyping is an essential part of design thinking and disciplined problem solving for three reasons: learning, risk management, and communication.

Prototype to Learn Prototyping is an experimental activity. A prototype embodies a hypothesis you've developed during the Ideate phase.[40] You build tangible prototypes to test your hypotheses. You run experiments by allowing users to interact with prototypes and collecting their feedback. Observing interactions with tangible artifacts typically provides richer, more thoughtful, and more reliable feedback than feedback based solely on verbal or written descriptions.

Developing prototypes also forces you to clarify your thinking. When confronted with translating our thinking into tangible form, we often realize how fuzzy our thinking was or discover gaps in how we imagined the solution. Prototypes serve the additional function of uncovering important problems and questions that are unexpected. We build to think.

Prototype to Manage Risk Prototyping reduces uncertainty about what works and what doesn't in solving users' problems. By resolving uncertainty before committing more resources to implementing solutions, you reduce the downside risk of failure and improve the odds of success.

Prototype to Communicate Prototypes enrich and facilitate communication with all stakeholders and internal team members. Because of the richness of interaction they provide, prototypes help you effectively communicate where you stand in your solution efforts. By using evidence from users to make design choices, prototypes reduce disagreements stemming from different opinions and perspectives about the solution. They also help diverse stakeholders discuss and negotiate the meaning, purpose, functionality, and performance of the solution.

How to Prototype?

For prototypes to provide these benefits, they must have a plan behind them. Below is a simple four-step planning method[41]:

1. *Define the purpose of the prototype.* Prototyping is an experimental activity. Knowing the purpose of an experiment is essential to designing it. Without knowing the purpose, you won't know what to get feedback on and from whom, making it difficult to determine what was learned. Before undertaking a prototype, state in writing what your team wishes or expects to learn from testing the prototype. You could frame this as one or more hypotheses in the form, "We believe that _____."
2. *Establish the level of approximation of the prototype.* Prototypes vary in their comprehensiveness (i.e., how many attributes and functions of the final solution they possess) and in their fidelity (i.e., how closely they match the look and feel of a finished solution). More comprehensive and higher-fidelity prototypes typically help users provide more useful feedback, but are more time-consuming and costly to build and less flexible to modify for later iterations. The level of approximation of the prototype reflects a trade-off between clarity and accuracy of feedback on the one hand, and affordability and flexibility on the other. A prototype should possess the minimal comprehensiveness and level of fidelity to generate useful feedback for the intended learning purpose you have defined in the previous step.
3. *Outline the experimentation plan.* The experimental protocol for running the experiment and analyzing the feedback generated should identify the type(s) and number of users involved in testing, the context in which the prototype will be tested, how feedback will be collected, and how it will be analyzed. We'll address these aspects of the experimental plan in the Test phase below.
4. *Create a schedule.* The final step before moving into testing is to create a schedule. This should identify when the prototype must be built, the time frame of when the prototype will be tested, and when the feedback will be analyzed. Prototype schedules help problem-solving teams stay focused and motivated.

Phase 5: Test

Prototyping and testing are intimately intertwined. They are consecutive steps in a disciplined experimentation process and they inform each other. What you're trying to test and how you'll test it are critically important to consider before developing a prototype. What you learn from testing one prototype helps you develop others.

The purpose of testing is to learn. You test with users to refine your solution and to refine your understanding of the people for whom you are designing and the problem they face. Don't limit the feedback you seek only to what users like and don't like about the prototype. Ask "why" a lot to uncover additional insights about users and the problem. Also ask for suggestions on how to improve the solution.

Testing prototypes gives serendipity a chance because it creates opportunities for unexpected feedback.[42] Interacting with a prototype in the context in which a solution will be used can inspire users to provide otherwise unimaginable input that leads to valuable improvements in the solution. But you must be alert and receptive to unexpected feedback and willing to explore why it happened to capitalize on serendipity.[43] As Louis Pasteur noted, "In the field of observation, chance favors only the prepared mind."

Prototyping and testing early and often seems time-consuming, but can actually speed up the overall solution development process. Testing allows teams to identify and weed out weak solutions earlier, and to unearth limitations of solutions before they get into advanced stages of development, when it takes more time and expense to address them.[44] Reflecting on this insight, IDEO's Tim Brown says testing prototypes early and often is paradoxical because "they slow us down to speed us up."[45]

How to Test?

Although prototyping and testing are entwined, planning and executing an effective test is a significant additional step after creating a prototype. We explain how to do it below.[46] The steps we outline start where we left off when planning for a prototype:

1. *Choose a setting and sample of users.* A critical aspect of testing prototypes is the choice of context and sample of users. These choices affect the richness and reliability of feedback. Test contexts can range from the controlled and artificial—such as a research laboratory or staged mock-up—to the actual,

natural setting in which the solution will be used. Sample users can be anybody, regardless of whether they face the problem you're solving or actual users who face the problem in meaningful ways.

To allow users to give you the most natural, detailed, and honest feedback, the test context and the people with whom you test should correspond as closely as possible to those of the real world. This typically means letting real users interact with the prototype in their natural setting. Putting a prototype in front of a user and asking for feedback, without allowing her to experience it as she naturally would, won't generate much useful feedback. For example, if you developed a prototype for an innovative travel mug, bringing a group of users together for a focus group in a conference room won't allow them to experience it like they normally would as part of their morning work commutes. Because their interaction with the prototype is decontextualized, their feedback will be less useful.

Be careful to avoid recruiting people predisposed to providing favorable, validating feedback, such as friends, family members, and enthusiasts— people passionate for the solution you're developing. This increases the risk of false positives. In contrast, recruiting only the most demanding and critical users for your test can lead to false negatives. To draw valid conclusions about your tests, avoid testing your prototypes with users who are either too easy or too skeptical.

A final factor to consider is the size of the sample. When testing early and rough prototypes, where the goal is to generate qualitative feedback rapidly, small samples of ten or so users are appropriate.[47] Later in the solution development process, when using high-resolution and comprehensive prototypes, much larger samples (typically in the hundreds) are needed to identify statistically significant results.

2. *Develop a feedback collection format.* To generate feedback about your prototype, you'll want to use a combination of observation and semi-structured interviews. For the latter, you'll need to develop questions using the principles of semi-structured interviews outlined in the Empathy phase. A simple and useful tool for capturing feedback from prototype tests is the *feedback capture grid.* This grid consists of four quadrants, each with a broad, open-ended question: "What worked?" "What didn't work?" "What didn't you understand?" (or "What questions do you have?") and "How could it be improved?"

3. *Communicate the prototype.* Plan on how your test users will encounter and engage with the prototype. The goal is to show them the prototype—allow them to interact and experience it—rather than tell them about it. Avoid explaining the thinking or reasoning behind your prototype. Think of yourself

as a host, helping users transition from reality to your prototype setting by providing the minimum context for them to understand what to do.

4. *Collect feedback.* Begin by actively observing how users interact with the prototype, how they use and misuse it. If the user gets sidetracked because he's misusing the prototype or doesn't understand it, then provide the minimal corrective feedback to help him continue. Have him think aloud as he experiences the prototype. As the host of the prototype experience, you can ask, "Tell me what you are thinking as you are doing this." This is similar to shadowing, which we discussed in the Empathize phase. It's important to have other team members acting solely as observers and recorders during feedback collection. If you can't do this, then video record the testing.

Be careful not to defend your prototype when you collect feedback about it. Because prototypes reflect our beliefs about what users want and involve substantial effort to develop, we can fall prey to confirmation bias, described in Chap. 3. We must embrace disconfirming or unexpected feedback because it can reveal unanticipated limitations of our solutions and provide opportunities to refine them. Test as if you will be wrong. Adopting this perspective reduces the temptation to defend your prototype and helps you accept disconfirming feedback, since you expect this.

5. *Interpret the feedback.* Return to the purpose of the prototype and the specific questions or hypotheses you developed. Use them to guide your analysis of the qualitative feedback you generated from your test. Synthesize what you learned about your questions and hypotheses, but don't limit your analysis just to these things. Because testing prototypes is another opportunity to empathize with users, synthesize what you learned about their needs and insights. The analytical toolkit described in the Define phase will be handy here.

6. *Reflect on the results.* Once you've analyzed and synthesized the feedback you collected, it's time to reflect on it. This is where you realize much of the value of testing. Discuss the results with your team and make sure they make sense to everyone. The critical questions to ask are as follows: How will we refine and improve the solution based on what we learned? What should we change? What should we keep? What should we tweak? Push your team to converge on the next iteration of prototype as you drive toward your final solution.

For simplicity, we've presented design thinking as a linear progression, from empathizing to testing. In the previous chapter, we showed you how to investigate the problem space by immersing yourself in how users actually experience the problem, and how to translate your observations into a guiding problem definition. This chapter switched the focus to exploring the solution space by imagining and creating possible futures for users, by generating and evaluating solution concepts and then prototyping and testing them.

But as you can now appreciate, the process isn't that simple. Design thinking is highly iterative, and necessarily so. An iterative, experimental process reduces the risks and improves your odds of developing an innovative solution. Iteration is a hallmark of good design and good solution development. You iterate by cycling through the entire process several times. You also iterate within stages, for example, by creating and testing multiple prototypes or moving through consecutive rounds of idea generation and concept evaluation. The objective is to home in on what the (final) solution should and should not do.

With all this iteration and refining, how do you know when to stop? The criteria for innovation we briefly discussed in the concept evaluation step of the Ideate phase offer an answer. Innovative solutions to challenging business problems exist at the intersection of three criteria: desirability, feasibility, and viability. An innovative solution must be desirable to users. This means users must view it as solving their problem more effectively than existing solutions, after accounting for the cost of adopting it. An innovative solution must also be feasible to provide. The technology must exist to reliably and efficiently implement the solution, and the solution provider must possess the resources and capabilities for implementation. Finally, an innovative solution must be economically viable for the solution provider—the economic benefits of development and implementation must exceed the costs. When you have sufficient confidence that your solution meets these criteria, you're ready to move to the "Sell" stage of the 4S method.

$$* \quad * \quad *$$

Design thinking, the focus of this chapter and the preceding one, is an abductive approach to solving complex business problems—you immerse yourself in understanding an existing problem to infer what the future solution should be. It provides an alternative, complementary toolkit to the hypothesis-driven and issue-driven approaches.

Approaching problem solving like a designer requires a different mindset and toolkit than the other approaches we described in Chaps. 4, 5, 6 and 7. A design thinking approach to problem solving emphasizes the *creation* of solutions—products, services, strategies, systems, and organizations. It is not solely about using brute intellectual force to decipher elegant answers to complex puzzles. Designers solve problems by bringing new artifacts into existence. They give physical form to thought. To do this, designers move fluidly between the abstract realm of mental models and the concrete realm of real people, experiences, and artifacts. To solve a problem is to create and to be creative.

Therein lies both the challenge and the promise of design thinking. Most people don't identify themselves as being particularly adept at creativity and often feel insecure about their creative abilities. This can manifest as a fear of failure, a fear of venturing into the unknown, or a fear of looking foolish. When people believe they're not creative, they lack the confidence to pursue creativity.

The promise of design thinking is that it demystifies creativity. It represents a disciplined process and a set of tools that can empower you to generate and pursue new ideas for solutions to challenging problems. To show you how to solve problems like a designer, we explored the process, methods, practices, and stories of design thinking. In doing this, we hope we've helped inspire you to use this approach and develop a sense of mastery over it.

In their aptly named book, *Creative Confidence*, Tom and David Kelley remind us that everybody is creative. In explaining the value of design thinking, the Kelley brothers conclude, "We know that if we can get individuals to stick with the methodology a while, they will end up doing amazing things."[48]

Regardless of how you solve the business problem you're tackling—whether it's through hypothesis pyramids, issue trees, or design thinking—you must persuade others of its value and feasibility. You'll need to develop and deliver a compelling story to sell your solution. To see how to do this, continue on to the next chapter and get ready to design the storyline for your pitch.

*   *   *

Chapter 9 in One Page

- Ideate, Prototype, and Test to explore the solution space:

  - *Disney World reimagined the customer experience by building full-scale mock-ups of the theme park customer journey.*

- Ideate = generate diverse solution concepts; choose the most promising for prototyping and testing.

- Ideation, step 1: volume and variety matter, average quality doesn't.

  - Pauling: *the best way to have good ideas is to have lots of ideas.*

- Guidelines: diversify the team, defer judgment, go for quantity

- Tools for ideation:

  - Analogical thinking: How is pediatric heart surgery like an F1 pit stop?
  - Brainstorming and brainwriting: use both for more and better ideas
  - Morphological analysis: spoon + fork = spork
  - SCAMPER questions: *Southwest Airlines reinvents the airline industry*

- Ideation, step 2: use a structured evaluation process to converge

  - Criteria: desirability (use design imperatives), feasibility, viability
  - Involve creative peers to minimize false positives and false negatives

- Prototype = create tangible approximations of solution for users

- We prototype to learn, manage risks, and communicate.

  - *The McDonald brothers rapidly and cheaply prototyped and tested "Speedee Service System" kitchen layout using chalk outlines on a tennis court.*

- How to prototype:

  - Define the purpose: What do you want to learn?
  - Determine how complete and finished it needs to be

- Test = get feedback about prototypes and analyze it to converge to a solution.
- Test early with rough prototypes: Tim Brown (IDEO): *prototypes slow us down to speed us up.*
- Pick a setting and sample: test in natural contexts; avoid fans and cynics.
- Design thinking isn't linear; be prepared to iterate.

Notes

1. The Walt Disney World story is based on three sources: Carr, A. (2015, May 15). The Messy Business of Reinventing Happiness. *Fast Company*. Retrieved from https://www.fastcompany.com/3044283/the-messy-business-of-reinventing-happiness.

   Kuang, C. (2015, March 10). Disney's $1 billion Bet on a Magical Wristband. *Wired*. Retrieved from https://www.wired.com/2015/03/disney-magicband/.

   Edson, J., Kouyoumjian, G., & Sheppard, B. (2017, December). More Than a Feeling: Ten Design Practices to Deliver Business Value. *McKinsey Quarterly*. Retrieved from https://www.mckinsey.com/business-functions/mckinsey-design/our-insights/more-than-a-feeling-ten-design-practices-to-deliver-business-value.

2. The Pauling Blog. Retrieved from https://paulingblog.wordpress.com/2008/10/28/clarifying-three-widespread-quotes/.

3. March, J.G. (1991). Exploration and Exploitation in Organizational Learning. *Organization Science, 2*, 71–87.

4. da Costa, S.D.P., Sánchez, F., Garaigordobil, M., & Gondim, S. (2015). Personal Factors of Creativity: A Second Order Meta-Analysis. *Journal of Work and Organizational Psychology, 31*, 165–173.

5. Page, S.E. (2008). *The Difference: How the Power of Diversity Creates Better Groups, Firms, Schools, and Societies*. Princeton: Princeton University Press.

   Singh, J., & Fleming, L. (2010). Lone Inventors as Sources of Breakthroughs: Myth or Reality? *Management Science, 56*(1), 41–56.

6. Williams, K.Y., & O'Reilly, C.A. (1998). Demography and Diversity in Organizations: A Review of 40 Years of Research. *Research in Organizational Behavior, 20*, 77–140.

7. Edmondson, A.C., & Lei, Z. (2014). Psychological Safety: The History, Renaissance, and Future of an Interpersonal Construct. *Annual Review of Organizational Psychology and Organizational Behavior, 1*, 23–43.

8. Ward, T.B., Smith, S.M., & Finke, R.A. (1999). Creative Cognition. In R.J. Sternberg (Ed.), *Handbook of Creativity* (pp. 189–212). New York: Cambridge University Press.

9. Diehl, M., & Stroebe, W. (1987). Productivity Loss in Idea-Generating Groups: Toward the Solution of a Riddle. *Journal of Personality and Social Psychology, 53*(3), 497–509.

10. Girotra, K., Terwiesch, C., & Ulrich, K.T. (2010). Idea Generation and the Quality of the Best Idea. *Management Science, 56*(4), 591–605.

11. Michalko, M. (2006). *Thinkertoys*. New York: Ten Speed Press.

12. Vernon, D., Hocking, I., & Tyler, T.C. (2016). An Evidence-Based Review of Creative Problem-Solving Tools: A Practitioner's Resource. *Human Resource Development Review, 15*(2), 1–30.

13. Franke, N., Poetz, M.K., & Schreier, M. (2014). Integrating Problem Solvers from Analogous Markets in New Product Ideation. *Management Science, 60*(4), 1063–1081.

14. Prince, G.M. (1968). The Operational Mechanism of Synectics. *Journal of Creative Behavior, 2,* 1–13.

15. Pollack, J. (2014). *Shortcut: How Analogies Reveal Connections, Spark Innovation, and Sell Our Greatest Ideas.* New York: Penguin.

16. Benyus, J.M. (1997). *Biomimicry: Innovation Inspired by Nature.* New York: Morrow.

17. Woolley-Barker, T. (2017). Teeming: How Superorganisms Work Together to Build Infinite Wealth on a Finite Planet. Ashland, OR: White Cloud Press.

18. This example is based on two sources: Greaves, W. (2006, August 29). Ferrari Pit Stop Saves Alexander's Life. *The Telegraph.* Retrieved from http://www.telegraph.co.uk/news/1527497/Ferrari-pit-stop-saves-Alexanders-life.html.

    Catchpole, K.R., De Leval, M., McEwan, A., Pigott, N., Elliott, M.J., McQuillan, A., Macdonald, C. & Goldman, A.J. (2007). Patient Handover from Surgery to Intensive Care: Using Formula 1 Pit-Stop and Aviation Models to Improve Safety and Quality. *Pediatric Anesthesia, 17,* 470–478.

19. Osborn, A.F. (1953). *Applied Imagination: Principles and Procedures of Creative Problem Solving.* New York: Charles Scribner's Sons.

20. Mullen, B., Johnson, C., & Salas, E. (1991). Productivity Loss in Brainstorming Groups: A Meta-Analytic Integration. *Basic and Applied Social Psychology, 12*(1), 3–23.

21. See the discussion of brainstorming research in: Vernon, D., Hocking, I., & Tyler, T.C. (2016). An Evidence-Based Review of Creative Problem Solving Tools: A Practitioner's Resource. *Human Resource Development Review, 15*(2), 1–30.

22. Santanen, E.L., Briggs, R.O., & De Vreed,G-J. (2004). Causal Relationships in Creative Problem Solving: Comparing Facilitative Interventions for Ideation. *Journal of Management Information Systems, 20*(4), 167–197.

23. Sutton, R.I., & Hargadon, A. (1996). Brainstorming Groups in Context: Effectiveness in a Product Design Firm. *Administrative Science Quarterly, 41*(4), 685–715.

24. Vernon, D., Hocking, I., & Tyler, T.C. (2016). An Evidence-Based Review of Creative Problem Solving Tools: A Practitioner's Resource. *Human Resource Development Review, 15*(2), 1–30.

25. Using this approach with six group members, generating three ideas each in six different five-minute rounds leads to the 6-3-5 brainwriting method (also known as the 6-3-5 method, or Method 635) originally developed by Professor Bernd Rohrbach in 1968.

26. Vernon, D., Hocking, I., & Tyler, T.C. (2016). An Evidence-Based Review of Creative Problem Solving Tools: A Practitioner's Resource. *Human Resource Development Review, 15*(2), 1–30.

27. Girotra, K., Terwiesch, C., & Ulrich, K.T. (2010). Idea Generation and the Quality of the Best Idea. *Management Science, 56*(4), 591–605.

28. Zwicky, F. (1969). *Discovery, Invention, Research—Through the Morphological Approach*. Toronto: The Macmillan Company.

29. Hargadon, A. (2002). Brokering Knowledge: Linking Learning and Innovation. *Research in Organizational Behavior, 24*, 41–85.

30. Vernon, D., Hocking, I., & Tyler, T.C. (2016). An Evidence-Based Review of Creative Problem Solving Tools: A Practitioner's Resource. *Human Resource Development Review, 15*(2), 1–30.

31. Some of the SCAMPER framework was first proposed by Alex Osborne, the father of brainstorming, and was further developed by Eberle, B. (1971). *SCAMPER: Games for Imagination Development*. Prufrock Press.

32. Serrat, O. (2017). Proposition 33: The SCAMPER Technique. *Knowledge Solutions: Tools, Methods, and Approaches to Drive Organizational Performance* (pp. 311–314). Singapore: Springer.

33. Vernon, D., Hocking, I., & Tyler, T.C. (2016). An Evidence-Based Review of Creative Problem Solving Tools: A Practitioner's Resource. *Human Resource Development Review, 15*(2), 1–30.

34. Ulrich, K.T., & Eppinger, S.D. (2016). *Product Design and Development* (6th edition). New York: McGraw-Hill Education.

35. This process is based largely on the six-step process identified in Chap. 8 of Ulrich, K.T., & Eppinger, S.D. (2016). *Product Design and Development* (6th edition). New York: McGraw-Hill Education.

36. Berg, J.M. (2016). Balancing on the Creative Highwire: Forecasting the Success of Novel Ideas in Organizations. *Administrative Science Quarterly, 61*(3), 433–468.

37. Brown, T. 2009. *Change by Design*. New York: HarperCollins Publishers. p. 92.

38. Kagan, E., Leider, S., & Lovejoy, W.S. (2018). Ideation-Execution Transition in Product Development: An Experimental Analysis. *Management Science*. Forthcoming.

39. Napoli, L. (2016). *Ray and Joan*. New York: Dutton.

40. Thomke, S.H. (2003). *Experimentation Matters*. Boston: Harvard Business School Press.

41. This process is based largely on the four-step process identified in Chap. 14 of Ulrich, K.T., & Eppinger, S.D. (2016). *Product Design and Development* (6th edition). New York: McGraw-Hill Education.

42. Horton, G.Y., & Radcliffe, D.F. (1995). Nature of Rapid Proof-of-Concept Prototyping. *Journal of Engineering Design, 6*(1), 3–16.

43. Gaughan, R. (2012). *Accidental Genius: The World's Greatest By-Chance Discoveries*. Toronto: Dundurn.

44. Thomke, S., & Reinersten, D. (2012). Six Myths of Product Development. *Harvard Business Review, 90*(5), 84–94.

45. Brown, T. 2009. *Change by Design*. New York: HarperCollins Publishers. p. 105.
46. These steps are based largely on the process identified in Chap. 9 of Ulrich, K.T., & Eppinger, S.D. (2016). *Product Design and Development* (6th edition). New York: McGraw-Hill Education.
47. Ulrich, K.T. & Eppinger, S.D. (2016). *Product Design and Development* (6th edition, p. 170). New York: McGraw-Hill Education.
48. Kelley, T. & Kelley, D. (2013). *Creative Confidence: Unleashing the Creative Potential Within Us All*. New York: Crown Publishing. p. 5.

10

Sell the Solution: Core Message and Storyline

It's time to move from problem solving to solution selling. Now that you've found a solution to the problem and conducted the analyses to support it, you can formulate recommendations. You'll then persuade the problem owner to follow your recommendations and take action. This is the climax of your mission and a new challenge. To accomplish it, you'll need to shift gears. Instead of digging deeper into the problem, you'll need to see how your solution fits into the problem owner's context and use this insight to sell it.

Forget about problem solving for a moment and step into the shoes of the problem owner who wants to learn about your solution. For example, imagine you're the CEO of Mustang Airlines, a low-cost air carrier operating in the USA.[1] You've asked a young executive to study an opportunity you're considering: to expand your fleet by purchasing five new Airbus A320neo airplanes. He's written a first draft of a memo that summarizes his findings. Here's what he says:

> As you requested, I reviewed the plan to buy five new Airbus A320neo airliners to expand Mustang's fleet and grow our profits. I first looked at the aircraft itself. The A320neo (new engine option) is a very good plane. One study found that it has lower operating costs than the Boeing 737, our current airframe, making it possible to recoup the price difference between the two aircraft in three years. This is essentially due to higher fuel efficiency. Consequently, it makes economic sense to modernize the fleet with this new aircraft. This would also help Mustang seize new growth opportunities, such as opening a new route to Mexico and destinations in Central America.

© The Author(s) 2018
B. Garrette et al., *Cracked it!*, https://doi.org/10.1007/978-3-319-89375-4_10

I then studied the impact of the decision on fleet management. As our fleet is exclusively composed of Boeing 737s, adding a new aircraft type would increase complexity, as well as maintenance and training costs, especially for pilots and technicians, without increasing our clients' willingness to pay. Although this impact is difficult to assess, my most conservative calculations suggest that the potential reduction in fuel expenses from the A320neo will not offset the increase in maintenance and training costs.

From a purchasing perspective, buying from Airbus would, for the first time, put competitive pressure on Boeing to strive for our business. This could help us negotiate better deals with both suppliers. Our purchasing department has had discussions with both vendors to determine how they would respond to a request for proposal for five new aircraft. Purchasing concluded that Airbus would offer a steeper discount per plane and better financing terms than Boeing.

However, based on my conversation with our commercial department, I realized that a bulk order of five planes is risky given the uncertainties surrounding air traffic between the USA and Mexico, especially since the recent declarations made by the new US administration. We therefore believe Mustang should continue its current policy of buying Boeing 737s one by one. Because of the risky nature of our industry, with many carriers seeking Chapter 11 protection, our shareholders value our cautious and incremental growth policy. Our CFO claims that announcing a bulk purchase of five aircraft in this environment might badly hurt our stock price.

In conclusion, my recommendation is to keep growing our fleet of B737s incrementally rather than purchase five A320neos.

However, it is worth noting that, if we considered a bulk purchase of new airplanes, the Airbus option would make sense for a larger order. My calculations show that—considering the impact on maintenance and training costs—the price and financing conditions offered by Airbus would provide significant benefits for us if we ordered at least nine or ten A320neos.

What do you think? Are you happy with the memo? Does the recommendation persuade you?

Don't Tell the Story of the Search, Tell the Story of the Solution

As you probably concluded, the memo is awful. We can improve it on several fronts. First, our young exec author needs to get straight to the point from the get-go. While he hedges his bet, he's essentially recommending that you not order the five A320neos. This is the core message. A major flaw in the memo is that this message is not readily apparent. It's buried near the end. We had to wait until the second-to-last paragraph to know the punch line. Aspiring journalists are told: "don't bury the lede." The lede (or "lead") is the most important part of the story being told, which should be concisely stated up front. Our memo writer has clearly violated this dictum of efficient and effective communication.

To complicate matters, we had to wade through countervailing, seesaw arguments to get to the recommendation. If you stopped reading after the first paragraph, you'd be left with the impression that the memo supports the project, which is misleading. As we continued reading, we learned the answer is complex as the writer lays out both pros and cons, never seeming to commit. Even after stating his recommendation, he hedges his bet in the last paragraph in a way that undercuts it. We simply don't get a straightforward answer, which is frustrating.

The origin of this frustration is reminiscent of US President Harry Truman's annoyance with two-handed economists. Although it may be apocryphal, Truman is reputed to have demanded, when frustrated by a lack of a clear policy recommendation, "Give me a one-handed economist. All my economists say, 'on the one hand … on the other hand.'" To be more persuasive (and less frustrating), not only must our memo writer state his core message from the top, making it easier to identify, but he must also provide a clear and compelling rationale for it.

How the author organizes and presents his thoughts contributes to the fuzzy and unconvincing rationale for the recommendation. As you read the memo, you may have struggled not only to guess the conclusion, but also to see how the arguments cohered to justify the recommendation. The memo lacks coherence.

The underlying flaw is typical: the writer is reporting his problem-solving process instead of explaining the recommendation and its rationale to the problem owner. The memo reads like an issue tree, not a recommendation for action. The writer starts by stating the problem, then covers the way he structured it, the analyses he performed and their results, without explaining how any of it supports the core message. For example, he mentions comparing the Airbus and Boeing offers for the purchase of five planes, which is irrelevant because he rules out a bulk purchase altogether in the following paragraph. For our junior exec, waiting for the end of the story to mention the recommendation may seem appropriate because he views the solution as the end of a bumpy road he followed to crack the problem.

This mistake is pervasive. Because we've spent so much time engaged in the problem-solving process, it becomes the de facto structure we use to articulate our solution. We may also be keen to demonstrate to the problem owner the hard work we've done and explain the difficult steps we went through to arrive at the solution we are presenting. It's tempting to tell the story of the search instead of telling the story of the solution.

This is, however, an ineffective approach to selling a solution. Decision-makers aren't like readers of crime novels, who enjoy identifying with the detective and his erratic thought process, and revel in waiting to find out whodunit. They don't want you to bury your core message in adventurous twists and turns. They aren't interested in hearing about the clever and challenging analyses you performed if this doesn't help sell your solution. They just want to hear your recommendation and be able to determine whether they agree with it and the reasoning behind it. They need a clear and compelling story that persuades them to buy what you're pitching. The "pyramid principle" is a tried-and-true way to do this.

The Pyramid Principle

Barbara Minto is a former McKinsey consultant and the creator of the "pyramid principle."[2] Her approach is based on an old and well-established insight—people can better understand and remember a set of ideas if they can mentally organize these ideas around a coherent pattern or logical structure. For example, since at least the Ancient Greeks, people have looked to the night sky and have seen collections of nearby stars as outlines of figures instead of just pinpoints of light. Imagining lines that link the stars together and using metaphors to animals and other creatures to make sense of these outlines helps us memorize and recognize constellations, because our minds need a pattern to comprehend and remember what we perceive. The same applies to ideas. To understand other people's thoughts and be convinced of what they are telling us, we must "see" how their ideas are connected in a recognizable structure. The tighter the connections and the simpler the structure—the stronger the coherence—the more convincing the story.

For business recommendations, Minto argues that the most efficient communication structure is a top-down pyramid that starts with communicating the core message—the "governing thought"—head-on, and then turns to a "key line" of arguments that support it, while also announcing the plan of the report. The core message must jump off the page immediately and pave the way for the later points that collectively justify or detail it. If you adopt this pyramidal communication strategy, the audience will see the big picture first and realize that all the ideas fit in a simple and visible pattern. This will free their minds and make them receptive to the core message and the overall content.

Figure 10.1 depicts the pyramid principle graphically.

In a pyramid-based report, the points in the key line, which lead to the different parts of the report, must be MECE, as defined in Chap. 5. You want the parts to cover the whole content, omitting nothing important, and you don't want them to overlap. To write the detailed report, you'll break down each key point into more elementary MECE components, pushing your most elementary findings at the lowest level of the pyramid.

When you give an oral presentation, you'll organize it along the same lines: you'll state the core message first and then present the key line, and then walk the audience through each "pillar" of the pyramid by discussing one by one the clusters of detailed points that support the key line. If you use visual aids, such as PowerPoint slides with charts and graphics, you must organize your slide deck accordingly. We'll discuss oral presentations and slide decks in the next chapter.

Let's apply the pyramid principle to the Mustang Airlines memo. Here, starting with the recommendation is easy. We just have to dig it out of the text and move it to the top of the page. So the governing thought would be something like this:

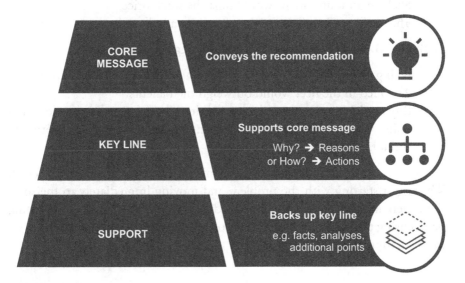

Fig. 10.1 The pyramid principle

Mustang Airlines should pass on ordering five Airbus A320neos and pursue instead its current policy of buying Boeing 737s one at a time.

Now, how can we cluster the ideas in the memo around a few key points? We can isolate two lines of reasoning in the text. The first one involves the comparison between the A320neo and the B737. It demonstrates that buying B737s is economically better for Mustang. The second line of reasoning questions the idea of purchasing several airplanes simultaneously because a bulk order would be too risky.

Comparing the two aircraft would be one of the first analyses to perform when investigating Mustang's fleet extension problem. This might be the reason our young executive put it first in the memo. If we compare the strength of the two points, however, we see the second one should come first: the company would put itself at risk by growing too fast, no matter which plane it buys. Once this point is established, choosing which aircraft to buy is much easier. The key line these arguments suggest is as follows:

1. Buying five airplanes simultaneously would be too risky.
2. Buying B737s is a better option than buying A320neos.

Once we've identified the points in the key line, we can justify them one after the other, with the required level of detail, using the following structure:

1. Buying five airplanes simultaneously would be too risky:

   a. Such an announcement would hurt the stock price.
   b. The traffic growth forecast doesn't justify a bulk order.

2. Buying B737s is a better option than buying A320neos:

   a. Flying only B737s creates a cost advantage. The costs of introducing the A320neo in the fleet would outweigh the benefits.
   b. Buying A320neos would be profitable only if we ordered at least ten units, which is too many (given anticipated needs and uncertainty about traffic growth).

We can rewrite the Mustang Airlines memo using the pyramid principle. We suggest starting with the problem and moving immediately to the solution, then announcing the key line, and, finally, rearranging the supporting points using the abovementioned structure. While we reorganize the flow, we can also improve the wording to make each point clear and specific:

As you requested, I reviewed the plan to buy five new Airbus A320neo airliners to expand Mustang's fleet and grow our profits. I recommend that Mustang pass on this project and pursue instead its current policy of buying Boeing 737s one at a time.

Two main points support this view:

- A bulk order of five airplanes would be too risky.
- Diversifying the fleet would jeopardize our cost advantage.

1. <u>A bulk order of five airplanes would be too risky:</u>

   a. Announcing a bulk order of five planes would hurt the stock price. Although Mustang is profitable and growing, it operates in a high-risk and loss-making industry. In this adverse context, our shareholders value our incremental and cautious growth strategy. Our CFO estimates that most of our investors and analysts would disapprove of an aggressive move that would increase our leverage and risk profile.

   b. In addition, our commercial department acknowledges that the volume forecast on which the project was based calls for drastic revision. With the change in the US administration's foreign policy, uncertainty is growing around future air traffic between the USA and Mexico, which was our main expansion opportunity.

2. <u>Diversifying the fleet would jeopardize Mustang Airlines' cost advantage:</u>

   a. Flying a standardized fleet of B737s creates a cost advantage for Mustang. Introducing the A320neo aircraft would hinder this advantage by generating a significant increase in training and maintenance costs. While Mustang can recoup the higher price of the A320neo in three years through the savings it generates on operating costs (mainly through lower fuel consumption), such savings can't offset the increase in training and maintenance costs. These factors would make the investment in the A320neo aircraft too difficult to recoup in a reasonable period of time.

   b. The discount and financing plan that Airbus offers on a five-plane order is better than Boeing's equivalent proposal, but is insufficient to tilt the cost-advantage in favor of the A320neos. Our simulations show we would need to order at least ten A320neo airplanes to make the project financially beneficial. Such a large order does not make sense in the current context.

In conclusion, we recommend that Mustang Airlines stick to the growth strategy that has made it so successful: the incremental expansion of a standardized fleet of B737s.

Pave the Way for a Dialogue

Stating the governing thought and the main points of your presentation from the get-go is critical to selling your solution effectively. Having a relevant core message isn't enough. It must also be concise and set a clear direction. Because you begin with it, you can't prepare your audience for it, so you can be sure it will trigger questions. You might think it's safer and more logical to keep the core message for the end, as a conclusive punchline that closes your narrative. We strongly disagree. While you save a punchline for the end of a speech to wrap it up, you state a governing thought from the get-go to pave the way for a dialogue in which you will answer the audience's questions. A governing thought sets direction, like a keynote in music or a compass in navigation. Use your core message as a governing thought that drives a conversation with the problem owner, instead of using it as a punchline that puts an end to this conversation.

From this perspective, we can think of our governing thought as the "elevator pitch" for our answer to the problem owner's initial question. Imagine you are the CEO of Mustang Airlines and you meet the junior executive you assigned to the A320neo opportunity in the elevator and you say something like, "Hi! Good to see you. So, what do you think we should be doing about the purchase of the five A320neos?" He has 30 seconds to say something and he (hopefully) doesn't want to squander this opportunity discussing minutiae about the problem. It's a priceless opportunity to prepare you for the formal presentation he'll give later. He may be tempted to answer something like, "Ah well, it's a tricky issue. The A320neo is a great plane but the traffic forecast is uncertain and the fleet maintenance costs will increase." But you, as the CEO, already know that. It's much more powerful for our young executive to take a stand and say, "The analyses we've conducted suggest at this point that we should give up the idea and continue to buy B737s one at a time."

As the CEO, you might object and ask questions (maybe just to see him squirm a bit). This might be intimidating and unsettling for him. But, if he's smart, this is what he should crave. A strategic recommendation is controversial by nature. Triggering a discussion is what it's supposed to do. Generating a dialogue—including objections—is nothing to fear, success is. Our young executive should want to trigger this discussion only when he can muster a bulletproof rationale. This is why the key line comes immediately after the core message. If you ask him why he thinks you should pass on the Airbus offer, he'd be prepared to say, "There are two main reasons. First, we believe the announcement of a bulk order would hurt the stock price. Second, the cost/advantage analysis shows that diversifying the fleet would hinder our cost advantage." This is when the elevator stops at his floor. He must exit while you continue up to your corner office at the top of the building. Before the sliding doors shut, you ask, "Are you sure?" To which he responds, "You'll hear all the details during our meeting on Monday afternoon."

What a great conversation! Had our junior exec been ill-prepared, his ability to make small talk might have saved him. With good preparation, he was able to take advantage of the situation to make real progress in sharing his views with you.

Using the pyramid principle to develop an elevator pitch means you must formulate your core message concisely and be able to answer in a few words the first questions that come to the mind of the problem owner. Broadly speaking, these questions typically belong to two categories: "why" and "how" questions. You'll be asked a "why" question if the problem owner remains unconvinced about your solution. You'll be asked a "how" question if she's convinced but wants to know more about how to implement the recommendation. The key line that supports the governing thought must contain the answers to these "why" and "how" questions. The key line has two functions: to establish the pyramid structure of your presentation and to answer the main questions the core message triggers. This will enable you to manage your conversation with the problem owner.

This idea of managing the conversation is very important. Monopolizing airtime by not allowing the problem owner to interject is ineffective and risky. You don't want to be seen as "preaching." Engaging in a dialogue is also risky, because it can get out of control. The core message must trigger a conversation, but a conversation you can drive. The best way to do this is to induce questions you can answer. Selling the solution isn't about giving a one-way lecture or about stirring a wide-ranging debate.

Design Your Storyline

The overall plan of the recommendation report you're putting together is called the "storyline." A complete storyline includes the core message, the key line, and all the elementary components of the presentation. If you're preparing a PowerPoint presentation, the storyline includes the complete list of slides you'll want to produce. You must design the storyline before creating slides. Otherwise, you'll risk developing unnecessary and inconsistent material.

When the time comes to sell your solution, the first thing you might be tempted to do is to switch on your computer, double-click on the PowerPoint (or some other presentation software) icon, and start designing slick slides that report your findings. This is not the way to proceed! The availability and ease-of-use of presentation software—including the ubiquitous PowerPoint—might lead you to produce slides as you assemble your findings, and to worry later about how to organize them. This is one of the reasons disjointed and incoherent presentations are delivered every day in boardrooms and conference rooms around the world.

The simplest advice we can offer on this issue is: *forget the presentation software for a while, and turn instead to your word processor.* Don't produce visuals before you've zeroed in on the story you want to tell. Start by building your storyline as a one-pager, as if you were writing a note, a memo, or the executive summary that will eventually become the first page of your full report. This will save you a lot of time and you'll end up with a much better presentation.

A Story of Two Pyramids

You may have noticed the commonality between the pyramid principle and the hypothesis pyramids we discussed in Chap. 5. If you've solved your problem by confirming a candidate solution, designing the storyline will be straightforward. It will be a close reflection of the hypothesis pyramid. Once you've refined and confirmed the solution, it will naturally translate into your core message. The first-level sub-hypotheses will only require some trimming and revision to give birth to the key line. At lower levels, you'll find support for your points in the set of elementary hypotheses you've validated through your analyses. You'll address limitations and constraints through the ideas you've invalidated.

Consider the Librinova example from Chap. 5. Figure 10.2 features the pyramid you could use to communicate your recommendation to the CEO of the company. Conveniently, it's a copycat of the hypothesis pyramid you've seen in Fig. 5.3! To create it, we simply assumed all the conditions held and we transformed them into findings, except the last one at the bottom right of the pyramid.

This example reinforces how efficient the hypothesis-driven problem structure is. Not only did it help confirm the solution, but it also provides the way to sell it. The story of the search gives you the story of the solution.

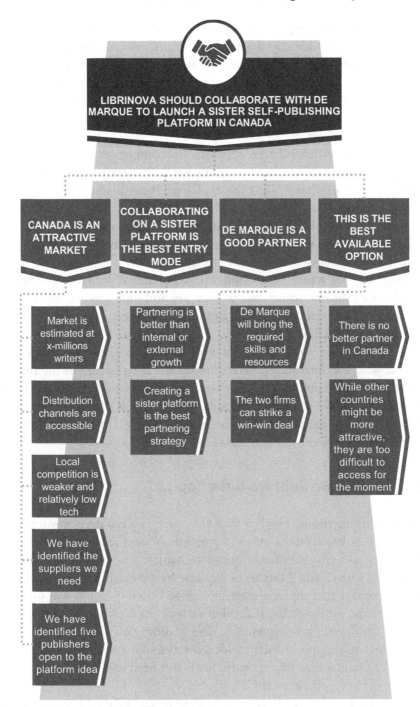

Fig. 10.2 Storyline on the Librinova case

From Chap. 2 onward, however, we've been suggesting that hypothesis pyramids are a double-edged sword because they combine the solution-confirmation pitfall with the miscommunication pitfall. What problem solver has never been tempted, for the sake of efficiency, to develop the final presentation from day one of the problem-solving effort? The core message merely reflects the pet solution suggested by the problem owner, and the storyline simply aims to bolster it.

If you adopt an issue-driven approach, in contrast, the problem-solving effort will be more robust, but the solution-selling narrative won't flow naturally from the issue tree. You can't expect an issue-driven problem-solving process to generate a core message by itself. When you have looked into all sub-issues, you're confronted with piecemeal findings that don't necessarily cohere into a solution to the problem or even into a single overarching conclusion. As we discussed in the previous chapter, a creative leap is sometimes necessary to go from findings to solutions. An additional leap is often required to go from a solution, which may be complex and multifaceted, to a governing thought, which must be simple and set a clear direction.

In the Librinova example, reviewing the issue tree we presented in Fig. 5.6 wouldn't be a good way to sell a solution to the CEO, no matter what the solution was. The final recommendation doesn't even appear in the tree, let alone the plan of action to implement it. In such cases, telling the story of the search is useless. We must shift gears and reorganize all the ideas to come up with a convincing narrative, as we did in the Mustang Airlines case. Let's discuss how to achieve this in more detail.

Pyramids Can Be Built from the Top …

If your governing thought is clear from the onset, you can develop your storyline top-down, based on the pyramid principle. Your core message, or governing thought, is the answer to the question that the problem owner has asked you. On this basis, you'll create the key line by answering the "why" and/or "how" questions that the core message induces. Each question will suggest a "pillar" for the pyramid. You'll develop each of these pillars by asking finer-grained "why" and "how" questions. The findings you've developed during the problem-solving phase will provide answers to these questions. Otherwise, additional analyses may be necessary. You'll also need to check that the items that support any point are MECE.

We implemented a top-down process when we revised the Mustang Airlines memo. This was relatively straightforward because the core message was easy to identify and entailed a "why" question almost mechanically. We identified that the answer to this question had two pillars: comparing how the two aircraft types fit in the existing fleet and questioning the size of the order. We therefore reorganized the memo into two main parts, introduced in order of importance.

... But Are More Often Built from the Bottom

Usually, however, the top-down approach is too difficult to implement. The governing thought doesn't appear clearly. The problem-solving effort has produced various analyses that have yielded disparate results. No one can see the big picture anymore. In such situations, it's more effective to build the pyramid bottom-up (as the analogy with actual pyramids suggests!). Instead of trying to invent a core message from scratch, you'll start with the elementary findings and try to group them in logically similar groups until they cohere into a consistent pattern. When such a pattern appears, you'll create your core message out of it. This is the essence of the approach we described in Chap. 8 for synthesizing qualitative data to build a bottom-up understanding of users during the Define phase of design thinking.

A practical way to implement this bottom-up process is to consider the elementary findings as building blocks you can rearrange and combine to build up the pyramid. In our problem-solving workshops, we often ask participants to write all their findings on different pieces of paper (such as Post-its) and then lay them out on a table or stick them on a wall. We ask them to express each finding as a complete sentence with at least a subject and a verb. This forces participants to focus on logic, causality, and potential actions, rather than on just topics. For example, "In the airline industry, announcements of bold organic-growth moves generally hurt the stock price" is better than "impact on stock price." Next, we instruct them to cluster these building blocks into a few groups or "buckets." To do so, they must identify ways that ideas meaningfully cohere. For each bucket or theme, we ask them to write a statement that synthesizes the ideas they have assembled. Again, they must write such statements as complete sentences, not just labels. The combination of these statements creates the key line, which they must synthesize in a governing thought.

Here's a real-life example, which involved one of us: Summit Water,[3] a utility company operating a large water and sanitation concession in an Asian capital, was considering a partnership with Cosyloo, a social business start-up, which had come up with an award-winning sanitation innovation targeting poor urban households.[4]

Sanitation at the "base of the pyramid" is a daunting challenge: 2.4 billion people globally, or two-fifths of the world's population, do not have access to sanitation. This creates huge health and pollution problems, especially in crowded megalopolis areas. Cosyloo's product was a stand-alone portable toilet that could be installed in houses and emptied weekly. This was a suitable solution for urban slum dwellers who had no access to public sewerage or septic tanks. Cosyloo's major technological innovation was a patented valve system, which controlled both the odor and back-splashing issues that plagued other portable toilet devices. In addition, as Cosyloo's technology involved small quantities of additives, it substantially reduced the weight of toilets for collectors, and most important, allowed for waste disposal in regular water treatment centers.

When presented with the project, Summit Water's VP for strategy and development was immediately interested. The company was desperately looking for this kind of solution as a response to the local authorities' pressure to extend sanitation to underserviced areas. The strategy and development VP was leaning toward a full-fledged launch of the new service. However, he knew that other members of the executive committee remained unconvinced. He had a small team examine the economic prospects for the project, which yielded the following findings:

1. A feasibility test demonstrated that the Cosyloo solution was technically viable. Households that participated in the experiment evaluated the service positively.
2. The ideal location to implement the new service was Laguna Bay, a suburban area not serviced by public sewage networks. In Laguna Bay, 90 percent of the households had septic tanks. The remaining 10 percent had no sanitation and therefore were potential users of portable toilets.
3. Most of the target households didn't have access to basic water distribution services either, which meant they weren't customers of Summit Water yet.
4. The official mission of Summit Water was to achieve 99-percent coverage in water distribution over the next five years. Offering running water and sanitation as a bundle could help achieve this objective.
5. Summit planned to charge a 20-percent markup on water bills for sanitation in Laguna Bay, no matter whether people would use septic tanks or portable toilets. This would amount to two dollars per household per month on average, which was deemed the maximum amount that low-income clients would be willing to pay for sanitation.

6. However, empirical evidence was missing to confirm such a willingness to pay.

7. A 20-percent markup would be too low to cover the cost of the portable toilet service, but it would be high enough to generate a significant margin on servicing septic tanks. Portable toilets must be emptied once a week, and septic tanks only once every five years. Financial simulations showed that the breakeven ratio was 7:1: Summit would need to service at least seven households with septic tanks to subsidize the service offered to one household with portable toilets.

8. The pricing and cross-subsidization billing plan had to win approval from local authorities.

9. Hiring and managing the teams in charge of waste collection was a new challenge for the company. This was a different, and much more labor-intensive, business than water distribution or traditional sanitation. In dense and crowded slums, the smallest vehicles could not get close enough to all homes. As a consequence, the most tiring part of the job had to be performed by individual "waste carriers." Summit Water planned to outsource the task to a local community organization.

10. In the septic-tank segment, the challenge was to dislodge current informal providers who offered the emptying service cheaply but unhygienically.

The basic question that may come to mind after going over this list is, *"So what?"* This is a question strategy consultants—and decision-makers of all kinds—ask several times a day. In other words, how can we make sense of these findings? What kind of recommendation can we formulate? Ultimately, what should the problem owner do? Reformulating, reorganizing, and summarizing the findings is useful but insufficient. We must go beyond the findings themselves to generate a sound recommendation. Summit's findings suggest that recommending a full launch of the portable toilet initiative would be risky. Killing the deal, however, would lead to discarding an opportunity that could help the company meet a blatant need that is part of its core mission. *So what?* It's by answering this question that we'll craft a storyline.

Let's try to build the pyramid bottom-up by grouping the elementary findings into a key line. The challenge is that the findings are somewhat contradictory. One cluster of findings supports doing the deal with Cosyloo because it's viable and fits Summit's mission:

- The deal would bridge a strategic gap in Summit's business (findings 2– 4).
- Cosyloo's solution is technically and commercially viable (finding 1).
- Cross-subsidization can make it financially viable (findings 5 and 7).

Another finding cluster emphasizes different areas of uncertainty Summit faces, which creates serious risks, working against the deal:

- The billing plan might not get approved (finding 8).
- The pricing might be wrong (finding 6).
- Significant operational and competitive challenges remain unsolved (findings 9 and 10).

The pyramid we are building here has two pillars that contradict each other. Let's imagine a discussion within the problem-solving team:

"So what do we do? It sounds like we're heading for a wishy-washy recommendation. 'Go for it—you'll look nice' but, 'not too much—you don't want to waste credibility and money.' That's not very useful. We have to deliver a compelling, action-oriented message!"

"What if Summit gave up on the idea?"

"Well, nothing serious would happen. They'd just pass on a weird but interesting innovation opportunity. Another one might come later. No big deal. On the other hand, this is a rare occasion to innovate in a domain in which most competitors are simply clueless."

"*So what?* Should we go for it? If we do, how should Summit Water implement this deal? We should try to make it as profitable as possible, right?"

"Correct. But, now that you mention it … based on findings two and seven, the economic incentive for Summit would be to grow the septic-tank service as quickly as possible, and to extend the portable toilet service as slowly as possible."

"*So what?*"

"Uh, well, provided we get the green light from the authorities on the billing system, we could launch the portable toilet service on a small scale, in a specific community for example, after making sure we've secured enough clients for the septic-tank service to fund it."

"How many clients?"

"Based on finding 7, we have to keep a 7:1 ratio. Let's say 9:1 to be on the safe side. A 9:1 objective is consistent with the overall proportion of households equipped with septic tanks in Laguna Bay anyway."

"Friends, I think we have our core message. Let me try to put it together: 'Sell the billing plan to public authorities as part of a pilot project in which Summit Water tests the portable toilet service in Laguna Bay, provided we've secured nine times as many clients for the septic-tank service.'"

"That's not very elegant …."

"We'll need to improve the wording. But the meaning isn't too bad!"

Although this is a simplified example, it illustrates the process of creating the core message by questioning the findings in a bottom-up approach. Again, summarizing isn't enough. You must synthesize findings and overcome contradictions by constantly asking the "So what?" question. In doing so, you can find new ways to cluster findings and make them cohere in a higher level synthesis, which is necessary to induce a core message.

Go for Either a Grouping or an Argument

What would the storyline look like in the Summit Water case? Based on the prior discussion, it would look something like the following:

> We recommend limiting the launch of the Cosyloo product to a target customer population in which Summit Water can serve nine households equipped with septic tanks for each household offered the portable toilet service. This recommendation is based on the following rationale:
>
> * Cosyloo offers us a deal that fits our strategic purpose:
>   - The deal bridges a strategic gap in our business.
>   - The solution is technically and commercially viable.
>   - We can make it financially viable through cross-subsidization with septic-tank services.
> * However we must overcome four hurdles:
>   - Winning approval from authorities for the billing plan.
>   - Testing and perhaps revising the 20-percent rate pricing.
>   - Solving operational and competitive challenges on waste collection from both portable toilets and septic tanks.
>   - Finding enough septic-tank service contracts to subsidize portable toilet contracts (we recommend nine for one).
>
> Hence, we recommend convincing the public authorities to let Summit Water experiment and refine the portable toilet service on a small scale and in combination with the septic-tank service, targeting a ratio of one portable toilet client to nine septic tank clients.

The underlying structure differs significantly from the one we used in the Mustang Airlines case. While we used a "grouping" pattern in the Mustang Airlines story, in the Summit Water example, we used an "argument" pattern.[5] We'll explain the difference.

In a grouping pattern, the key line consists of points of the same kind that collectively support or detail the core message. For example, in the Mustang Airlines example, the two points—the size of the order and the diversification of the fleet—both support the recommendation to pass on the Airbus offer. Their order can be inverted without changing the logic, and we have chosen the order that makes the communication more efficient. As mentioned earlier, the key line and the clusters of sub-points in each pillar of the pyramid must be MECE.

A grouping storyline is the best way to present a solution supported by several reasons in parallel. It also suits a recommendation that entails a process or a list of actions to take, such as:

The company can cut costs by €50 million across the board:

- *The following actions will save €25 million on purchasing:*
  - *action 1 (€10 million).*
  - *action 2 (€7 million).*
  - *...*

- *Headquarter expenses can be reduced by €20 million:*
  - *idea 1 (€8 million).*
  - *...*

- *Other opportunities are worth €5 million and include:*
  - *...*

When ordering the different points in the key line and at lower levels in the pyramid, we recommend always starting with the most important items. In the cost-cutting example, it's preferable to present the categories of savings in decreasing order of magnitude. When magnitude or importance is irrelevant, the order must still make sense, at least intuitively. For example, if the grouping describes a process to follow, the steps in the process should be listed in the order they're performed. Many presentations are cumbersome just because they ignore this elementary rule.

Here's another caveat: it's indispensable to ensure the grouping is MECE at each level. If your supporting points overlap, your audience will wonder whether your thinking is clear, or whether you're saying the same thing twice to sound more persuasive. But, by far, the most challenging part of MECEness is the "collectively exhaustive" condition: when building a grouping of reasons, we must make sure that, when taken together, they're sufficient to support the governing thought. We highlighted this point in Chap. 5 when we discussed hypothesis pyramids. It also applies to storylining, but it's easy to overlook. When using a grouping pattern, it's essential to have the mental discipline to ask, "If my audience agrees with all the points in the key line, can it still disagree with the governing thought?" Only when the answer to this question is "no" will you know your grouping is truly MECE. In the example of the three sources of savings that add up to €50 million, this is as simple as adding three numbers. In most cases, asking this question will reveal gaps in the logic.

While the grouping pattern is the most popular way to build a storyline, another option is possible: the "argument" pattern illustrated by the Cosyloo storyline. An "argument" follows a key line of reasoning that goes from premises to conclusions. The core message results from a stream of arguments in which each new point is logically connected to the prior point. Such a linear logic differs from groupings, in which every key-line point is connected to the core message, but independent from the other points in the key line.

The most convenient and common way to build an argument is to use the "situation–complication–(question)–resolution (SCR)" key line. This is actually the one we've used in the Summit Water example. Such arguments are organized in the following way:

1. Start with a statement describing the situation that triggered the problem you're addressing. In the example, the *situation* is: *Cosyloo offers us a deal that fits our strategic purpose.*
2. Then explain why things are more complicated than expected—why you can't give a simple answer immediately. In the example, the *complication* is: *However, we still must overcome four hurdles.*
3. At this point, you can include a reformulation of the initial *question* that considers the complication. This step can be omitted if the question is easily inferred from the context. In the example, we could have said: *So, how can we mitigate the risks of testing Cosyloo's technology?*
4. Finally, answer this question with a core message that solves the problem. In the example, the *resolution* is: *We recommend limiting the launch of the Cosyloo product to a target customer population in which Summit Water can serve nine households equipped with septic tanks for each household offered the portable toilet service.*

You might have noticed that, in the Summit Water example, both the situation and the complication are each supported by sub-points that are organized as groupings: the situation is bolstered by three reasons why the Cosyloo deal is attractive, and the complication is decomposed into four implementation hurdles. In practice, you can choose between an argument and a grouping at each level and in each pillar of the pyramid. A grouping key line can lead to other groupings at the lower level, which was the case in the

Mustang Airlines example, but it can also include one or several arguments. However, decomposing an argument into sub-arguments can be tedious: the audience might get lost in the pyramid if you make them walk through a maze of several sub-arguments.

Grouping or Argument?

Groupings and arguments each have their fans. Those who find that grouping patterns come more easily to them may find argument patterns unnatural and contrived. Conversely, many people prefer arguments, finding groupings too blunt and unsubtle for their taste.

Each pattern has its pros and cons and each is appropriate to different situations. To be an effective communicator, you must master both. The two patterns are summarized in Fig. 10.3, with their respective pros and cons.

Groupings are the workhorses of storylines. They're robust: if your audience disagrees with one of several reasons you're giving for your governing thought, it may still agree with the overall message (assuming the weak point didn't undermine your credibility). And groupings are easy to put together: lists of reasons ("why"), ways, or steps ("how") are easy to compile once we have a governing thought in mind.

The primary weakness of groupings isn't a logical one (assuming they're properly structured and supported)—it's tactical. Consider again the Mustang Airlines example, but with a twist. Instead of imagining yourself as the CEO of the company, you're now playing the role of the junior executive tasked with investigating the problem and providing a recommendation. (Don't think of it as a demotion, think of it as a reprieve from the stress of running a company.)

In your new role, you pitch your recommendation to the CEO along with the two main reasons to support it (a grouping). Suppose the CEO advocated the bulk purchase of five A320neos in the first place and you have reason to believe she still thinks it's an attractive option. Maybe the Airbus offer was made during a convincing one-on-one meeting between your CEO and the Airbus CEO at the Paris Air Show, leading her to view the deal favorably. Knowing this, would you still want to communicate your recommendation in such a blunt way? Maybe not. Enumerating a list of reasons why the CEO's plan is ill advised, without even acknowledging the idea's merits, goes straight to the point—but may be too brutal. Using a grouping structure with an audience that initially disagrees with you can be perceived as too blunt, or downright rude.

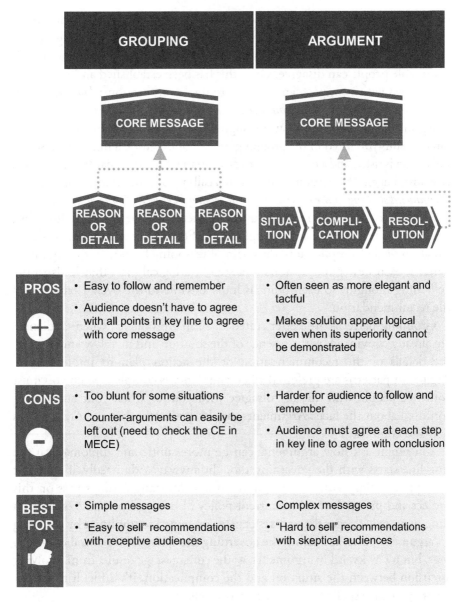

Fig. 10.3 Storyline patterns

The alternative argument pattern can help you address this tactical difficulty. The "situation" that forms the first pillar of the argument, here, might be: *The offer we have received from Airbus, which we've carefully analyzed, has many advantages.* This "situation" can be supported by a list (or grouping) of reasons why the offer is attractive, including the technical and economic advantages of the new A320neo, and the commercial incentives offered by Airbus. Such a "situation" states the reason for the debate to take place, acknowledging that the recommendation is not a "no-brainer," but a difficult decision on which reasonable people can disagree. Once this has been established and your audience agrees with you, you can move on to the "complication": *However, making a bulk purchase of five Airbus aircraft raises serious difficulties.*

Again, this complication can be supported by a grouping of reasons—the same reasons you listed in the grouping version of the story: a financial reason (a bulk order is risky) and a technical one (diversifying the fleet jeopardizes Mustang's cost advantage). The tension you've created calls for a "resolution": *As a result, we recommend sticking to the current policy of buying Boeing 737s one at a time.*

As this example illustrates, argument patterns can be more tactful. This, incidentally, is also the risk with arguments: if the audience disagrees with the situation or the complication, the chain of reasoning breaks. In the argument pattern, each new point appears as a step in a logical path that leads to the governing thought, so each point is indispensable to the overall rationale of the recommendation.

Grouping patterns are better suited to simple problems, where audiences are already convinced by the essence of the solution and merely want to know the details of the recommendation or the action plan to implement it. Argument patterns are preferred when your story is complex, when you must convince people who initially disagree with you, or when your audience is confused about the facts. Arguments should dominate when your rationale is rich and complex.

You might ask how arguments can be more subtle and diplomatic if the storyline starts with the governing thought anyway? Admittedly, if you start your presentation with "We recommend that Mustang Airlines pass on this project and pursue instead its current policy of buying Boeing 737s one at a time," you may trigger the very resistance you hoped to minimize by choosing an argument pattern. Putting the governing thought first is natural in groupings, but it's awkward in arguments: as the core message results from resolving a tension between the situation and the complication, it's difficult to state it before you have spelled out these first two pillars.

To overcome this challenge, a good practice is to depart from the rule we stated at the beginning of this chapter when we advised you to make the core message short and crisp. Instead, you may want to summarize the entire argument in the governing thought. Using the Mustang Airlines example, the first paragraph of the storyline could read:

The offer we have received from Airbus, which we have carefully analyzed, has many advantages, particularly the technical edge and the fuel efficiency of the new A320neo. However, making a bulk purchase of five Airbus aircraft would increase our financial risk and net operating costs. As a result, we recommend sticking to the current policy of buying Boeing 737s one at a time.

Consider the Summit Water example again. There, you could start your recommendation memo as follows:

We have looked into the opportunity for Summit Water to team up with Cosyloo to launch a portable toilet service. Such a deal would fit with Summit's strategic objectives and we can make it viable. However, it raises significant legal, financial, and operational hurdles. This is why we recommend limiting the launch of the Cosyloo product to a target population in which Summit can serve nine households equipped with septic tanks for each household offered the portable toilet service.

The rest of the report will detail the SCR argument. This will be made easier by the fact that the reader is expecting to hear the details of a balanced, nuanced recommendation, not just a list of concurring reasons.

*   *   *

The ultimate objective of solution selling isn't to gain intellectual support for your solution, but to trigger action. Your recommendation report should convey actionable recommendations, not mere analyses or reassessments of the problem. The guidelines we've presented in this chapter will prove useful when you keep this essential point in mind.

These guidelines serve as a backbone for any presentation, one-page memo, detailed report, slide deck, or any other form used to communicate your message. Our experience has taught us that crafting the core message and putting together the storyline is *always* the main challenge in business communication, no matter how recommendations are delivered. It's true that the choice of medium, the quality of the visual aids, the style of delivery, and the oral skills of the presenter play a significant role. It's also true that some of the best presenters—or "storytellers" as fashion now dictates they call themselves—don't just present a recommendation dryly supported by a well-structured rationale. They use stories and anecdotes, play with the emotions of their audience, and make their presentations enjoyable and memorable. In reality, most business presentations don't fail because they lack such embellishments, but for much more basic reasons. Even the most compelling speaker, using the most inspired communication techniques, needs a clear message and a strong rationale. We'll discuss how to deliver such a message in the next chapter.

Chapter 10 in One Page

- To sell your solution, use the pyramid principle: governing thought first, followed by a few key-line points:

  - *Mustang Airlines: pass on project to buy five A320neos, and maintain current policy of buying Boeing 737 s one at a time, because:*

  1. *A bulk order of five airplanes would be too risky.*
  2. *Diversifying the fleet would jeopardize cost advantage.*

- *Governing thought:* crisp (ideally, your recommendation in one sentence); sets the general direction; triggers questions that the key-line points will answer.

- The key line is the structure of your *storyline*:

  - Based on your hypothesis pyramid if you used the hypothesis-driven path
  - Otherwise, built bottom-up by grouping your findings into clusters

- Two patterns of storylines: groupings and arguments

- Grouping: all key-line points support or detail the governing thought

- Argument: the key-line points are organized in a logical sequence—each is connected to the prior one, and the last one leads to the conclusion.

- The typical argument pattern is the "SCR" triad:

  - *Cosyloo SCR:*

  1. *The deal with Cosyloo would fit with Summit Water's strategic objectives …*
  2. *However, it raises significant legal, financial, and operational hurdles.*
  3. *Thus, we recommend limiting the launch of the Cosyloo product to …*

- Choose groupings for "easy sells" and arguments for more difficult ones:

  - Prefer a grouping when your audience expects your recommendation and mainly needs detailed reasons or steps to implement it.
  - Go for an argument when a grouping might be too blunt or when the subject is complex and needs to be introduced gradually.

Notes

1. The company is fictitious, but the problem realistically applies to most low-cost airlines, such as SWA in the USA or Ryanair in Europe.
2. Minto, B. (2002). *The Pyramid Principle* (3rd edition). Upper Saddle River, NJ: Prentice Hall.
3. The company names have been disguised for confidentiality reasons.
4. Brossard, S., & Garrette, B. (2016). *The Cosyloo–Summit Water Partnership: Innovation at the Base of the Pyramid*, HEC Paris case study, Retrieved from https://www.thecasecentre.org/educators/products/view?id=138010.
5. Minto, B. (2002). *op. cit.*

11

Sell the Solution: Recommendation Report and Delivery

Once you've crafted a compelling core message and a "pyramidal" storyline, you know the story you want to tell. The time has come to bring your story to life in concrete form by developing a written and visual presentation, which you'll use to pitch your solution to the problem owner and other stakeholders.

Whenever we teach the 4S method to MBA students, they're visibly relieved when we reach this point in the course. They know the time has come to play with PowerPoint and design fancy slides with impressive graphics, a game they believe they're good at. They think it's easier and more fun than constructing issue trees, crunching numbers, and struggling with groupings and arguments. A major takeaway from their brief professional experience seems to be that the only legitimate way to give a business presentation is to talk over PowerPoint slides projected on a screen. The irony is that as an audience member, one is bored to death by this approach.

This is the curse of PowerPoint: we hate attending PowerPoint presentations, but as presenters, we'd feel "naked" if we had to step into a meeting room and present without slides. Despite the scorn heaped upon it, the default approach to presenting recommendations in most business settings remains the slide deck.

We'll be honest: we aren't going to show you how to rid yourself of the security and comfort of using "slideware" such as PowerPoint to help deliver your solution pitch. That might be a bridge too far for many of us. What we will do is explain the mechanics of how to design an efficiently structured, easy-to-understand, and persuasive presentation that doesn't put your audience

© The Author(s) 2018
B. Garrette et al., *Cracked it!*, https://doi.org/10.1007/978-3-319-89375-4_11

to sleep. We'll begin by explaining how to prevent your "ta-dah!" moment—when you reveal your solution to the audience—from becoming an "uh-oh" train wreck.

Manage Communications Throughout the Process

If you're about to pitch your solution to the problem owner, it shouldn't be the first meeting you've had with her since she entrusted you with solving the problem. On rare occasions, a business leader might give you a problem to solve and tell you to come back a month later with a solution. This is a trap you should avoid.

The final presentation of your recommendation (if there is one) shouldn't be a "big reveal" where you've built up suspense by withholding information about the solution, only to reveal it in the final meeting. Instead, your final presentation should be the culmination of an ongoing conversation with the problem owner and other stakeholders. You should have laid the groundwork with them so that the content, including your recommendation, comes as no surprise. While this approach helps the problem owner and other audience members avoid surprises, it also helps you, as the solution seller, avoid being surprised by a skeptical and unreceptive, if not outright hostile, audience.

To avoid surprises, schedule intermediary checkpoints with the problem owner during the problem-solving process. Checkpoints allow you to update the problem owner on the status of your progress and get feedback. They serve three crucial purposes. First, they provide an opportunity to reconfirm with the problem owner that you remain aligned on how you understand and define the problem, which can change over time. Second, each occasion to talk to the problem owner is an opportunity to share your intermediary findings and get early reactions. This gives you a chance to hear objections you didn't anticipate and prepare your audience to hear difficult messages that will need time to sink in. Finally, checking in with the problem owner is an opportunity to test some of the slides you're developing and determine whether you'll include them in the final report and presentation.

Checkpoints can take many forms, from formal update meetings to short phone conversations or exchanges of text or email messages, depending on your relationship with the problem owner, the complexity of the problem, and scheduling and logistic constraints.

Checkpoints are especially useful when there is more than one problem owner or if the problem owner wants other stakeholders in the final meeting. In such cases, preparatory meetings with stakeholders (individually or in small groups) give each person a chance to understand your views and make objections and comments that can help you improve your storyline, or even change your recommendation. This approach is often called "pre-wiring" the final meeting.

Ideally, when you step into the final meeting, no one will be surprised by your analyses and facts or disagree with them. This doesn't mean everyone will agree on everything. The final meeting is often when different people defend different interpretations of a situation or suggest alternative recommendations. But if disagreements occur, they should be grounded on a shared understanding of the facts and respectful of the work you've done assembling them. With sufficient preparation, you'll create an environment where everyone can share their views in good faith. Without adequate pre-wiring, you risk facing a barrage of unexpected objections or even becoming a scapegoat for the lack of consensus.

Beware the PowerPoint Curse

The slide-based approach to communicating recommendations was originally invented by management consultants, long before software such as PowerPoint existed. In his book *The McKinsey Way*, Ethan Rasiel describes the first pieces of equipment he was given when he joined McKinsey in 1989: "a box of mechanical pencils, an eraser, and a set of ruled plastic templates with cutouts for various shapes: circles, rectangles, triangles arrows, etc." to draw his slides by hand.[1] One of us—Olivier—joined McKinsey's Paris office the same year and still owns the same rulers, even though he hasn't used them in a long while.

When slides were costly, time-consuming, and difficult to produce, only consultants who could rely on a support staff of skilled visual aids designers used them, and then only to produce slides that were necessary to substantiate their recommendations. "Saying it with charts" was a differentiator for management consultancies.

The widespread adoption of PowerPoint in the early 1990s changed everything. Suddenly, it became easy and cheap for anyone to produce slides. Nowadays, hundreds of thousands of personal computers equipped with PowerPoint or other slideware are spitting out billions of slides every year. Business people are drowning in an ever-growing tide of fancy visuals used to deliver often-incomprehensible presentations.

Using PowerPoint can be an effective way to deliver your message, if you have one. However, the fundamental problem with the proliferation of PowerPoint slides is that many presenters seem to confuse the means with the ends. Instead of using slides as visual aids that support a message, they compile fancy illustrations of unrelated facts first, and worry about their implications later (if at all). In the hands of people who have only a fuzzy idea of their core message, slides produce the same effect as singing a song when you've forgotten the lyrics: it vaguely reminds your audience of something, but what is it, really?

The most important thing to remember about PowerPoint presentations is when to prepare them—or rather, when *not* to: not before you have a storyline. As mentioned in Chap. 10, the first step is to express your ideas in text format and organize them hierarchically.

Create an Effective, Modular Report

Your report typically serves two purposes: it's a slide deck for your oral presentation, but it's also a written report the audience can read ahead of the meeting and take away as a record of the work and a source for future reference. In developing your final report, you therefore have two objectives. You want visually compelling slides that grab the audience's attention and convey the core ideas of your storyline, without being littered with small text the audience can't read. These slides, however, will have insufficient written explanation to be used as a handout without your oral elaboration. As a printed handout, you want your presentation to look like an illustrated report that functions as a self-explanatory document—but if you project these slides in the meeting, they'll make for a boring, and often unintelligible, presentation.

A logical solution, advocated by many communications experts and coaches, is to develop two documents: a slideshow for presentation, and a full report to be left behind as reading material. This approach is costly and time-consuming and may also be a waste of time because few problem owners will read a full report from cover to cover if they're satisfied with the presentation. Unless the presentation and report are professionally produced for a high-profile event, this solution is rarely implemented.

We must be pragmatic and strike a balance between simplicity and detail. Like all compromises, this has drawbacks, but our experience shows it's manageable. The guiding principle is to *build a modular document that mirrors your storyline.* While the whole document will provide exhaustive coverage of the storyline, you can use selected pages for a presentation or discussion. Because you can use the document as either a report or a presentation, we'll consider pages and slides as the same thing.

The storyline must provide the overall structure of the report, as depicted in Fig. 11.1. The governing thought and its supporting key line become the executive summary. Each key-line point, with its supporting messages, becomes a section. Each elementary message in the storyline becomes a page in the report or slide in the presentation.

If you follow this principle, your report will include four kinds of pages (or slides):

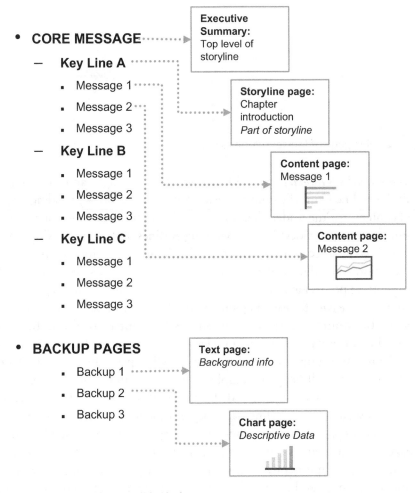

Fig. 11.1   From storyline to slide deck

Executive Summary

This report examines the project of ordering five new Airbus A320neo airliners to expand the Mustang Airlines fleet. Our recommendation is to pass on this project and pursue instead the current policy of buying Boeing 737s one at a time.

Two main points support this view:

- A bulk order of five airplanes would be too risky.

- Diversifying the fleet would jeopardize Mustang Airlines' cost advantage.

Fig. 11.2 First page of Mustang Airlines report

1. The *executive summary page* with the governing thought and the key line. Each key-line item will announce a section in the report—providing a table of contents for the reader. Figures 11.2 and 11.3 show examples of executive summary pages (slides) for the Mustang Airlines and Summit Water cases, respectively. These examples illustrate that it's easy to write the first page of the report once the storyline is set because the core message and its main supporting points have been developed during the storylining stage.

2. One *storyline page* for each key-line point. This type of page, which appears at the beginning of a section, announces the content of the section and introduces the pages that feature elementary messages. Figures 11.4 and 11.5 present examples of the first two storyline pages for Summit Water. We'll present a full-fledged example in the next chapter. Occasionally, your presentation may be simple and short enough to forgo different sections and you won't need storyline pages beyond the initial executive summary.

3. One *content page* for each elementary message. Most (but not all) of these pages will use charts to present facts, analyses, and illustrations in a visual way. Each page must convey only one elementary message that serves as the title for the page and the report should comprise as many content pages as there are messages in the storyline. The rule is simple: *one slide per message,*

Executive Summary

This report investigates the opportunity for Summit Water to team up with Cosyloo to launch a portable toilet service.

- Such a deal would fit Summit Water's strategic objectives and we believe we can make it economically viable.

- However, the business model raises significant legal, financial, and operational risks which we have to mitigate.

- This is why we recommend limiting the launch of the Cosyloo product to a target customer population in which Summit Water can serve 9 households equipped with septic tanks for each household offered the portable toilet service.

Fig. 11.3 First page of Summit Water report

one message per slide. For example, a PowerPoint implementation of the Librinova storyline we created in Chap. 10 would include 11 content pages, as there are 11 boxes at the lowest level of the pyramid depicted in Fig. 10.2.

This is a rule you can bend. Occasionally, you might include two related points on a single page, under a two-part message, or you might need two pages to support a single point, if two pieces of evidence are used to support it. But the general rule should apply in at least 80 percent of cases.

4. As many *backup pages* as needed. You may need to include additional information, document your work, add backup, and provide source material for further research. Since this material is unnecessary to support your storyline, relegate it to backup pages, grouped in an appendix.

Together, the executive summary and storyline pages reproduce your entire storyline in a modular format. They form the backbone of your report and ensure that someone who didn't attend the presentation can read and understand it. Modularity has another advantage: for a presentation, you can select which parts of the storyline you want to discuss and which ones you don't. We'll return to this point later in the chapter.

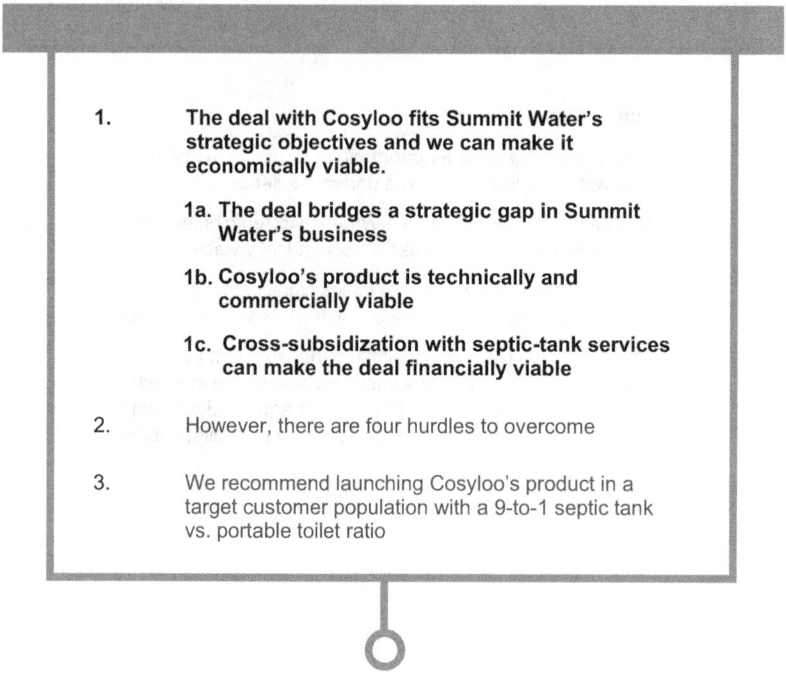

1.   **The deal with Cosyloo fits Summit Water's strategic objectives and we can make it economically viable.**

   1a. The deal bridges a strategic gap in Summit Water's business

   1b. Cosyloo's product is technically and commercially viable

   1c. Cross-subsidization with septic-tank services can make the deal financially viable

2.   However, there are four hurdles to overcome

3.   We recommend launching Cosyloo's product in a target customer population with a 9-to-1 septic tank vs. portable toilet ratio

Fig. 11.4   First storyline page of Summit Water report

Develop the Content Pages

Most pages in your report will be content pages, which support the key-line points by providing the results from your analyses. Figure 11.6 provides an example, based on the Mustang Airlines case we discussed in Chap. 10. This page belongs to the part of the storyline that argues that buying B737s is a better option than buying A320neos because the cost of introducing the A320neo would outweigh the benefits.

The slide depicted in Fig. 11.6 features three main components:

1. The action title: "The payback period of investing in an A320neo instead of a B737 would be too long."
2. A tracker indicating the specific point in the storyline, which is the "2a" on the top left.
3. The content itself, illustrating the analytical finding.

The *action title* concisely conveys the message. A message title is like a headline in a magazine, not an item in a table of contents. For instance, "Payback of switching to the A320neo" is brief, but conveys no message. Action titles are full sentences, including a verb, that make a point.

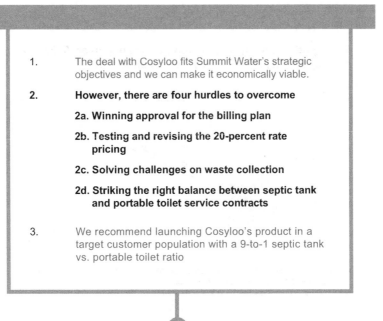

1. The deal with Cosyloo fits Summit Water's strategic objectives and we can make it economically viable.

2. **However, there are four hurdles to overcome**

   2a. Winning approval for the billing plan

   2b. Testing and revising the 20-percent rate pricing

   2c. Solving challenges on waste collection

   2d. Striking the right balance between septic tank and portable toilet service contracts

3. We recommend launching Cosyloo's product in a target customer population with a 9-to-1 septic tank vs. portable toilet ratio

Fig. 11.5 Second storyline page of Summit Water report

As you create each content page, each action title should match the corresponding message in the storyline (except perhaps for dropping a few words to be brief). A good way to check that your presentation aligns with your storyline is to review the pages in the report and read the action titles aloud without looking at the content of the slides. If what you hear matches the storyline, your report is telling the right story.

Trackers help to keep the audience on track. The role of the tracker is to locate each page within the overall plan of the presentation. In Fig. 11.6, the "2a" tracker refers to the numbering in the previous storyline page. An alternative option is to use a visual tracker, for example a set of arrows representing the sections, highlighting the section under discussion. A third option is to use a descriptive tracker with a keyword or a short phrase. In Mustang Airlines, we could, for example, mention "A320neo vs. B737" at the top of all slides that deal with the second part of the storyline.

Finally, the *content* is the heart of any content page. The chart featured in Fig. 11.6 supports the title message by quantifying the payback in a simple financial model.[2] The chart focuses on the result of the financial analysis, rather than on the calculations that have been done or the details of the financial model that an Excel table would provide.

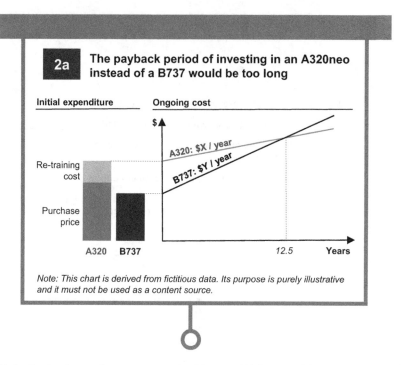

Fig. 11.6   Content page in a report on the Mustang Airlines problem

Charts are much more effective at conveying evidence than long chunks of text—a picture paints a thousand words—or data in tabular form. In our example, the extra cost of including A320neo airplanes in Mustang Airlines' fleet is easier to grasp if it's displayed in a bar chart than written in a table.

Some people disagree with this chart-based view because charts hide the underpinning numeric models and preclude discussions on assumptions and calculations. Critics argue that you must present the details of your calculations and let the audience understand for itself how you got to your numbers. There's merit to this objection: not every presenter has the credibility for his hypotheses and calculations to be accepted without explanation. If a problem owner has entrusted you with performing analysis, she probably doesn't want to review every detail. You'll need to find middle ground.

One option is to show the chart and have the details at the ready in the backup pages if someone asks for them. This approach may not work if your reasoning is based on non-obvious assumptions the audience doesn't know. An alternative is to spell out (and perhaps justify) your key assumptions in a slide that precedes the one depicting your model. This is a situation where you'll break the "one slide per message" rule. The title on the first page could be "To calculate payback, we have created a model with four key assumptions," followed by a second page entitled "Based on these assumptions, we find that...."

You don't need quantitative charts for all of the content pages in your report. Most content pages should show facts, but not all facts are numbers to be shown in chart form. For example, three quotes from consumer interviews may make a crucial point about quality of service more effectively than whatever numbers are available. A map of a retailer's outlets, a picture of a competitor's product, a side-by-side comparison of features in the offerings of two players, and an organization chart are important facts, but not quantitative charts. Relevant non-numerical facts beat irrelevant numbers.

In the rare cases where your content pages don't display facts, they should illustrate a conceptual insight. Use concepts where needed—for instance, scales showing that benefits outweigh drawbacks in the qualitative analysis of a proposal. But, like quantitative charts, keep conceptual charts simple and relevant.

You'll find examples of both quantitative and conceptual charts, and pages displaying more qualitative evidence in text form, in the case study we present in the next chapter.

Because charts are an essential part of recommendation reports, we'll take a closer look at how to design better charts. We'll limit our discussion to basic guidelines. For a more in-depth examination, take a look at *Say It with Charts*, by Gene Zelazny.[3]

Make Quantitative Charts Relevant and Simple

Quantitative charts, which synthesize numbers or display results from numeric calculations, are the workhorses of business presentations. This is to be expected: most business leaders rightly believe decisions should be supported by data, numbers, and quantitative analyses. For instance, investments or new endeavors of any kind usually require a "business case" proving there is a sound business opportunity, reflected in sufficient financial returns, that makes sense for the company. You'll need more than numbers to win approval, but you can't make your case without them.

An advantage of numbers is that, because they represent quantities, you can easily establish comparisons between them—such as percentages, rankings, or changes over time—that are easy to represent with computer graphics. As soon as you have numbers in a table, Excel can generate a chart that visualizes these numbers and makes orders of magnitude, proportions, trends, correlations, and more jump off the page.

The key to effective data visualization is to know *what* you want to see jump off the page. What analysis do you want the data to illustrate? Is it the change in a quantity over time—for instance, your sales? Is it the comparison of that quantity with another quantity—your sales compared to your main competitor's? Is it the way various components contribute to that quantity— your sales by product line? A data table could include all the numbers to answer these three questions, but a graph requires you to choose an "angle" to look at the numbers—a specific analytical result you want the data to show. Figure 11.7 illustrates six types of generic analyses you can perform on quantitative data and nine chart templates to convey the corresponding results.

Time Series One analysis you will visualize frequently is the variation over time of a variable, such as sales or profit. Displaying the change in a variable over time is one of the most common visualization tasks you'll perform. You want to show whether sales have increased, decreased, or fluctuated. Statisticians call such data a time series. We typically represent time series data graphically as a line or a column chart in which time progresses from left to right. For example, the column chart in Fig. 11.8 displays sales in successive years, while the line chart on the right-hand side of Fig. 11.6 compares two sets of cost data (one for the A320neo and one for the B737). While a line suggests a continuous trend, a column chart indicates that the same variable (sales) is measured at regular time intervals (yearly, for instance).

Split Another popular visualization is to compare different parts in a whole. The classic template is a pie chart that depicts the split (in percentage or actual values) of a variable across categories, such as sales across different countries, as shown in Fig. 11.9. This is a static representation. If you want to show how the sales split evolves over time, comparing several pie charts will be awkward and difficult to interpret. Stacked columns work better. Here, you may want to express the values in percentages rather than in raw numbers because the totals can differ over time, making comparisons difficult. You compile the percentage of sales in the different countries in a column, indicating the countries by different colors or patterns, and repeat this column for every year.[4] Comparing the columns will illustrate how the sales split across countries evolves over time (demonstrated in Fig. 11.9).

Waterfall You might want to decompose a total value into both positive and negative components, such as inflows and outflows of cash, or positive and negative sources of change in a number. Traditional split charts can't do the job. A "waterfall" chart works well. For instance, the waterfall chart in Fig. 11.10 shows how the sales of a company have grown over a year through winning new clients and losing existing ones. Items are added to the picture

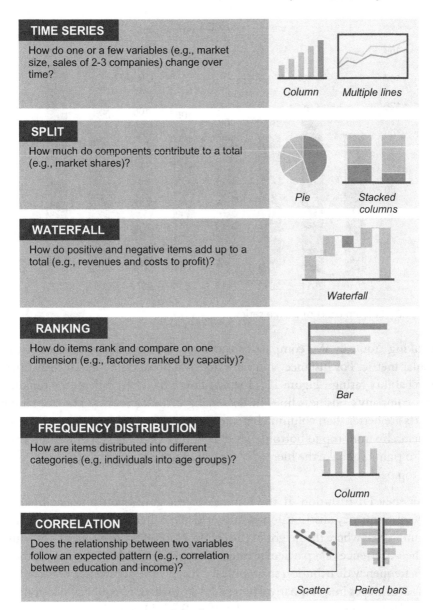

Fig. 11.7 Quantitative chart templates

from left to right, appearing as chunks of columns that start where the preceding column has stopped. Positive items appear as chunks that climb upward, while negative items fall downward. This gives the impression of a cascade of items that get you from the original number on the left to the final number on the right.

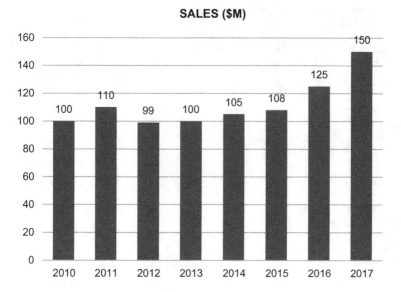

Fig. 11.8 Column chart of a time series

Ranking You can also compare categories by ranking them based on a particular metric. For instance, you can rank rival products based on their prices or reliability ratings. Figure 11.11 shows how a bar chart reflects the rankings of a company's business lines in decreasing order of profits. Horizontal bar charts are better than column charts for rankings because a bar chart suggests a hierarchy from top to bottom, while a column chart suggests variation from left to right. To make the hierarchy explicit, place the top-performing item on the top bar.

Frequency Distribution If the number of categories you must compare is large, a frequency distribution is appropriate. A frequency distribution is a column chart where the height of the column indicates the frequency or count of the occurrence of a particular category in a variable. For example, you can use a frequency distribution to graphically display the occurrence of categories of ages or wages in a company. Figure 11.12 provides a frequency distribution of students in a course earning grades of A, B, C, D, and F.

Correlation You might also want to compare two variables rather than one to show whether the relationship between them follows an expected pattern. For example, you can rank business lines based on both sales and profits to check whether greater sales levels correlate with higher profits. A paired bar chart will fit this purpose: the business lines are ranked in decreasing order of sales

DISTRIBUTION OF SALES (2016)

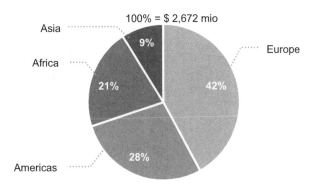

DISTRIBUTION OF SALES (2010-2016)

(%, $millions)

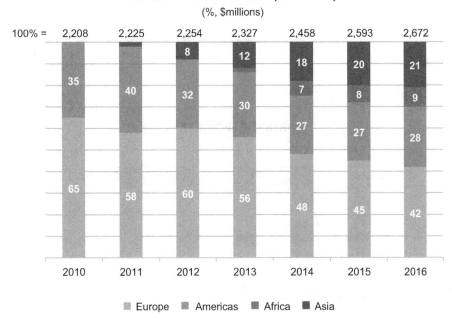

Fig. 11.9 Pie and stacked columns charts

as bars on the left side, and the corresponding profit levels are reported in parallel on the right side (see Fig. 11.13). The inverted-pyramid shape of the graph suggests a correlation: profits decline as sales decline.

A more traditional way to represent a correlation is to plot each variable as a dot on a scatter graph in which the two variables (e.g., sales and profits) are represented by two perpendicular axes. A correlation appears if the dots align

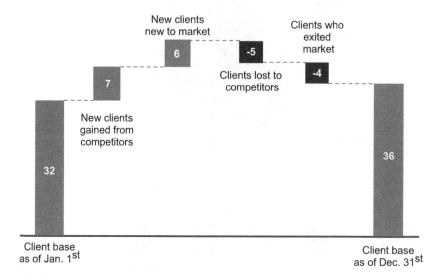

Fig. 11.10 Waterfall chart

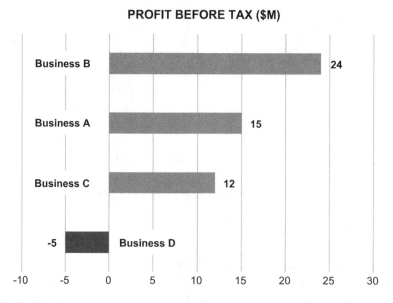

Fig. 11.11 Bar chart

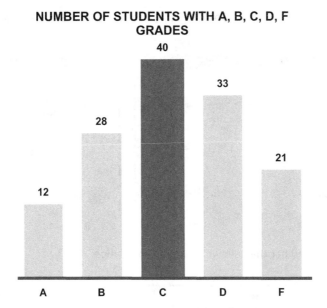

NUMBER OF STUDENTS WITH A, B, C, D, F GRADES

Fig. 11.12 Frequency distribution

more or less close to a straight diagonal line, which represents a perfect correlation. A famous example is the "learning curve" popularized by the Boston Consulting Group (see Fig. 11.14). The learning curve theory claims that a firm's production costs decrease by a constant percentage each time the firm doubles its accumulated production, resulting in a negative correlation between the logarithms of cumulative volumes and production costs.[5]

We've limited our list to simple numeric analyses and chart templates to provide you with guidelines about how to select the simplest charts that fit the most frequent quantitative analyses. The world is a complicated place and some analyses require advanced data visualization techniques to be understood.[6] For most business presentations, however, the findings you must visualize are relatively simple, and these nine basic patterns will cover most of your needs. Occasionally, you must combine two patterns on one chart to make your point: Fig. 11.6 combines a split and a time series. In general, however, resist the urge to create a complex page when a simple one will do.

Likewise, resist the temptation to embellish visuals with unnecessary colors, animations, 3D or perspective effects, transitions, and other gimmicks. Making the charts visually arresting is misguided. Your slide deck isn't meant to hypnotize your audience. Instead, it provides the foundation for a productive conversation. On each page, the visual serves a single message, and the messages, taken together, serve your recommendation.

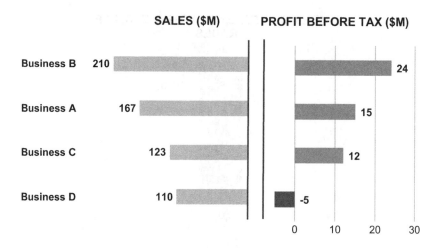

Fig. 11.13 Paired bar chart showing ranking correlation

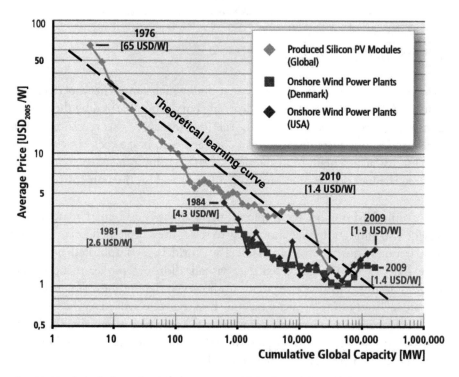

Fig. 11.14 Correlation of price per watt and installed capacity of renewable energy sources

Use Conceptual Charts Sparingly

Conceptual charts are visuals that illustrate qualitative reasoning and ideas, such as frameworks, structures, relationships, or processes. They make it possible to visualize non-quantified links between variables, such as causal or temporal relationships between factors and outcomes. You can create them using PowerPoint's library of shapes. One of the most popular examples of a conceptual chart is an organization chart that shows hierarchical links among people or departments in an organization. Conceptual charts can be used for other purposes, such as representing an issue tree or a hypothesis pyramid, as we did in prior chapters. Conceptual charts can also prove useful in showing the big picture while explaining the details. For example, displaying an action plan as a flow chart that features four connected arrows representing the four major steps in the plan helps the audience follow the steps while keeping an eye on the overall plan.

However, we recommend using conceptual charts sparingly. If you use a conceptual chart where a data-based chart is needed, you risk coming off as speculative or lazy because you didn't take the time to gather the necessary evidence to validate your point. If you use a conceptual gimmick to illustrate an idea that you could convey in plain language—for instance, inserting a grocer's scale drawing to illustrate "striking the right balance between price and quality"—you risk looking childish. Classic concepts that your audience is familiar with, such as flow charts and organization charts, are welcome when appropriate. Use new visual concepts as you would use newly coined words: rarely.

We provide a library of basic conceptual charts in Fig. 11.15. We've organized the templates based on the connections they create between variables. For example, flow charts show items in a temporal or causal sequence, while structure charts emphasize static connections.

Trim the Deck Ruthlessly

You now have a full report that follows the structure of your storyline. It's a perfect tool to leave behind or to send in advance to your audience. The trap is that you may have fallen in love with the slides you've produced, believing you must present every one of them. But that would be a mistake.

Presentations with fewer slides are better. They leave more time for discussion. Focusing on fewer messages helps ensure your audience understands all the points you're making. You'll appear more authoritative and confident with

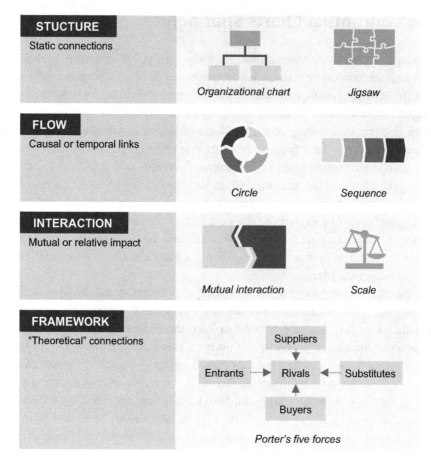

Fig. 11.15 Conceptual chart templates

fewer slides. If you can tell your story with 30 slides, try 20, not 40. Your audience will be grateful. As the French writer Antoine de Saint-Exupéry wrote: "Perfection is attained not when there is nothing more to add, but when there is nothing more to remove."

Why do most presentations include many more slides than necessary? A cynic might say that consultants must justify the substantial fees they charge. Many "in-house" problem solvers make the same mistake. They feel compelled to "show the sweat" they've put in, and a thick report is better in that respect than a thin one. There's also comfort in taking cover behind a big pile of slides. "They may not like what I have to say, but at least I've done my job!" It takes a brave presenter to walk into the arena with a slim set of slides: "Will they take me seriously? What if they have a question I can't answer?"

The modular structure we've proposed offers a comforting compromise. You only need to select the subset of 20 slides you *must* present. Once you've identified them, you can isolate this subset from the other pages, which you'll keep as backups. With backups at the ready, you won't feel naked if someone asks a detail question that isn't addressed in your core deck. If you have the time (or if you fear your pages are too detailed for on-screen presentation), create simplified versions of the 20 pages you've selected. To do so, suppress redundant words and details, and ruthlessly focus each slide on the title message and the chart that supports it.

This modular approach ensures that a subset of presentation slides serve as purely visual aids. They don't tell the entire story: in the presentation meeting, *you* will. Your presentation is a resource you will use to steer the conversation. Since you'll hand out the complete report anyway, the rest won't be lost, and someone who does not attend the meeting can get a complete record of your work.

Quality Control

You've managed the communications process. You've defined the structure of your presentation and prepared its contents. But you're not yet ready to walk into the big meeting. Now is the time to quality-check your presentation for legibility, spelling and grammar, calculations, and internal consistency. While you're at it, double-check that you observed *all* the guidelines we suggested above. The checklist in Fig. 11.16 recaps 18 questions you should ask before an important presentation. Take the time to go through it.

Beyond Slide Presentations

Although we've described an approach to translate your storyline for a solution pitch into a slide deck, good slides aren't sufficient for a good presentation. They aren't even necessary: Martin Luther King Jr. didn't need PowerPoint to describe his "dream," and no one (we hope) ever used slides to propose marriage. Slides are simply crutches for presenters—a cheat sheet that helps us remember what to say and appear in command of the meeting.

Many experts have argued that the overuse of slideware is detrimental to effective communication, as it undermines logic, depth, and critical thinking.[7] They claim that breaking every line of reasoning into bullet points and

	CHECK BEFORE DELIVERY
Process	❑ Problem owner knows what to expect in the meeting ❑ Key facts have been shared with all participants
Structure	❑ Storyline is clear and compelling ❑ Report follows storyline : Storyline = Executive Summary + chapter introductions ❑ There is one message per page, one page per message (with few exceptions) ❑ Trackers or visuals help the audience remember where it stands
Content	❑ Action titles correspond to storyline and can be read in sequence ❑ Facts presented in each page support the action title ❑ Assumptions are spelled out as needed ❑ Relevant backups are included as appendices ❑ You have selected a maximum of 20 key pages for presentation ❑ Quantitative charts are chosen for message, not for effect ❑ Conceptual charts are rare and relevant ❑ No useless animations, transitions, 3D effects, images or colors distract from your messages
Quality control	❑ No font smaller than 16pt is used, except in footnotes ❑ A fresh and competent pair of eyes has checked grammar and spelling ❑ You have checked all the calculations; all percentages add up to 100 ❑ You have checked labels and scales, sources, footnotes, tracker and page numbers

Fig. 11.16 Report and presentation checklist

cramming complex analyses into simplistic charts destroys nuance, flattens the relative importance of findings, oversimplifies or ignores interconnections between ideas, and hinders open, critical debate. This critique attracted public attention when US General H.R. McMaster banned PowerPoint presentations from all war-room briefings, blaming "slideware" for an insidious erosion of strategic vision.

Why not then, at least occasionally, try to break the mold of the formal, slide-based presentation, and aim for an interactive conversation instead? Be bold: don't use slides for the final meeting!

There—we've said it. But just like the 20-slide goal, we know this is likely to remain an aspirational idea, not a daily practice. Rather than going for the radical zero-slide approach, we have two practical suggestions to change the tone of your recommendation meeting.

Tell a Story to Launch the Conversation

Your aim in your presentation isn't to read your slides, but to engage the audience in a conversation. If that wasn't the case, you'd just submit your report and cancel the meeting. But holding the meeting is the right choice: adults learn by discussing, not solely by listening or reading.

An effective way to open a conversation is to start with a story. Begin with the core message, as the pyramid principle dictates, and then immediately tell a story that will grab the problem owner's attention and stimulate interaction—a concrete, realistic illustration of the main message you're delivering. People are generally more engaged and more receptive to vivid, real-life stories than to calculations and analyses.[8] Well-chosen examples and analogies are powerful persuasion tools that complement dry, rational reasoning. Stories capture attention and elicit reactions, moving the meeting into conversation mode. It's then easier to use your modular, well-organized slide deck to answer the pyramid of questions the core message and the illustrative story have created in your audience's minds.

Suppose, for example, you're recommending to the CEO of Mustang Airlines not to buy the new A320neo aircraft. You could begin the presentation by telling her a story of two airlines: one that went bankrupt because of shortsighted fleet development choices and one that thrived through sticking to a strict low-cost business model.

There are risks with this approach. The first is that the story must be an appropriate one, not a superficial or manipulative analogy. Using the story of Steve Jobs launching the iPhone every time you recommend a new product launch will damage your credibility.

Second, this approach will work well with some decision-makers, but may fail with others—for instance, people who pride themselves on demanding facts and figures and studying them religiously. While some executives love war stories, others want to see an Excel table before forming any opinion. You must understand the preferences of the problem owner and adapt your approach accordingly.

Third, the time to look for stories is *after* you've defined your message, not before. Stories are here to illustrate the message and bring it to life. They shouldn't be the basis for defining it—that would be falling into the miscommunication pitfall we discussed in Chap. 2.

Having said all that, if you can use good stories to help people relate to your talk, you will have created a conversation, not a mere presentation. Some people might not agree with you, but at least you're maximizing the chances they'll listen and participate. If your audience participates in a conversation, they're much more likely to remember (and agree with) what you say. And who knows? By telling a compelling, relevant story, maybe you won't need the 20 slides.

Let the Audience Absorb the Content

Some highly regarded business leaders, such as Jeff Bezos at Amazon, forbid the use of PowerPoint presentations in their companies. When Amazon executives have ideas to communicate, they write up their views in a 4- to 6-page memo, which the company calls a "narrative."[9] They take the memo to a team meeting, where the first 20 minutes are spent reading the narrative. The presenter then fields questions from the rest of the team.

If you've written a storyline before designing your slides, as we recommend in this book, you'll have no difficulty producing such a narrative, perhaps supported by a few attached slides for handing out, wherever analytical findings really must be visualized. The advantage of this memo-based approach is that the narrative structure emphasizes the flow and depth of ideas, instead of juxtaposing piecemeal facts in a smorgasbord of slides. The audience has time to absorb the content of your storyline, and can then discuss both its logic and the supporting evidence.

A more radical way to stimulate audience participation is to let it absorb the data you've gathered and the analyses you've conducted, without sharing your storyline. In this spirit, some consultants use "walk-through" presentations: they turn their key slides into posters hung on the walls of the boardroom, and ask the members of the management team to walk around and discover them. Participants can ask questions, discuss in small groups, and add comments by placing stickers on the posters. Then a plenary discussion, facilitated by the consultant, allows all participants to share their views.

This inductive approach does the opposite of what we advocate in this book: it lets the audience construct its own storyline from the facts, rather than being guided by the problem solver. It should be reserved for skilled presenters and educated audiences able to step back from the data and to resist the temptation to jump to conclusions from isolated findings.

* * *

The purpose of any communication is to convey a message. The backbone of any solution selling is a compelling storyline. Without it, visuals are useless, which is why we insist that the storyline precedes the slides. This seems to be common-sense advice, but given the way many problem solvers develop the content of their presentations, it is often ignored.

For the storyline to be persuasive, it needs to be supported by easy-to-understand, visually conveyed evidence. When your storyline is complete, with an action-oriented core message and a clear key line, you can select the findings you want to present and invest time in designing charts to communicate them. As we explained in Chap. 10, you can develop a storyline from the bottom-up, but writing the final report is a top-down process. The investment you make in developing the storyline pays off handsomely in the time you save creating the final report. When you have the full report in hand, your mind is free to carefully select the pages you want to present to steer the conversation to the ultimate goal of selling your solution.

In the next chapter, we'll walk you through an application of the entire 4S method to a real-life case.

Chapter 11 in One Page

- There's more to solution selling than a good storyline and a fancy PowerPoint presentation. You must steer a constructive conversation with the problem owner.

- Avoid the "big reveal": use checkpoints to manage communications with the problem owner during the entire problem-solving process. Avoid surprises.

- Build the report along the storyline, respecting the pyramid principle:
  - *Executive summary* = overview of the storyline, with core message and plan for the overall report (each item in executive summary is a section).
  - Sections start with a storyline *page* that presents the next level in the storyline.
  - Items in the storyline page announce one or several *content pages* in the section. *Each content page* conveys one message and one message only, with an action title, in sentence form.
  - Reading aloud the action titles of the content pages = your storyline
  - Put everything else you may need in *backup pages.*

- Use the report and presentation checklist before your meeting.

- Use no more than 20 slides from the report for your presentation (plus text pages and backups).

- Engage the audience: tell a story to launch the conversation.

Notes

1. Rasiel, E.M. (1998). *The McKinsey Way.* New York: McGraw-Hill.
2. This model is based on fictitious data.
3. Zelazny, G. (2001). *Say it with Charts* (4th edition). New York: McGraw-Hill.
4. Given this objective, it makes senses to use "100%" bars and to show the percentages in each column, as in Fig. 11.9. Such charts are prone to misinterpretation, however, as a declining percentage of a growing whole can occur even when the absolute value of the item increases, and vice versa. To avoid such confusion, it is indispensable, at a minimum, to mention the "100%" total value at the top of each bar. In some cases, you may want to resort to stacked columns in absolute values, which make the contributions of components harder to compare, but are more faithful to reality since they are not distorted by being converted to percentages.
5. BCG has become famous by producing charts that showed, in industry after industry, that this correlation held. Accordingly, this is a case in which correlations support an explicit theory. However, when using this type of chart without such a preexisting theory, keep in mind the dangers of taking correlation for causal evidence, as we discussed in Chap. 7.
6. See, for instance, presentations by the late Hans Rosling. Retrieved from https://www.ted.com/speakers/hans_rosling.
7. Tufte, E. (2006). *The Cognitive Style of PowerPoint: Pitching Out Corrupts Within.* Cheshire, Connecticut: Graphic Press.
8. Heath, C., & Heath, D. (2007). *Made to Stick: Why Some Ideas Survive and Others Die.* New York: Random House.
9. Stone, M. (2015, July 28). A 2004 email from Jeff Bezos explains why PowerPoint presentations aren't allowed at Amazon. *Business Insider France.* Retrieved from http://www.businessinsider.fr/us/jeff-bezos-email-against-powerpoint-presentations-2015-7/.

12

The 4S Method in Action

It's now time to bring the entire 4S method to life. We'll apply the method to a real-life case and walk through the development of the problem statement, issue tree, solution, storyline, and recommendation report. For confidentiality reasons, we've disguised the name of the companies, the geographies, the time frame, and some financial data, but we've remained faithful to the actual problem-solving initiative that took place. We start with a brief description of the company and the issue at hand.

Case Study: The Kangaroo Opportunity

"Cherry Holdings" is a family-run company that operates several fashion apparel and textile businesses in various Central and Eastern European countries. Founded as a small manufacturing operation by the great-grandfather of the current owners, it engaged in an aggressive strategy of external and international growth a decade ago. Cherry Holdings has built a reputation as a smart acquirer. It excels at identifying small, privately held acquisition targets that it can buy, revamp, and grow within the group. Their acquisition strategy draws on superior management processes and some back-office synergies.

Cherry Holdings is currently contemplating the acquisition of "Kangaroo," the leader in the men's underwear market in "Syldavia." Cherry's top executives are unfamiliar with Kangaroo's line of business and the country in which it operates. Given their tight time constraints, Cherry is asking for assistance in evaluating the attractiveness of Kangaroo as an acquisition target. They

© The Author(s) 2018
B. Garrette et al., *Cracked it!*, https://doi.org/10.1007/978-3-319-89375-4_12

provide us with the memorandum they received from Kangaroo's current owner. This memo contains relevant background information and is reproduced in the following section.

Information Memorandum on Kangaroo
Kangaroo products and brands

Kangaroo produces and sells men's underwear under two brands: Kangaroo and Alligator. The company has focused on this business since its creation 50 years ago. In 2018, men's underpants (boxers and briefs) account for 74 percent of Kangaroo's sales and up to 87 percent of its operational profit. The rest of the business comes from men's undershirts and, to a lesser extent, pajamas.

Kangaroo is the leading brand in the department store and specialty retail channels, while Alligator addresses the mass merchandise channel. Taken together, the two brands command 16.1 percent of the domestic market for men's underpants. The largest competitor has a 9.6-percent market share. Kangaroo generates 14.6 percent of its net sales in exports.

Core business strategy

Kangaroo quickly became the leader in Syldavia and expanded internationally soon after its creation in the 1960s. In 1992, the company launched the Alligator brand to penetrate food retail chains that were thriving at that time in Syldavia. The move was a great success: the new brand benefited from the strong growth of mass merchandisers replacing small distributors of basic products.

Kangaroo gained its reputation and market leadership by offering high-quality products based on technical innovation. However, it had some trouble in the 2010s because it didn't adequately adapt to the changing market environment. Kangaroo realized it focused too much on production issues and not enough on marketing strategies. A major revamp initiative was launched in 2015, with the assistance of a leading management consultancy. The company revised its strategy and restored its financial balance in one year. In 2017, net sales accounted for §350 million[1] and generated an operating margin of 6 percent.

The company employs 709 people, including 350 people in manufacturing. It outsources about 75 percent of its production to lower-cost countries. The new managing director of Kangaroo, who joined two years ago, developed a new strategy for the company and a comprehensive marketing approach for the two brands. In particular, she improved internal procedures, strengthened the marketing department, and streamlined the company's product range. Kangaroo now has 15 to 30 percent fewer products than the competition.

The growing pressure from mass merchandisers has forced the company to improve its cost structure to retain profitability. In parallel, Kangaroo has *emphasized efficient procurement, distribution logistics, and professional merchandising. As a result, Kangaroo outperforms its competitors in these key areas, making Alligator the reference brand for mass retailers.*

Product Diversification

For many years, the company's two brands have grown outside its core men's underwear business by launching complementary products:

- *Kangaroo nightwear (pajamas, dressing gowns) and leisurewear (swimwear, T-shirts/polo shirts, pullovers)*
- *Alligator nightwear (pajamas) and leisurewear (swimwear, active wear)*

These product-line extensions are perceived as consistent with the brands' territory and have been well-received by both trade partners and consumers. However, Kangaroo never considered diversification a priority and didn't develop dedicated product concepts, roadmaps, and budgets. Given this, the success achieved in the marketplace was remarkable.

Strategic plans for the Two brands

The company has a five-year strategic plan, which emphasizes four main priorities:

- *Finalizing the positioning of both brands in line with their respective image and market potential*
- *Pursuing the product diversification strategy in line with the positioning of each brand*
- *Supporting product diversification with product and brand communication*
- *Enhancing commercial services to retailers and consumers to support the brand strategy*

In essence, the plan aims at achieving different market positioning for the two brands while relying on a single back-office organization for procurement, distribution, and general services. Since Kangaroo doesn't expect to achieve significant growth in its core underpants and undershirt business, it plans to boost its organic growth through product-line extension. The two brands will clarify their relative positioning and develop different products.

The Kangaroo brand will target the growing segment of men over 40 years of age, who have reached a certain level of prosperity, wish to remain young and healthy, and spend more time on leisure activities. Such consumers look for coherent product offerings in a meaningful brand universe, ask for first-class service at the point of sale (e.g., specific shop atmosphere, home delivery, product-range consistency, etc.), and are willing to pay a premium for such upscale offerings.

Consequently, the Kangaroo brand will provide elegantly styled, high-quality products made from brand-specific fabrics that deliver superior comfort. Kangaroo will become the brand for comfortable leisurewear. A significant part of the future Kangaroo collection will consist of different types of shirts and pullovers complemented by jackets and trousers for indoor and outdoor leisure. The brand will also offer accessory products such as swimwear, dressing gowns, and belts.

Kangaroo-branded products will sell through upscale retail channels, ranging from boutiques in department stores, corners in specialty stores, to franchise stores, allowing it to control the distribution of its products and how the brand is presented to consumers. Once Kangaroo has anchored its new concept in the domestic market, it will export it into neighboring countries where the brand has managed to achieve a positive image and remarkable client awareness in spite of its low market share.

By contrast, the Alligator brand will focus on offering excellent value-for-money in mass retail outlets. Although the brand retains a rather young and sporty image, thanks to its past communication campaigns, it has not yet established a truly specific market positioning. Its success results mostly from the technical and logistical expertise of the Kangaroo Company, associated with the significant growth in the mass merchandiser channel over the past 20 years.

Alligator develops collaborative relationships with mass retailers to help them grow their non-food sales in Syldavia, while expanding into neighboring countries where retail formats recently started to change. To leverage these collaborative ties further, the company will continue to improve the supply chain for Alligator, shortening the response time between production and demand at the point of sale, and enhancing its competitive position in mass retail.

In parallel, Kangaroo will promote the Alligator brand and expand its product range into sporty leisurewear products such as T-shirts and sweatshirts, Bermuda shorts, and swimwear. Alligator's communication, both at the point of sale and through sponsored events, will anchor the brand as a sporty, fresh, and dynamic label. It will emphasize the healthy side of engaging in activities such as jogging, biking, hiking, and so on. The brand will benefit from the association between sport and comfort, and between sport and leisure. Comfortable products are not only a prerequisite for good performance in sports, but also for staying well every day. Featuring popular athletes engaging in the aforementioned sports will personify the positioning.

Potential Acquisitions

Kangaroo also considers external growth through the acquisition of small, usually family-owned companies with well-established international brands or specific product expertise. Some target companies are available because they are either too small to survive on their own or confronted with succession problems. The objective of such acquisitions would be to achieve synergies in product procurement and other back-office functions, to accelerate international expansion, and to increase bargaining power with retailers.

What Is the Problem?

Cherry Holdings' management team considers the acquisition of Kangaroo favorably, but executive committee members have different perspectives on Kangaroo. Albert, the CEO, likes the Kangaroo brand a lot and believes in its expansion potential. Evgeny, the CFO, is positive about the deal, based on the financials, which he thinks are attractive. His team has conducted a discounted cash-flow analysis of the five-year business plan of Kangaroo, combined with the potential synergies the acquisition can generate with some other of Cherry's businesses. This analysis results in a valuation that greatly exceeds the acquisition price. However, Brenda, the marketing and operations officer, is more cautious. She's insisted that the data currently available aren't sufficient to reach a decision, and she wants to establish a project team to gather additional insights through market research, competitive analysis, trade interviews, expert interviews, and so on.

Cherry Holdings doesn't need a recommendation on the acquisition price, the structure of the deal, or the synergies with its other businesses. What the firm wants is a strategic analysis that assesses the attractiveness of the market for men's underpants and Kangaroo's strategic plans. Specifically, a conversation with Brenda points out the following areas for investigation:

- The market for men's underwear and its evolution in Syldavia. Brenda worries about slow market growth, as unit prices have been declining and the volume trend looks flat.
- Kangaroo's market position, brand image, and market-share evolution. Brenda is concerned with the past decline in Kangaroo's sales, which led to a restructuring plan a few years ago.
- The competitors, present and potential.
- The retail sector and its likely evolution.
- Kangaroo's growth plans, in particular its project to expand into adjacent product categories.

This conversation suggests limiting the scope of the study to analyzing the market, the industry, and Kangaroo's five-year strategic plan. Unlike other problems that we've mentioned in this book, the issue doesn't look too complicated. The problem is atypical because it is relatively straightforward.

To define the problem, let's look at the TOSCA checklist:

- There is no *Trouble* in the literal sense. The symptom is an acquisition opportunity rather than a trouble, which is not totally unusual, as mentioned in Chap. 4. What can be called a "trouble" is that Cherry Holdings fears overestimating Kangaroo's potential. Brenda seems somewhat suspicious about the market attractiveness and Kangaroo's strategic plans.
- The *Owner* of the problem is mainly Brenda. The two other decision-makers are convinced already. The purpose of the problem-solving effort is either to convince Brenda to approve the deal or to provide her with solid arguments to reject it. The main piece Brenda is missing is a strategic audit of Kangaroo. Moreover, since Evgeny has computed discounted cash flows to value the acquisition, she'll be in a better position to take a stand if we provide her with a strategic assessment to which she can easily relate. In other words, we must focus on Kangaroo's ability to generate future cash flows in a steady and predictable way.
- *Success* isn't determined by whether Cherry Holdings pursues or terminates the deal. It rests on our ability to give Brenda a convincing view of whether she should approve the deal or not. We can consider ourselves successful when Brenda is able to take a clear stand on the Kangaroo deal, in a way that is convincing and acceptable for Albert and Evgeny. With this in mind, our scope is limited to the strategic appraisal of the company, as defined by the questions Brenda asked in our conversation with her.
- The main *Constraint* is that we have little time to conduct the project. This constraint is offset by the limited project scope. Within this scope, the external component (market trend, industry analysis, competitive benchmark, etc.) seems particularly important. In addition, we won't have access to the management and the current owners of Kangaroo.
- The main *Actors* are the three decision-makers.

We can state the problem in the following way: *Is Kangaroo's business attractive enough and its strategic plan convincing enough to justify Cherry Holdings' interest in acquiring it, assuming a fair agreement on the other aspects of the deal?*

The main way to confirm or disconfirm Cherry Holdings' interest is to substantiate or question Kangaroo's ability to generate cash in the coming years.

Structuring the Problem

Given the problem statement and the data we gathered from the information memo, we view the scope of the project as twofold:

- Examine whether Kangaroo's current men's underwear business is likely to generate a steady and predictable stream of cash in the upcoming years.
- Look into the strategic moves Kangaroo is considering in its five-year plan, in particular the product diversification strategy, and assess their likely impact on future performance.

This scope suggests an issue tree with two main branches, as represented in Fig. 12.1. The first branch deals with Kangaroo's current business assessment, with an emphasis on market and industry analyses, drawing on Porter's Five Forces model. The second branch addresses Kangaroo's strategic plans, especially its product diversification project. This issue tree doesn't cover all possible aspects of the problem, but it fits the scope of the study quite well, given the time constraints and the priorities defined by Brenda.

Solving the Problem

In the course of the problem-solving effort, the ongoing conversation with Brenda leads the project team to drop the external-growth issue from the scope of the problem. Cherry Holdings believes it will be able to deal with this topic later if it actually acquires Kangaroo. Deciding on acquisitions is much more the prerogative of a firm's main shareholder than of its management. In addition, it seems pointless to spend time at this stage speculating on potential acquisition targets. The main focus should be on Kangaroo's fundamentals rather than on its potential for external growth.

To perform the required analyses, the project team gathers data mainly from market studies, retailer panels, and industry reports. The team also conducts a series of interviews with retailers, industry experts, and consumers.

Overall, the findings suggest the industry structure is sound and stable. Established brands such as Kangaroo and Alligator should be able to generate comfortable profit margins in the foreseeable future. Through their interviews, however, the team members identify an important issue: mass retailers' private labels may create a threat to Kangaroo's sales and profitability. The

Fig. 12.1 Issue tree on the Kangaroo case study

distribution-channel mix has shifted in favor of mass retailers (hypermarkets and supermarkets), and these mass retailers have created their own private labels that eat into the sales of established brands such as Kangaroo. The team concludes that launching the Alligator brand, with its value-for-money positioning, was a smart move to counterattack on this front, and that private-label products have probably reached a plateau and are unlikely to gain additional market share in the future.

Regarding Kangaroo's strategic plan, the project team engages in a series of case studies of small- and medium-sized companies in similar industries that have recently tried to expand their product lines under the same brand umbrella. This benchmark exercise reveals that Kangaroo's plans seem overly optimistic. Most comparable companies haven't reached the growth target Kangaroo expects to achieve in five years. However, interviews with retailers and consumer focus groups suggest that, while the project seems oversold, it might create positive spillovers for the core business.

Selling the Solution

The core conclusion of the problem-solving team is that Kangaroo is attractive enough to justify Cherry Holdings' interest, which should alleviate Brenda's concerns. However, the appraisal of Kangaroo's strategy remains unclear. The business is attractive, and Kangaroo's strategic plan doesn't create major risks, but the diversification project seems a bit oversold and unrealistic.

Based on the insights and findings they drew from the analyses, the team puts together the following storyline, in which the page numbers within parentheses refer to the first section of the final recommendation report presented in the Appendix.

Storyline of the Kangaroo Opportunity

Core message and key line (report version p. 1; presentation version p. 2):

Kangaroo's business is attractive enough to justify Cherry Holdings' interest in a potential acquisition, in spite of some doubts on the chances of success of Kangaroo's expansion plans:

1. The industry structure favors high and stable profitability for established brands.
2. Kangaroo is well positioned for the future.

3. Expansion plans are uncertain but entail low risk.

Detailed storyline:

1. The industry structure favors high and stable profitability for established brands (report version p. 3; presentation version p. 4):

   (a) Demand is stable in men's underpants key segment:

     – Consumers are loyal, because of inertia and low commitment to purchasing decision (p. 5).
     – Volume trend is flat (p. 6).
     – Average unit prices are stable (p. 7).

   (b) Branded competition is not intense:

     – There are few large brands, and they do not compete aggressively (p. 8).
     – New brand entry has failed consistently (p. 9).
     – Some current players might exit (p. 10).

   (c) Retailers' private labels (PL) are not a major threat:

     – PL have grown big (p. 11), particularly in more mature segments (p. 12).
     – But they have probably reached a plateau (p. 13).
     – And they have not really hurt the leaders anyway (p. 14).

2. Kangaroo's core business is well positioned for the future:

   (a) Change in distribution-channel mix will not hurt anymore:

     – Mass retailers have taken a growing and dominant share in the distribution-channel mix.
     – This change has hurt the Kangaroo brand, especially in the domestic sales of briefs.
     – However, it favors Alligator, and both brands have progressed in their respective distribution channels.
     – The Alligator brand fits mass retailers' expectations.

   (b) Both brands have upside:

     – Good consumer image
     – Good trade image
     – This despite underinvestment

3. Expansion plans are uncertain but entail low risk:

   (c) Success in product-line extensions is rather unlikely:

      – Plans are ambitious versus comparables.
      – Early customer feedback is negative.
      – Kangaroo has no distinctive skills.
      – Kangaroo management may be overextended.

   (d) But risks are low:

      – Plans are not costly compared to core-business cash flows.
      – Plans can be evolved/fine-tuned overtime (no "big bets").

   (e) Even failing may benefit the brand in the core business

*　*　*

This storyline follows a grouping pattern, with three key-line points: (1) industry structure and market attractiveness, (2) Kangaroo's current position in its core business, and (3) Kangaroo's expansion plans.

As the problem is relatively simple and calls for little creativity, the structure of the storyline mirrors the issue tree. There's no creative leap between breaking the problem into sub-issues and supporting the core message with key-line points. The core message is very close to the problem statement, and the supporting points are similar to the sub-issues and the elementary analyses. The main difference is that the stream of research on acquisitions that was initially envisaged in the issue tree was disregarded, as mentioned earlier. Other differences reflect a focus on the insights that help bolster the core message, while pieces that yielded poor or insignificant results, such as the analysis of profitability by segments or internationalization by country, are deliberately ignored.

We present the first section of the final report in the Appendix. This report is an example of what the output of a relatively simple problem-solving effort might look like. Note, in particular, the executive summary and storyline pages (pp. 1–4) which we present in both report and presentation versions. As suggested in Chap. 11, the report versions are self-contained: any reader can read and understand them without external elaboration. In contrast, the presentation slides are simplified versions that the presenter uses as a support to announce the structure of the presentation and keep the audience on track with the storyline.

The report follows the pyramid principle: each key-line point is developed as a mini-pyramid, with the storyline page summarizing the corresponding segment of the story (p. 3) and the content pages presenting the elementary findings (pp. 5–14). These mini-pyramids cohere into the pyramidal pattern of the full report, with the executive summary presenting the whole story (p. 1) and each storyline page introducing a pillar of the pyramid.

All content pages have two headlines: the action title, which conveys the message (the "so what?") of the page as part of the storyline, and a capitalized headline that presents the chart content in purely descriptive terms. You'll also see that the report contains a variety of quantitative, qualitative, and conceptual charts, based on different templates, which should shed light on various ways to convey analytical findings and more qualitative evidence with both text and visuals.

Appendix: First Section of a Report on the Kangaroo Case Study

EXECUTIVE SUMMARY

Our study suggests that Kangaroo's business is attractive enough to justify Cherry Holdings' interest in it as a potential acquisition, in spite of some doubts on the chances of success of Kangaroo's expansion plans.

1 **The industry structure favors high and stable profitability for established brands**, with no major risk in the predictable future. Indeed, the demand is stable and the slow-moving industry structure creates only limited and manageable threats (essentially through the rise of mass retailers and private labels).

2 In this favorable context, **Kangaroo is well positioned for the future**. It has built a sound and solid position around its two brands while maintaining a low level of investment. Therefore Kangaroo's core business can continue to generate steady streams of cash flow in the coming years.

3 **Kangaroo's expansion plans are uncertain but entail low risk.** Based on the reactions of consumers and retailers and on a study of similar strategic moves, Kangaroo's targets appear overly ambitious. However, the plan requires limited investments, and even if it does not generate the expected revenues, it might in fact benefit the brands' image in the core business.

1

EXECUTIVE SUMMARY

Kangaroo's business is attractive enough to justify Cherry Holdings' interest, in spite of some doubts on Kangaroo's expansion plans

1 **Industry structure favors established brands**
- Demand is stable and predictable
- Branded competition is not intense
- Private labels are not a major threat

2 **Kangaroo is well positioned for the future**
- Change in distribution-channel mix will not hurt anymore
- Both brands have upside

3 **Expansion plans are uncertain but entail low risk**
- Success in product-line extensions is rather unlikely
- But risks are low
- Even failing may benefit the core business

2

1. The industry structure favors high and stable profitability for established brands

- Demand for men's underpants, which account for 74% of Kangaroo's sales and 87% of operational profit, is very stable and predictable.
    - ✓ Consumer behavior is characterized by strong inertia, with high brand loyalty and low commitment to the purchasing decision (p. 5)
    - ✓ The market trend is flat in volume, at least since 2012 (p. 6)
    - ✓ Average unit prices remain stable thanks to a shift in consumer preferences from briefs to boxer shorts (p. 7)
- Branded competition is not intense
    - ✓ There are few large brands, and they do not compete aggressively (p. 8)
    - ✓ New brand entry, including through licensed brands, has failed consistently (p. 9)
    - ✓ Some current players might exit (p. 10)
- Retailers' private labels are not a major threat
    - ✓ Low-price products have increased their market share significantly (p. 11) particularly in more mature segments, e.g., briefs (p. 12)
    - ✓ Most retailers believe their private labels have reached a plateau and will not progress anymore (p. 13)
    - ✓ In addition, the rise of private labels has not hurt the best-established brands, which is consistent with past experience in other categories (p. 14)

3

1. Industry structure favors established brands

- Demand is stable and predictable
    - ✓ Consumer behavior characterized by strong inertia
    - ✓ Market flat in volume since 2012
    - ✓ Unit prices stable thanks to shift from briefs to boxers
- Branded competition is not intense
    - ✓ Few large brands, moderate competitive intensity
    - ✓ No successful new brand entries
    - ✓ Exits possible
- Private labels are not a major threat
    - ✓ Low-price products growing, esp. in mature segments
    - ✓ Private labels at a plateau…
    - ✓ … and not hurting established brands

4

Consumer behavior is characterized by strong inertia, with high brand loyalty and low commitment to the purchasing decision

CONSUMER BEHAVIOR FOR THE PURCHASE OF UNDERPANTS

Brand loyalty

- *"Once a man has found comfortable underpants that he likes, he doesn't switch to rival products"* – Hypermarket manager

- *"Very high brand loyalty, which is exceptional for textile products"* – Industry expert

- *"Buyers who like the comfort of a particular brand remain loyal for life"* – Specialty store manager

Low commitment

- *"There are in fact 3 types of buyers for men's underwear: mothers who buy for kids and teenagers, young adults (20-35 years old) who buy for themselves, and wives who buy for husbands"* –Supermarket manager

- *"Women who order for their husband and sons buy to replace worn-out or too small pieces. They focus on price, not on brand. Young adults are more sensitive to looks and brands"* – e-commerce vendor

- *"Purchasing decisions are essentially rational, mainly to replace worn-out pieces. Nevertheless there is a small market for more fancy products"* – Retailer

Source: Interviews

5

The market trend is flat in volume, at least since 2012

MARKET FOR UNDERPANTS

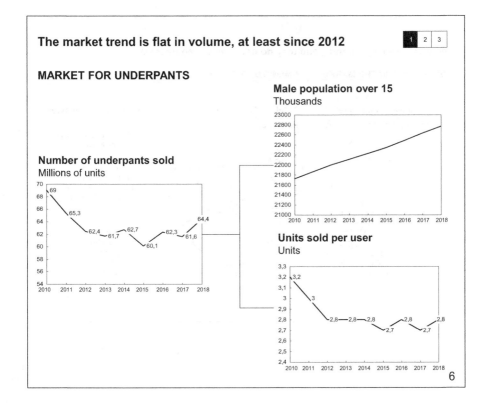

Number of underpants sold
Millions of units

Male population over 15
Thousands

Units sold per user
Units

6

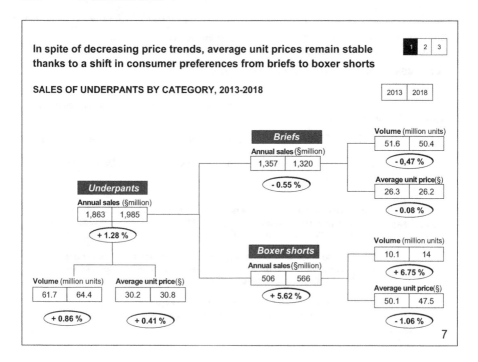

In spite of decreasing price trends, average unit prices remain stable thanks to a shift in consumer preferences from briefs to boxer shorts

| 1 | 2 | 3 |

SALES OF UNDERPANTS BY CATEGORY, 2013-2018

| 2013 | 2018 |

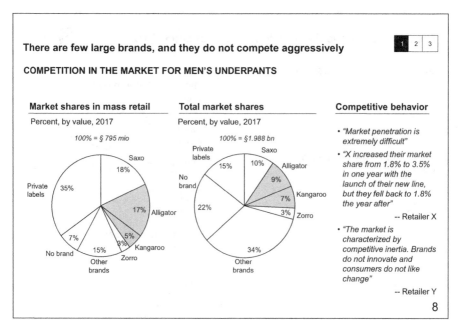

There are few large brands, and they do not compete aggressively

| 1 | 2 | 3 |

COMPETITION IN THE MARKET FOR MEN'S UNDERPANTS

Market shares in mass retail

Percent, by value, 2017

100% = § 795 mio

Private labels 35%
Saxo 18%
Alligator 17%
Kangaroo 5%
Zorro 3%
Other brands 15%
No brand 7%

Total market shares

Percent, by value, 2017

100% = §1.988 bn

Private labels 15%
Saxo 10%
Alligator 9%
Kangaroo 7%
Zorro 3%
No brand 22%
Other brands 34%

Competitive behavior

- *"Market penetration is extremely difficult"*

- *"X increased their market share from 1.8% to 3.5% in one year with the launch of their new line, but they fell back to 1.8% the year after"*

  -- Retailer X

- *"The market is characterized by competitive inertia. Brands do not innovate and consumers do not like change"*

  -- Retailer Y

8

New brand entry, including through licensed brands, has failed consistently

COMMENTS ON NEW MARKET ENTRIES

• *"New entrants never managed to take up significant market share"* -- Industry expert

• On the specific threat of licensed brands:

  –*"The impact of the entry of generalist brands on the men's underpants market is very simple to assess: there is no impact whatsoever"* – Supermarket manager

  –*"Generalist labels have launched products under license, which animates the market a bit, but at the end of the day, the clients go back to the traditional brands anyway"* – e-commerce retailer

  – [Their gains are] *"limited to large cities and high end shopping malls"* – Mass retailer executive

  –*"The impact of global "high end" brands has been to stir the competition to some extent, but their product quality is too low to gain any significant position"* – e-commerce retailer

• Overall:

  –*"The bulk of sales remains with traditional white briefs, period"* – Hypermarket manager

  –*"The basic brief still is the cash cow in this market"* -- Mass retailer executive

Source: interviews

9

Some current players might exit

COMMENTS ON POTENTIAL EXITS

  • *"Some players will throw in the towel very soon"* – Mass retailer executive

  • *"The Zorro and Charlie brands are doomed to fail and disappear from the shelves"* – Mass retailer executive

  • *"Rumors say Zorro and Charlie are to exit the men's underpants market. I believe Navyblue is also on a glide path to exit"* – Hypermarket manager

  • *" Zorro and Charlie have simply failed to rejuvenate the brand"* – e-commerce retailer

  • *"Charlie will exit Syldavia for sure"* – Industry expert

Source: Interviews

10

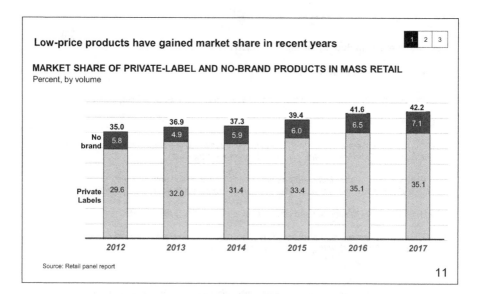

Low-price products have gained market share in recent years

MARKET SHARE OF PRIVATE-LABEL AND NO-BRAND PRODUCTS IN MASS RETAIL
Percent, by volume

Source: Retail panel report

11

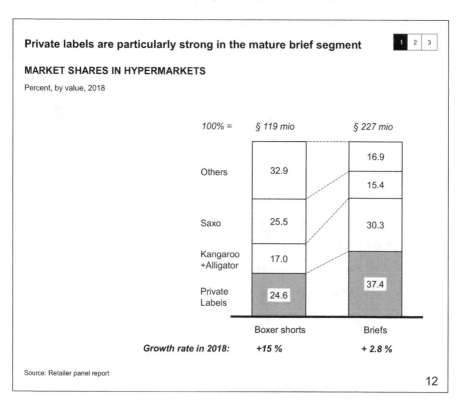

Private labels are particularly strong in the mature brief segment

MARKET SHARES IN HYPERMARKETS

Percent, by value, 2018

Source: Retailer panel report

12

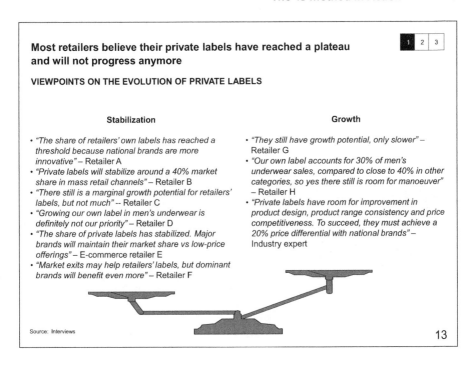

Most retailers believe their private labels have reached a plateau and will not progress anymore

| 1 | 2 | 3 |

VIEWPOINTS ON THE EVOLUTION OF PRIVATE LABELS

Stabilization

- *"The share of retailers' own labels has reached a threshold because national brands are more innovative"* – Retailer A
- *"Private labels will stabilize around a 40% market share in mass retail channels"* – Retailer B
- *"There still is a marginal growth potential for retailers' labels, but not much"* -- Retailer C
- *"Growing our own label in men's underwear is definitely not our priority"* – Retailer D
- *"The share of private labels has stabilized. Major brands will maintain their market share vs low-price offerings"* – E-commerce retailer E
- *"Market exits may help retailers' labels, but dominant brands will benefit even more"* – Retailer F

Growth

- *"They still have growth potential, only slower"* – Retailer G
- *"Our own label accounts for 30% of men's underwear sales, compared to close to 40% in other categories, so yes there still is room for manoeuver"* – Retailer H
- *"Private labels have room for improvement in product design, product range consistency and price competitiveness. To succeed, they must achieve a 20% price differential with national brands"* – Industry expert

Source: Interviews

13

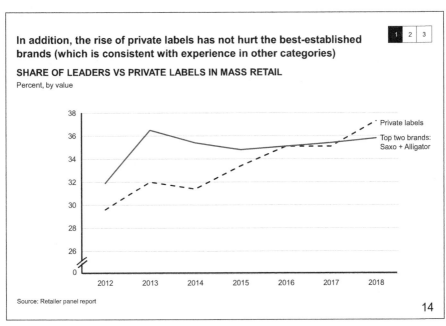

In addition, the rise of private labels has not hurt the best-established brands (which is consistent with experience in other categories)

| 1 | 2 | 3 |

SHARE OF LEADERS VS PRIVATE LABELS IN MASS RETAIL
Percent, by value

Private labels

Top two brands: Saxo + Alligator

Source: Retailer panel report

14

Note

1. The symbol § represents the currency used in Syldavia.

13

Conclusion: Becoming a Master Problem-Solver

We started this book by describing five problem-solving pitfalls—traps we're prone to fall prey to when we face challenging problems. Some see these pitfalls as evidence that human input in problem solving must be minimized and look forward to the day when AI will take care of all problems, from the mundane to the most vital. Thanks to reams of big data and ever-smarter machine learning algorithms, they claim, no problem will be too complicated for AI to solve. Others agree with this prediction, but fear it will have disastrous consequences for humankind.

Whether it's formulated with a techno-optimist mindset or offered to support apocalyptic prophecies, we disagree with this increasingly widespread view. AI promises to replace experts in many fields, ranging from medicine to financial advice. But complex and non-routine problems can't be solved by expertise alone: they must be defined and structured first. Of course, technology has a part to play. AI and big data will change how we solve problems, just like calculators and computers did. But such analyses are a small part of the problem-solving process, not the whole approach. It takes a human to identify and frame problems, to structure and monitor a comprehensive problem-solving effort, to plan analyses, to critically assess and interpret evidence, to imagine novel solutions, to use judgment to evaluate them, and to convince decision-makers to implement them. We believe it always will.

Although we used business illustrations in this book, the critical thinking principles we explored apply to problems in most human activities. A recent study, for instance, examined the link between critical thinking skills and "negative life events," ranging in severity from mild (e.g., missing a flight, getting into a shouting argument, or letting food go bad in the fridge) to serious

© The Author(s) 2018
B. Garrette et al., *Cracked it!*, https://doi.org/10.1007/978-3-319-89375-4_13

(e.g., getting a ticket for drunk driving or filing for bankruptcy). It showed that people with strong critical thinking skills experience fewer of these negative real-world outcomes,[1] suggesting that critical thinkers can utilize their skills in many walks of life.

It's easy to see why. Wouldn't it be valuable, for example, when thinking about your personal financial strategy for retirement, to structure the complex issues it raises? What about having the five problem-solving pitfalls in mind to help you think more critically about provocative posts on your favorite social network or the platforms of political candidates in the next election? Likewise, the solution-selling tools we introduced don't just apply to business settings. You can use them to structure any pitch you need to make. Enhancing our problem-solving and solution-selling skills not only makes us better business people, but it can also help us manage our lives better and be more responsible citizens.

There is, however, a reason problem-solving and communications skills are difficult to teach and to learn: they require practice. The chapters of this book have introduced you to defining problems rigorously, building issue trees and hypothesis pyramids, leveraging frameworks, conducting rigorous analysis, using design thinking techniques to generate creative solutions, and building storylines and persuasive reports. These things are not pieces of knowledge, like the periodic table of chemical elements; they're skills, like riding a bike. As a child, you didn't learn to ride a bike by reading the owner's manual. Instead, you got on the bike, pedaled, fell off, and got on again—until you shouted, "Look, Dad, no hands!"

That's what you must do now—practice. One advantage of working in business—any business—is that opportunities abound to solve problems and sell solutions. Almost by definition, a manager or executive is someone who deals with problems. Every day brings a fresh supply of headaches, large and small. These are your practice opportunities, and they make problem-solving skills easier to develop than in most other settings. If you're not a manager or executive, find someone in your organization facing a challenging problem and volunteer to help solve it. If that's not possible, find business case studies on the Internet, from publishers like Harvard Business School, Ivey, or the European Case Centre, and practice cracking them.

Treat these challenges as opportunities to learn. Start small: even a simple, familiar problem that lies within your domain of expertise is an opportunity for practice. Ordinarily, you may not give it a minute's thought, maybe because you'd solve it by analogy to past problems. But pause for a moment. If you knew nothing about this problem, how would you state it? What are the Trouble, the Owner, the Success criteria, the Constraints, and the Actors?

What is the core question? Should you build a hypothesis pyramid? An issue tree? Do you need frameworks? Design thinking tools? The beauty is that you already know the answer (or think you do), so you have nothing to lose. This is like riding your first bike—with the stabilizers. Who knows, the problem-structuring effort may lead you to see a new solution to a familiar problem.

The same learning approach applies to solution selling: pick a communication need you don't regard as challenging—so simple that you gave it little thought. Perhaps it's a simple e-mail to a coworker or an oral progress report on a project in a staff meeting. You know how to do it and your approach works just fine. But in the spirit of practicing your skills, try to build a simple storyline, using a grouping or an argument. Maybe you'll discover your governing thought is not as crystal-clear as you thought it was. Chances are, even in a straightforward case, your communication can become more effective with minimal effort.

Another essential aspect of becoming a better problem solver is to practice with others. As we've pointed out throughout the book, flaws in problem-structuring logic, in analysis, and in communication are easier to detect in others than in ourselves. What flaws aren't? An indispensable way to improve your skills is to share the results of each stage of your problem-solving efforts with coworkers who can provide feedback and constructive challenge. Even better, practice as a team: join forces with a colleague, develop the same work products separately, then compare notes, and construct, together, a problem statement, an issue tree, or a storyline that combines the best of your respective approaches. When you're on the receiving end of solution selling that looks like it could be improved, offer your help (tactfully).

Working in teams will remind you of a point we've illustrated in several examples in this book: there are many ways to find and communicate the wrong answer, but no single way to get it right; and no way to always get it right the first time. Remember those iterate arrows in Fig. 3.1? It may not feel natural, at first, to revisit each step in the 4S method after you've progressed to the next one. Our training as productive business professionals values "getting it right the first time." Good problem solving, however, rarely works this way. Working with others will force you to see problems and solutions as they do—differently. This is the best way to learn the importance of remaining open-minded at every step of the problem-solving process.

What can this constant, collegial practice accomplish? To answer this question, we only need to look at some of the best problem solvers we've been privileged to meet. While their problem-solving skills impress us, it's not necessarily because they're incredibly smart or creative. Instead, they've mastered the tools we've described in this book. Like chess champions who can play multiple games simultaneously, great problem solvers recognize the value of using multiple lenses on the same problem at once. They've stated, structured, and solved so many issues, large and small, that they can reconcile different approaches to the same problem. They're not only able to define a complex problem rigorously, but they can juggle multiple problem statements of the same issue. They're as comfortable with hypothesis- and issue-driven approaches as they are with the empathetic and experimental disciplines of design thinking. They juggle functional and industry frameworks to look at the same issues and sub-issues from different angles. Finally, they can distill the essence of an emerging solution into a compelling governing thought supported by a clear storyline, yet remain open to revisiting this solution in the light of new facts.

We wrote *Cracked It!* to set you on the path to becoming a master problem solver. Whether you're new to solving complex business problems or an old hand, a disciplined, structured process is key. We developed the 4S method and the toolkit that goes along with it for this purpose. Processes like the 4S method may not be sexy, but the guidance and discipline they provide can give you the confidence to tackle seemingly insurmountable challenges. With practice, you'll be able to solve difficult problems and persuasively sell your solutions. Few things in life can provide the same sense of satisfaction as when you look back on a thorny, complex problem you've worked on and know you cracked it.

Note

1. Butler, H.A. (2012). Halpern Critical Thinking Assessment Predicts Real-World Outcomes of Critical Thinking. *Applied Cognitive Psychology, 26,* 721–729.

Index[1]

---

[1] Note: Page numbers followed by 'n' refer to notes.

© The Author(s) 2018

B. Garrette et al., *Cracked it!*, https://doi.org/10.1007/978-3-319-89375-4